Praise for *You: Part*

'Forget the cardigan and slippers and buy t̶h̶i̶s̶ ̶i̶n̶s̶t̶e̶a̶d̶.̶ ̶A̶ ̶c̶l̶e̶a̶r̶ ̶h̶e̶a̶d̶.̶
invigorating and inspiring guide to t̶h̶e̶ ̶r̶e̶s̶t̶ ̶o̶f̶ ̶y̶o̶u̶r̶ ̶l̶i̶f̶e̶
Kirsty Young, broadcaster

'Campbell and Jane have translated midlife anxiety into a calm playbook.
Embracing life's transitions with positivity can be a game-changer'
Jeremy Snape, former England cricketer and founder of Sporting Edge

'This book gets straight to the heart of what we all need to find fulfilment, joy
and purpose in the second half of life: a pause to focus energy, embrace change
and overcome fears. An essential, life-enhancing read'
Celia Dodd, author of *Not Fade Away: How to Thrive in Retirement*

Campbell Macpherson is an international business adviser, change specialist, keynote speaker and author. His first book, *The Change Catalyst* (Wiley 2017), is about leading change and was the 2018 Business Book of the Year. His second book, *The Power to Change* (Kogan Page 2020), is about embracing personal change. *You: Part Two* is his third.

Via his consultancy, Change & Strategy International, Campbell helps leaders to build strong leadership teams, align their people to a clear strategy, create change-ready cultures and lead successful and sustainable change. He runs 'Leading Change' workshops and webinars for leaders at all levels of organisations, and 'Embracing Change' workshops and webinars for employees to help them to embrace change and look for the opportunities. He is also an Executive Fellow of Henley Business School.

For more than twenty-five years, Campbell has been helping leaders and leadership teams align their people to a clear strategy, build change-ready cultures and lead successful and sustainable change. His list of careers and clients is a lengthy one. Campbell started his career flying aircraft (badly) in the Royal Australian Air Force. He still holds the record for being the worst pilot ever to make it through to jets.

www.changeandstrategy.com
www.campbellmacphersonspeaker.com
www.campbellmacphersonauthor.com

Jane Macpherson is fully qualified as both a yoga teacher (IYAT 500 hours) and yoga therapist. She has been helping her clients transform their lives for more than sixteen years.

Prior to yoga, Jane had a successful career in marketing, brand strategy and sponsorship for a variety of international organisations including Ogilvy & Mather, Pepsi, Westpac Bank and Barclays. She was the Head of Sponsorship and Donations for Westpac during the Sydney 2000 Olympics.

Jane runs yoga retreats in the UK, India and Europe and conducts face-to-face and online classes, one-on-one yoga therapy and private yoga sessions from her studio in Cheltenham or wherever she happens to be at the time thanks to Zoom.

As well as being co-author of *You: Part Two*, Jane also co-wrote the chapter 'The Power of Yoga' in *The Power to Change* (Kogan Page 2020).

www.janemacphersonyoga.com

Jane and Campbell met in Sydney in 1991 and were married in 1992. They have two remarkable adult children and live in Cheltenham, England.

They give keynote speeches and conduct workshops, webinars and online programmes based on the topics in *You: Part Two* – for anyone who wishes to shape their own Part Two and for organisations wishing to help their employees to do the same, as well as those businesses that are seeking to improve their relationships with lucrative 'second half' customers.

To find out more, visit www.you-part-two.com (don't forget the hyphens).

You: Part Two

Thriving in the second half of your life

by Campbell Macpherson
and Jane Macpherson

•••••••••••••••••••

A How To book

ROBINSON

ROBINSON

First published in Great Britain in 2021
by Robinson

10 9 8 7 6 5 4 3 2 1

A CIP catalogue record for this book
is available from the British Library.

ISBN: 978-1-47214-558-1

Typeset in Sentinel and Scala Sans
by Ian Hughes

Printed and bound in Great Britain
by Clays Ltd, Elcograf S.p.A.

Illustrations by Liane Payne

Papers used by Robinson are from well-
managed forests and other responsible
sources.

Robinson
An imprint of
Little, Brown Book Group
Carmelite House
50 Victoria Embankment
London EC4Y 0DZ

An Hachette UK Company
www.hachette.co.uk

www.littlebrown.co.uk

How To Books are published by
Robinson, an imprint of Little, Brown
Book Group. We welcome proposals
from authors who have first-hand
experience of their subjects. Please set
out the aims of your book, its target
market and its suggested contents in an
email to howto@littlebrown.co.uk.

Contents

Jane was on a ten-day trek to Machu Picchu in Peru.

Towards the end of this life-affirming adventure, the expedition paused to rest in a tiny village on the side of a remote mountain. In front of one of the simple, ancient houses sat an old woman, quietly and proudly preparing her family's evening meal. She exuded calmness, contentment, health and purpose. Jane was drawn to her and introduced herself.

During the short conversation that followed,
Jane said to her, via an interpreter:
'I hope you don't mind me asking, but how old are you?'

The woman looked directly into Jane's eyes,
smiled and gave a simple yet profound response,
'I don't know, but I am well.'

Introduction

Welcome to Part Two.

It promises to be quite a ride. We Part Two-ers can expect to live longer than previous generations and have vitality to spare. We are setting off on an exciting new chapter; full of change, possibly even meaning, and yet so many of us simply do not know who to trust when it comes to advice on thriving in the second half of our lives.

If the thought of consulting a 'life coach' right now leaves you a little cold, even if you can't quite articulate why, and yet you could do with more than the purely financial guidance you receive from your financial adviser – this book is for you.

It is designed to be the start of a discussion about your Part Two and by the time you have finished reading, we hope you feel it has not only been helpful and informative but also entertaining, because very little worthwhile in life is worth doing without a chuckle or three.

The book is a genuine husband and wife collaboration. Jane was the content director of *You: Part Two*, while I, Campbell, was the chief scribe. As well as collaborating on content throughout, Jane's other critical role was to make sure the book didn't become a 'man in his fifties writes about (not) retiring' tome.

The idea for the book came to me a little later than it should have, to be honest: I had already well and truly embarked on my second half adventures. The book's genesis was the event of my fifty-fifth birthday. On that day, an invisible switch in cyberspace was flicked and an entire army of cyber-marketing sleeper bots sprang into action to mark the occasion. My computer and phone were suddenly abuzz with pension companies wanting me to transfer my pension or pensions into one of theirs or to alert me that I could now start to draw down funds from my pension savings or enticing me to calculate how much money I needed to 'retire', whatever that word actually means – a subject we will delve into several times throughout the book. Some investment firms invited me to ponder whether a quarter of a million, half a million or a million would be enough for me to live on. I didn't click any of them; I sensed I wasn't going to like the answer. Ads for Viagra and Tena Men adult nappies seemed to pop up out of nowhere. One email asked me if I wanted to subscribe to a magazine I had previously never heard of called *The Oldie*. I have since discovered it is excellent: 'a light-hearted alternative to a press obsessed with youth and celebrity'. But I digress.

The images I was being presented with, especially from financial services firms, were visions of white-haired, wistful couples sitting on benches overlooking the ocean. I presumed they were waiting for Nurse to come and collect them. Or it was of ruddy-cheeked 'grey hairs and no hairs' happily tending to their gardens, beaming up at the camera from their InSassy Garden Kneeling Pads. Or impossibly perfect, air-brushed, three-generation Californian families all slim, fit and tanned with perfect teeth, perfect hair and everyone from grandma to grandkids dressed head to toe in white. Even one company's image of a sixty-something on a Harley made me cross. I can't explain why. At least that particular firm had identified the issue and was trying its best.

In the game of life, marketing directors across the globe seemed to have moved me to a part of the board marked 'old and irrelevant'. They were politely informing me that my time was up, that it was time to bring my pedalo in from the middle of the lake and let the young'uns get on with things from here. You've tried your best. Better luck next time.

I was incensed!

In terms of my career, I was only just getting going. After thirty-four years in business, I had finally worked out which way was up, what I was good at and what I could now stop pretending I would ever be any good at. I was still the same person I had been a few decades earlier, but now I had skills, knowledge and experience that had taken time to acquire. I had recently begun an exciting new chapter: restarting my consultancy and publishing my very first book with a global publisher, which even won an award. I had recently returned from giving a keynote speech at a client's conference in Vegas and was about to hop on a plane to do the same thing in Singapore. This was my time.

In fact, it was our time. The kids had left home. Jane's yoga business was blossoming, and she was planning her next round of yoga retreats in Mallorca, Kerala and Marrakech. We were both well and very happy together. Don't talk to us about taking a back seat.

A few months later, I saw the image that would spur me into action on an enormous billboard within the spotlessly clean, futuristic labyrinth that is Zurich airport. It was an advertisement for UBS Private Banking: a photograph of a fit, tanned, good-looking and confident silver-haired man in his sixties at the helm of his yacht. He was squinting slightly into the wind; in control, vital and full of life with a long, healthy future ahead of him. The ad asked me in gigantic letters: 'Is 60 the new 40?' and then in smaller font: 'What does that change? Do I have the right plan?'

'That's how they should be marketing to us,' I said out loud, much to the surprise of the lady in front of me on the escalator.

While the idea for the book had occurred to me a few months earlier, this image strengthened my resolve to do it. That evening, I started to map it out. The next month I was lucky enough to secure the services of literary agent extraordinaire, Jonathan Hayden, and pitched the idea to him. He loved it. Once it was in a shape for Jonathan to pitch to publishers, Little, Brown fell in love with it, too.

But when I showed Jane the UBS ad that had inspired me, she shuddered. 'I really don't like "60 is the new 40",' she declared. 'It's so trite. And it is so male. And I can see why you like that image, but it does nothing for me. But then, it isn't aimed at me. UBS obviously decided that wealthy men are its target audience. Women wouldn't even notice that ad.'

She was only just warming up.

'You know, to women, all "60 is the new 40" says is that younger is better. Looking younger is better. Being younger is better. It is used by advertisers to tell us that if we dress a certain way, if we exercise in a certain way, if we eat certain foods or if we use certain "anti-ageing" beauty products, and don't get me started on "anti-ageing" beauty products, then we can turn back the clock. The phrase is an insult to sixty-year-old women. It's not about being young again; that's impossible. Ageing is fine. We just want to age well. That incredible lady I met in Peru had the right attitude. Age is just a number and the number is not important.'

The ad obviously triggered something in Jane too!

It was an invaluable 'men are from Mars; women are from Venus' moment that proved why husband–wife collaboration on this book was so crucial. To me, '60 is the new 40' spoke of vitality and a longer life ahead. To Jane, it spoke of an obsession with youth and age. I had never even thought about it that way.

We wanted this book to appeal to everyone – men, women, career people, people without careers, parents, entrepreneurs, leaders, managers, workers, painters, artists, musicians, doctors, nurses, carers ... anyone who is looking to make the transition to their particular Part Two.

It had to be thought-provoking yet practical. Obviously, we need to address the financial aspects of the next phase, but there is so much more to life than money. Besides, money is no guarantee of happiness, vitality or 'success'. Many people with buckets of cash have difficulty finding their feet after their self-defining full-time career has come to its natural conclusion.

We also had to confront the other pandemic that runs rampant through our Western societies: ageism – and the best way to vaccinate ourselves against it is attitude. The wrong attitude can not only make life miserable; as we will explore, it can shorten it considerably.

We also need to discuss ways to extend our prime, because living longer is not good enough. We need to live well for longer.

Part One of the book, 'This is our time', explores all of these elements of living well in our second half, from attitudes to ageism to making this prime time last as long as possible.

Part Two of the book is all about change, as this is the time of our lives when almost everything seems to be changing or is about to change. We are entering a phase when multiple life-altering changes will all be happening at the same time – at work, at home and within – and sometimes we need help to see these changes as the opportunities that they are.

We compare the menopause with the much paler male midlife crisis that a friend of ours once labelled 'MenoPorsche'. We discuss how so many of our relationships are changing: our relationships with our partners, our parents and our children are all entering new phases. We are the sandwich generation. Our kids are returning to roost, finding it tough to get on the first rungs of either the career or housing ladders, and our parents are, generally, living longer.

But Part Two of the book doesn't merely talk about *coping* with change, it provides you with proven, tried and trusted techniques for *embracing* it, drawing from my decades of helping business leaders to lead sustainable change, and our joint experience in helping individuals to cope with and embrace personal change. I run workshops, webinars and online courses with employees on the subject based on my second book, *The Power to Change* (Kogan Page 2020). Jane helps her one-on-one yoga therapy and private yoga clients to cope with and accept change in an even more powerful way; and the topic is the ever-present, subtle subtext that runs through every one of her classes, workshops and retreats.

We obviously had to talk about the word I try my best to avoid saying out loud: 'retirement'. So, we kick off Part Three, 'Rethinking the "R word"', with a discussion about how an increasing number of us are redefining the concept completely. 'Retirement' no longer means either stopping or fading relevance. In fact, as we shall see, the traditional concept of retirement can be bad for your health, even life-shortening! For many, *not* retiring is a financial necessity, for others it is a choice. For more than a few of us, it is a little bit of both.

More of us are continuing to work deeper into our second half than ever before. More of us are changing jobs, even careers, later in life – sometimes several times. More of us are becoming self-employed – through redundancy, personal choice or both. An increasing number of us would like to start our own business, but we are hesitant to take the plunge. Part Three explores all of these topics, including why older workers are invaluable, the fact that older entrepreneurs are more successful and how to start your own business. We have also included some stories and tips from a trio of successful second half entrepreneurs.

Part Four is about an issue that the whole world needs to come to terms with, and the majority of us will need to address in some shape or form: the challenge of finding and funding aged care – for our parents and perhaps one day for each other or ourselves (gulp).

Of course, we all need to fund our second half, so Part Five of the book is a collection of tools, tips and observations on the subject of money from someone who has been working in and with the financial services industry for much of the last thirty years. Its purpose is to de-mystify the world of financial services and money as much as possible. We discuss financial planning for the second half in the chapter called 'And then a miracle happens'. We talk about pensions and the lack of them for many of the post-Boomer generations. I suggest keeping things simple, mixing it up, not panicking, paying attention to fees and finding an adviser you trust. We end the Money section exploring why so many financial services firms have got it so wrong in the past and an introduction to a few of the firms that I have admired after three decades of hovering around the industry.

In Part Six, we come back to you: your purpose, your goals, your strengths, your weaknesses, your opportunities and, if you wish, your plan for a simply sublime second half.

This book is designed to help you to pause and reflect; to help you determine what you want from your next act and to start to make it happen.

We hope it is valuable. We hope it contains more than a few useful nuggets of insight for you as you think about your Part Two.

But most of all, we hope you enjoy it.

Campbell and Jane.

PART ONE:

This is our time

'Tell me, what is it you plan to do
with your one wild and precious life?'
Mary Oliver, 'The Summer Day'[1]

We are setting off on a new adventure, equipped with decades of experience and unshackled by outdated misconceptions relating to age and vitality. We have spent Part One experiencing, perhaps even learning.

Part Two is our time to shine.

In these chapters we will explore how now is the perfect time to pause for reflection, the fact that age is only a number and that with the right attitude we can combat or simply ignore the subtle and not-so-subtle ageism that is rife within Western societies and live long, healthy and fulfilling lives.

[1] American poet and Pulitzer Prize winner (1935–2019).

CHAPTER 1:

Interval

'For a month, Michelle and I slept late, ate leisurely dinners, went for long walks, swam in the ocean, took stock, replenished our friendship, rediscovered our love, and planned for a less eventful but hopefully no less satisfying second act.'

Barack Obama, *A Promised Land* [1]

Is it half time already? How on earth did that happen?

We don't feel any different, do we? Well, not on the inside anyway. That young dreamer is still there, a little buried perhaps under layers of time and experience. But he's still there. She's still there. They're still there. Recently, I caught sight of myself in the mirror as I was leaving the house on my way to a client meeting and time froze for a few seconds. I was taken aback by the person who returned my gaze: the laugh-lines, the converging wrinkles either side of the eyes, the corrugated brow, the greying temples, the receding hairline and yet the undimmed brightness of eyes I recognised from long ago. It was the face of someone with experience; someone who looked as though they knew what they were doing. 'So that's how others see me!' I proclaimed aloud. And chuckled at the revelation.

We all need moments like these. Moments to pause, to reflect, to take stock. Now is the perfect moment.

It's like an interval at the theatre; that point of the evening when we visit the bathroom, stop by the bar for some refreshments and take a few minutes to reflect upon the first act of the show before wondering what may unfold during the second. We can guess what may happen in Act Two. We can extrapolate personality traits and behaviours we have

---

[1] USA's 44th President (1961–). From the opening paragraph in his book, *A Promised Land* (Viking 2020).

seen the characters display in the first half, but we are bound to be wrong. The second act inevitably serves up a few twists and turns that we didn't see coming. It rarely turns out as we had expected. And it is almost always more exciting.

This book is your interval.

In this particular show, you are the main character. To some degree, you are also the director – but with far less control over the actors than the kind you'd find on Broadway. You can influence the action on stage, but you can't control it. Once the curtain rises and the lights blink into action, the actors are on their own.

The first act was setting the scene, developing the characters and commencing the narrative. The second act is where it all happens – full of new experiences, highs, lows, love, laughter, joy, fear, passion and tragedy.

There is absolutely nothing we can do about the first half. It's gone. It's over. The good, the bad and the ugly are all in the past. Some of their ghosts will inevitably linger in the background of our lives and their impact may even be felt influencing our thoughts and decisions, but they only really exist in our memories, in our minds. The degree of influence that these memories have over what we do in our second half is entirely up to us. We can keep them in the past where they belong, or we can drag them around like an anchor weighing us down – it is our choice. The great decisions we have made, the damn awful decisions we have made, the triumphs, the howlers, the agonies and the ecstasies . . . there is nothing we can do about any of them. All we can do is learn whatever we can from our multitude of experiences and move on. And move on we should – because this is our time.

Obviously, this is not always easy to do. For some, past experiences are so horrible, so unfair and so life-altering that their influence will be ever-present. But even these, with a great deal of help, can be put into perspective. Whatever is in our past, none of it need define us.

I met a taxi driver in Vegas in 2018 and the encounter will stay fresh in my memory for a long time. Dawn was breaking as I strode out of the Aria hotel, where I had given a conference speech the night before. I was dragging my suitcase, heading for the airport. At the taxi rank stood a battered yellow cab and out of it clambered the most dishevelled cabbie

I have ever seen. He was dressed in a filthy track suit and looked as though he had spent the entire night in his taxi's boot. His unwashed hair radiated from his scalp as if it was trying to escape and he sported a thick, brush-like grey moustache. My first thought was, *Boy, The Lorax[2] has fallen on hard times!*

During the fifteen-minute ride to the airport, he told me his life story. 'I suppose you are wondering why I am drinking water,' was his opening remark as he took a swig out of a two-litre bottle. I wasn't. Drinking water wasn't the most outlandish thing I had seen in this town, to be honest.

'I used to be twice the weight I am now. I had a terrible childhood, abusive father, God-awful family life. I was on all sorts of drugs and drinking two bottles of vodka a day. I would go through at least two of these big bottles of Coke every day, too. I was a mess.' This wasn't the casual conversation I had expected at 6:05 in the morning as the sun slowly rose above The Strip. I was suddenly very much awake.

'So, what happened?' I asked. 'What made you change?'

'You know,' he mused. 'I was fifty-three and I just woke up one day and thought: *It's about time I stopped blaming my parents for everything!* So, I threw all my drugs away, threw my booze away and I have drunk nothing but water ever since.' He then went on to talk about how he only had four teeth left and was saving up for some new ones.

Thankfully, most of us have been luckier in life than my new taxi-driver friend. We have blundered through the innocence of childhood, the confusing insecurity of adolescence, the fake adulthood and experimentation of our late teens and the mad indestructibility of our twenties. We may also have been lucky enough to experience the zombie-like fog of young parenthood and the bittersweet joy of sharing a house with teenagers who are simultaneously trying to discover who they are while utterly convinced that their parents know absolutely nothing.

When we get to the age we are now, we have discovered what we are good at and what we are spectacularly bad at. We have taken on multiple new identities, new labels: girlfriend, boyfriend, sports person,

---

[2] One of my favourite Dr Seuss creations, The Lorax is a little character with the most preposterous moustache and a mischievous but knowing glint in his eye. He 'speaks for the trees' and confronts The Once-ler, who is bent on environmental destruction. *The Lorax*, Dr Seuss (Random House, 1971).

swot, student, clown, artist, musician, actor, dancer, wallflower, professional, partner, wife, husband, father, mother, teacher, friend, enemy, winner, loser. We have made friends and we have lost friends. We have forged careers, often in completely the wrong direction. We have made money. We have lost money. We have done things we regret, and we have done things we are proud of. We have loved and lost and loved again. Perhaps many times. And we have come through it all, not completely unscathed – where would be the fun in that – but we have come through it, nonetheless.

With this treasure trove of experience, knowledge and hopefully at least one or two nuggets of wisdom firmly in the bank, we can now turn to face a future that is ours. Ours for the making. Ours for the taking.

The interval is the time to pause and reflect before cracking on with the second half.

It may be the time to take stock of our relationships, our physical health, our mental well-being. It could be time to assess our current choice of career, our work–life balance, what makes us happy, what's important to us, what isn't, what we think about ourselves and why, our habits, where we live, how we live, why we live.

It is certainly the time to review what we would ideally like to see in Act Two. It is also the time to take stock of our financial situation – as boring and as daunting as that phrase may sound.

And while we do all of this, we must suspend judgement of ourselves. We need an honest appraisal of where we are now before we can sketch out any sort of flexible plan for our future – but one without recriminations or blame. 'Flexible' being the operative word. Because the only thing that is certain in the future is uncertainty. Let's not forget that alongside every successful plan with its diligent preparation and hard work sits a massive dollop of fortune. Yes, we do make our own luck to a certain degree. As Tiger Woods once said, 'The harder I practise, the luckier I get.' But it is equally true that stuff just happens –good things happen to bad people and bad things happen to good people. Things happen that no amount of planning can possibly predict or prevent. Any plan we may compile for the next few decades cannot possibly be a roadmap, as the road is yet to be laid. Any plot we sketch out for Act Two is guaranteed not to go as planned. But a general direction of preferred travel; a general synopsis of the second act – yes, that may be helpful.

However, planning is not for everybody. In seeking input for this book, a good friend of ours replied, 'I see life as "minority: action; majority: reaction" with massive side-orders of luck, opportunism and serendipity.' To Jim, the most important thing about life is how you react to the challenges and opportunities it throws your way. He makes a profound point.

If you concur with Jim and the very thought of a 'plan', however flexible it may be, seems utterly pointless to you, then perhaps what you want is a philosophy, an attitude, an approach to life that underpins your thoughts, your feelings and your reactions to the inevitable opportunities, challenges and changes that will come your way throughout the second, magical half of your life.

If that last paragraph is more you, then rather than asking yourself 'What would I like to achieve in the second half?', it may be far better to ponder 'How do I want to feel about myself? When I am sitting on the proverbial rocking chair in another forty or fifty years, what memory will make me smile; what will I be most proud of; what will I regret not having done?'

But no matter if we are detailed planners or radical acceptors, we could all take this time to pause and ask ourselves:

- What do I want to *change* in the second half?
- What do I want to *keep* in the second half?
- What do I want *less* of? What do I want *more* of?
- What do I want to *do* less of? What do I want to *do* more of?

Because this is our opportunity to change. And change is inevitable.

After reading this book, you may decide that no adjustments are required. Alternatively, you may come to the conclusion that this is indeed the moment for dramatic transformation. The decision is entirely up to you. There is no right answer.

Are you looking forward to the second half with excitement? If not, why not? You are well and vital with years of experience that you can leverage to write several new and exciting chapters.

Are you looking forward to the second half with a little

apprehension? If you weren't, you wouldn't be human. After all, even good change is tough. New challenges, new purposes, new roles, new directions all sound very exciting but how do I prepare? Where do I start? How do I fund this? How do I make it happen? Do I have the energy?

Every silver lining has a cloud. What concerns you most when it comes to the second half of your life? Money? Relationships? Unfulfilled success (however you define that ethereal concept)? Your social standing? A change of identity? Finding a new sense of purpose? Changing careers? Your family's happiness? Taking care of your parents? Staying well yourself? Staying mentally agile? Or simply staying sober like my Vegas taxi driver?

And what dreams do you have for this exciting new chapter?

Are they *grandiose dreams* of incredible career success, global travel, fame and fortune?

Are they *grand dreams* of a loving, life-long relationship and contentment? Are they dreams of helping your children through education, secure a foothold on the job ladder and get on their way? Perhaps of enjoying future grandchildren?

Are they *exciting dreams* of starting your own business; of quitting your job and doing something completely different?

Are they *calmer dreams* of doing less, appreciating life and enjoying the moments?

Or are they simply dreams of financial survival, caring for ageing parents and searching for ways to fund it all?

Perhaps they are none of the above. Perhaps they are a combination of several of them.

Whatever your dreams may be for the second half of your life, this is a book about facing the future with confidence. It is about overcoming obstacles. It is about coping with, embracing and even instigating personal change. It's about thriving in the second half.

This isn't the beginning of the end. It's merely the end of the beginning.

Bring it on!

CHAPTER 2:

It's only a number

'Age is a just an abbreviation for experience.'
Spoken by a BBC news reporter whose name we didn't capture

There is nothing stopping us from reinventing ourselves at forty, fifty, sixty, seventy or any age – apart from ourselves.

Sure, we are physically slower than we once were – a truth we have no choice but to accept. This fact was hammered home to me in fine style in April of 2020 as I left the house for a mid-pandemic 5km run. Well, slow jog as it turned out. A couple of kilometres into it, I was thinking how pleased I was with how I was doing: no aches and pains, the plantar fasciitis was behaving itself, no twinges in the knees, the ankles were faring well without the ankle braces, the rhythm was good, the speed was good. Or so I thought. With no warning whatsoever, I was overtaken by a tall hipster in his early twenties lolloping gracefully past me, sweat-free, dancing on the balls of his feet, earphones firmly embedded and completely oblivious to the rapidly deflating ego of the fifty-something he had left so effortlessly in his wake.

And it is not just our physical speed that declines with age. Our problem-solving skills, our conceptual reasoning ability, our memory and our brain's processing speed have all been on a steady decline since our early twenties. BBC Two's *Horizon* episode 'The Great British Intelligence Test', which aired on 4 May 2020, examined the responses of more than 250,000 people to an interactive online quiz and, with the help of researchers from the Department of Brain Sciences at Imperial College London, showed how our problem-solving and conceptual reasoning skills peak in our twenties and then decline steadily and continually as we get older. It found that the average forty-year-old has the same pure problem-solving abilities as a twelve-year-old! The worse news is that our ability to solve problems declines even further beyond forty.

Yet if we think about it, we already know this. Who do we call when we can't get the Smart TV to do what we want? A teenager. Who do we call when we can't work out how to get our recurring Zoom webinar to record automatically, in HD, in Speaker view and starting with everyone muted except for our panel of experts? A twenty-something.

So, with the danger of plagiarising that scene from *Monty Python's Life of Brian*: apart from a decline in physical strength, physical speed, the ability to recover from injuries, problem-solving skills, conceptual reasoning capabilities, memory and our brain's processing speed ... What has ageing ever done for us?!

Well luckily, problem-solving and decision-making in the real world also requires experience and insight. Twenty-somethings may possess superior cognitive capability, but they lack the knowledge, context and experience to know whether their proposed solution is even vaguely feasible. Our synapses may be firing at a slightly lower rate than they once did, but we know a rubbish idea when we hear one.

At least we think we do, for experience can also be a barrier to change. I have seen this many times in the world of business: older, experienced managers dismissing new ideas with the phrase, 'We tried that ten years ago.' Not helpful. Perhaps the newbie has a different spin on what was attempted a decade previously. Perhaps the time wasn't right ten years ago, and circumstances have changed. Sometimes with experience comes complacency, sometimes even a touch of arrogance, or fear. We look back on our twenty-year-old self and realise how little they knew. So, we automatically think the twenty-something standing in front of us today knows naff-all as well. That is completely the wrong way to think about it. The fact they don't yet know what they don't know could be an advantage.

Richard Branson has a term for it: 'intelligent naivety'. The inherent complacency that comes with experience infects all successful organisations and industries. Virgin was able to exploit this phenomenon by entering established industries with new, customer-centric businesses with the simple thought that there must a better way. All innovators do this – Uber, Tesla, Microsoft, Airbnb, Netflix, Huffington Post, Lenovo, Amazon, Google, Soho House, the list goes on.

While writing this, I had what Jane calls a 'BGO', a Blinding Glimpse of the Obvious. Why don't all companies set up 'problem-solving units' or 'innovation hubs' comprising a swarm of excited twenty-somethings with synapses firing rapidly in all directions, loosely shepherded by a couple of seasoned execs? But few do. Executives in successful, market-dominating organisations involuntarily kick back against anything that could alter the status quo, because they know that innovation inevitably means disruption and that disruption could spell short-term disaster for their careers – and their share options. It may be the right thing for the long-term future and value of the company but in my experience, not enough leaders genuinely think about the long term – especially the closer they get to the end of their career.

It also screams to me that if we want to start our own businesses, we should form a mutually respectful partnership with a twenty-something. We would be unstoppable.

FIT FOR LIFE

Meanwhile, other research suggests that if we look after ourselves, there is not that much difference between a forty-year-old brain and the brain of an eighty-year-old. Argye Hillis MD, the director of Johns Hopkins Cerebrovascular Center (she studies blood flow in the brain – I looked it up), tracked six thousand people aged between forty-four and eighty-four over seven years. She found that those who made positive life changes – those who, for example, had stopped smoking, followed a Mediterranean diet, did regular exercise and maintained a healthy weight – decreased their chances of dying in the time period by 80 per cent. Eighty per cent! If we add to that list quality sleep, continually challenging our brains, adopting a positive mental attitude and enhancing our resilience to change, we can help to slow down the ageing process even further – on the inside and the outside. It is the inside that really matters.

The link between lifestyle and longevity makes complete sense, seeing that some of the biggest killers for those of us between the ages of fifty and sixty-four are lifestyle related. The top six killers include heart disease, respiratory diseases, cirrhosis and other diseases of the liver, cancer of the colon, lung cancer and breast cancer. The good news is that we are statistically too old to die of testicular cancer or suffer from dysmenorrhea or lupus. Every cloud . . .

Gym membership among us 'second halfers' has increased significantly. In fact, Nuffield Health reports that the over sixty-fives are their most frequent gym users.[1] Just step into any health club outside of a city centre and you will find that the spin classes and weights rooms, the swimming pools and cardio areas are teeming with people in their forties, fifties, sixties and beyond. A fact that hit me front-on a few months back when I burst into the men's changing room of our local gym to be greeted full-frontal, close-up and personal by a gentleman who was well into his seventies standing tall and proud, stark-bollock naked, dressed in nothing but his socks and sandals. To this day, I have no idea whether he was in the process of getting dressed and decided to start with his footwear, whether he was getting undressed and somehow managed to remove his trousers and Y-fronts over his Birkenstocks in some personal homage to Mr Bean, or another even stranger third process that I am yet to mentally untangle.

The very next day, we bought a running machine for home.

Yoga has never been more popular, and not only because of its incredible physical benefits. The number of Americans practising yoga has doubled to almost 40 million since 2012. Another 40 million say they intend to.[2] Yoga in Japan is up four-fold in just five years, and more than half a million Brits now practise yoga regularly. It's not just women; more than one in four yogis are men. Robert Downey Jr., Woody Harrelson, David Beckham, Colin Farrell, Matthew McConaughey, Jon Bon Jovi, Ryan Giggs, Barack Obama . . . when these guys start to talk about 'getting on their mats' and the career-prolonging and life-affirming benefits of yoga – even we mere mortals start to take notice.

As a gang, we are fitter, more energetic, younger at heart and better prepared to meet life's challenges, according to research commissioned by SunLife UK of fifty thousand people aged fifty and over.[3] On average,

[1] https://www.nuffieldhealth.com/article/rise-of-the-active-over-65s-figures-show-those-aged-72-are-uks-most-regular-gym-users
[2] https://bookretreats.com/blog/yoga-statistics
[3] SunLife's 'Big 50' online research of 50,004 individuals aged between fifty and seventy-five conducted by Critical Research between November 2016 and January 2017.

the respondents felt ten years younger mentally and four years younger physically than their current age. Mind you, how they came to that conclusion is beyond me, but let's go with it anyway. Almost two-thirds declared they had more time and enjoyed life more than they used to. The majority were more relaxed and had more money to spend on themselves. I have a feeling those last two might be related. But best of all, 78 per cent said they now cared much less about what others think. Love it.

Forty-six per cent said that life was more exciting. It is.

And it will probably be longer, too.

INTO OUR EIGHTIES – AND BEYOND!

Human life expectancy has more than doubled in the last 120 years. Thanks to clean water, immunisation, antibiotics, better nutrition, globalisation, enhanced medical treatments and techniques, improved agriculture methods, our ability to get food to parts of the world that need it and, believe it or not, far fewer deaths from war (well since 1945 anyway), average global life expectancy has soared from not much more than thirty-two in 1900 to more than seventy-two today.[4]

The rise in life expectancy in some countries has plateaued over the last few years thanks mainly to an epidemic of obesity (more than 40 per cent of American adults are obese and the numbers in Australia and the UK are nearing 30 per cent, whereas mainland Europe is in the low 20s). Life expectancy may continue to plateau for a few years thanks to COVID-19. As I write this, the official global death toll from COVID-19 has exceeded 3.2 million people at a median age of eighty-two.

But global pandemics and obesity notwithstanding, the magic of immunotherapy, gene therapy and further enhancements in medical care will surely see life expectancy increase further in the future. Take, for example, advances in the way medical professionals deal with strokes: the mortality rate for this condition has halved in just ten years. We are now able to replace faulty heart valves without open-heart surgery, enabling people in their late eighties to receive this life-prolonging operation. According to an article published in the medical journal, *The Lancet*, in 2009, every second baby born today in industrialised nations should expect to live to one hundred.

[4] https://ourworldindata.org/life-expectancy

Obviously, increases in life expectancy have not been uniform across the world. Average lifespans in a few parts of Africa are still hovering in the fifties while your average Japanese woman can expect to live to eighty-seven. The mean in South Korea is eighty-four. It's seventy-seven in China and only slightly higher in the USA. Throughout much of Europe, Australia and New Zealand, the average life expectancy is in the low eighties. Why women live longer than men is a great mystery to me. In Jane's case, I assume it will be from living such a stress-free, calm, no-surprises life! (Though Jane says she hates to disappoint me, but it's the yoga.)

When it comes to life expectancy, the USA lags conspicuously behind its peers. The average forty-five-year-old American male can expect to live to seventy-nine[5] while the average forty-five-year-old Australian male can expect to live to eighty-two[6], according to both nations' official actuarial tables. The OECD ranks Australia as ninth in the world in terms of average life expectancy while the US, the richest and most powerful nation in the world, comes in way down at number twenty-eight.[7]

While differences in obesity rates may account for a tiny part of the gap, perhaps the main reason why the US is ranked so low in terms of life expectancy is its mystifying obsession with not having a universal public health system. The US healthcare system is the most expensive system in the Western world.[8] The 'land of the free' spends almost twice as much per capita on healthcare than Canada, Germany, Australia, the UK, Japan, Sweden, France, the Netherlands, Switzerland or Denmark.[9] And yet, the system obviously fails so many of its people. The obscene costs and insurance-based nature of the heavily privatised US healthcare system can be an early death sentence for those who can't afford health insurance; and if you lose your job, odds are you either lose your health insurance or can no longer afford to keep it going. Unemployment can increase the cost of insurance more than four-fold, according to the

[5] https://www.ssa.gov/oact/STATS/table4c6.html
[6] https://www.aihw.gov.au/reports/life-expectancy-death/deaths/contents/life-expectancy
[7] https://data.oecd.org/healthstat/life-expectancy-at-birth.htm#indicator-chart
[8] https://www.hsph.harvard.edu/news/hsph-in-the-news/the-most-expensive-health-care-system-in-the-world
[9] https://www.cnbc.com/2018/03/22/the-real-reason-medical-care-costs-so-much-more-in-the-us.html

Kaiser Family Foundation,[10] and the cost of healthcare for someone who does not have insurance can be outrageous. So outrageous that a diagnosis of cancer can also mean a diagnosis of bankruptcy, or premature death, or both. In 2019, 25 per cent of US adults reported that they had skipped medical care because they couldn't afford it.[11] And that was before forty-two million Americans filed for unemployment benefits during the first wave of the COVID-19 lockdown.[12] And yet there remains an ingrained aversion to 'socialist medicine' (as a board member of one of my American clients labelled Britain's NHS in a discussion over dinner one night) among so many otherwise caring Americans. I will simply never understand it.

But assuming we have a few shekels put away for a rainy day, have access to good healthcare and are capable of eating well, exercising and keeping our minds and brains healthy, we are likely to live long lives well into our eighties, perhaps even beyond.

The critical thing is to stay as well as possible for as long as possible. The older we get, the more essential it is that we look after ourselves. Living longer sounds wonderful. Living longer with mobility issues, health issues or advanced dementia does not.

Our grandparents were old at fifty

Think back to your grandparents when they were the age you are now. They were old! When I look at photographs of my grandparents when they were in their fifties, I am astonished at how old and old-fashioned they were. They looked like old people. They certainly dressed like old people. They had the air of a generation that was winding down. Mind you, I think my grandfather was born looking old. Old, kind and lovely. I can still smell him if I close my eyes. It's a musty, safe smell infused with clouds of roll-your-own tobacco. And of fresh tomatoes on the vine. I can still hear his warm chuckles and feel his bony frame as I hugged him. He died in his late seventies after twenty years of gasping for air due to smoking-induced emphysema. I am surprised he hung on for that long.

[10] https://money.usnews.com/money/personal-finance/family-finance/articles/how-to-get-health-insurance-when-youre-unemployed
[11] Federal Reserve Board issues Report on the Economic Well-Being of U.S. Households. 14 May 2020.
[12] https://fortune.com/2020/06/04/us-unemployment-rate-numbers-claims-this-week-total-job-losses-june-4-2020-benefits-claims

He was six foot one and a half tall and as thin as a beanpole. My grandmother was four foot ten, no matter which way you looked at her. They made quite a couple.

Nanna lived into her nineties and she pretty much looked and acted the same way for the entire second half of her life. She had a highly entertaining naughty streak that may have been one of the things that kept her going for so long. It was just before her eightieth birthday when Nanna first met Jane and she thought it would be hilarious if she greeted us at her front door in her bra and knickers. 'Put them away, Nan!' I laughed. 'And put some clothes on!' She then proceeded to hold Jane's hands in one of her hers while patting the other in a consoling manner and declared to my soon-to-be-fiancée, 'Campbell's last girlfriend was such a lady.' I could fill a book with mad memories and the 'Nanna-isms' of my delightfully barmy grandmother. Throughout her life, or at least the forty years of it for which I was around, she would simply say whatever she wanted, whenever she wanted – and the older she got the more she got away with. In her late sixties she was diagnosed with a massive brain tumour but even its removal didn't slow down the off-beam, often outrageous comments. In the last few months of her life, she described her latest morning routine to me. She would wake by first opening just one eye. Then she would tentatively take a look around until she realised where she was and that she was still with us. Once those facts had sunk in, the first word of her day would be: 'Damn!' Upon confessing that to me, we both burst into laughter.

My grandmother may have already looked old to a younger me when she was in her forties and fifties, but in terms of her attitude and behaviour, she didn't age one bit throughout all the decades I knew her. Which made we wonder: How old is old?

How old is 'old'?

According to the WHO, old age starts at sixty. Most European countries peg the start at around sixty-five.[13] What a load of nonsense!

The World Economic Forum (WEF) recently redefined old age as beginning once you have fifteen years left to live. This means that in Sierra Leone, old age starts in your late thirties and a Japanese woman

---

[13] https://www.agedcareguide.com.au/talking-aged-care/what-age-is-considered-old

won't enter old age until she is in her seventies. While I guess that actuaries and statisticians may find that definition enlightening, I am not all that sure what to do with it.

The definition of 'old' obviously depends upon who you ask. People in their twenties and thirties reckon that old age starts at fifty-nine, according to a 2017 study by US Trust.[14] People in their forties are more inclined to agree with Europe and say that old age starts at sixty-five, whereas those of us in our fifties and beyond reckon that we won't be old until well into our seventies. It seems that the younger you are, the likelier you are to think that old age starts well before it actually does. The consequences of this understandable but incorrect assumption pervade too many societies across the globe, as we will discuss. It is bad for the health of our nations, and the health and longevity of all of us as we get older.

Dr Sergei Scherbov, author and lead researcher of a multiyear study on ageing, states in his book *Prospective Longevity: A New Vision of Population Aging*[15] that the definition of 'old' has changed as lifespans have increased. 'Someone who is sixty years old today is middle-aged,' writes Dr Scherbov. His view is that for Americans, old age roughly starts at seventy for men and seventy-three for women, although 'your true age is not just the number of years you have lived.' He goes on to say that 'today's sixty-five-year-old is more like a fifty-five-year-old from forty-five years ago.'

Frankly, his conclusion should have been that numbers are irrelevant as they only prompt us to make meaningless comparisons. I am also surprised that it took a multiyear study to arrive at his startlingly obvious conclusions. Sergei was born in 1952. He will be seventy soon.

He could have just asked his friends.

[14] https://www.nytimes.com/2018/12/13/well/mind/age-aging-old-young-psychology.html
[15] Warren C. Sanderson & Sergei Scherbov. Harvard University Press, 19 November 2019.

CHAPTER 3:

Ageism: the biggest 'ism' of them all?

'Young people are just smarter.'
Mark Zuckerberg, CEO Facebook

'If the global "over-fifties" population were a sovereign state ... it would be the third-biggest economy in the world and ... growing the fastest,' declares Mary Bright, Age Adviser and Public Policy Manager of The Phoenix Group, the UK's largest long-term savings and retirement provider.[1]

And yet, ageism is everywhere.

A recent report commissioned by the Royal Society for Public Health[2] decreed that 'ageism is the most commonly experienced form of prejudice and discrimination in the UK and Europe'. It is a similar story in so many other Anglo-Saxon countries. Incidentally, ageism appears to be nowhere near as prevalent in many Caribbean nations or Asian nations where older people are valued; where respect for, and care of, elders are integral parts of the way people in those societies think and operate.

This was a bold statement by the Royal Society: declaring that ageism is more common than racism, sexism or all of the other 'isms' used to describe discrimination on the basis of sexual preference, disability, choice of religion ... the lot!

Yet the World Health Organization concurs. Its 'Global Report on Ageism'[3], published in March 2021, declared that every second person in the world is believed to hold ageist attitudes – leading to poorer physical and mental health and reduced quality of life for older people, and costing societies billions of dollars a year.

[1] International Longevity Centre UK webinar 'Why is longevity important to business?' 17 September 2020
[2] https://www.rsph.org.uk/static/uploaded/a01e3aa7-9356-40bc-99c81b14dd904a41.pdf
[3] https://www.who.int/news/item/18-03-2021-ageism-is-a-global-challenge-un

A 2020 study in the US estimated that ageism in the form of negative age stereotypes and self-perceptions led to excess annual costs of US$63 billion for the eight most expensive health conditions.

The UN report also cites Australian estimates that if 5 per cent more people aged fifty-five or older were employed, there would be a positive impact of AUD$48 billion on the national economy annually.

The land of my birth seems to have a surprisingly negative attitude towards ageing, even though average life expectancy in Australia is one of the highest in the world. Only 29 per cent of Australians are optimistic about ageing compared to a global average that is still low at 33 per cent, according to www.agedcareguide.com.au. I wonder why. Every nation has its myths. Perhaps the image of the fit Aussie surfers, world-class sportspeople and rugged jackeroos and jillaroos have seeped so deeply into the national psyche that it colours all other ideas of what an Australian should look like.

AgedCareGuide.com.au reported that more than half of Aussies say they are worried about ageing, even though almost three-quarters also say they are prepared for old age. So, they are prepared – but worried, nonetheless.

Of course, it's not just Australia. As the UN has discovered repeatedly, negative attitudes toward older people are widespread across the globe. According to a 2015 survey by the World Health Organization, nearly two-thirds of the eighty-three thousand people they polled of all ages from fifty-seven countries 'did not respect older people and the lowest levels of respect were found in wealthier Western nations such as the US'. The WHO also commented that older people pick up on this pervasive ageism and it affects their physical and mental health.

'It is time to stop defining people by their age,' wrote John Beard, WHO's director of ageing and life-course in 2015, then aged sixty. Oops. Couldn't help myself.

COVID-19 LAID BARE THE PERVASIVE AND INSIDIOUS NATURE OF CASUAL AGEISM

The number of deaths in the UK during the first quarter of 2020 was no different to the average of the last five years for that time of year. But then COVID-19 hit and more than sixty-three thousand 'excess deaths' were recorded across the United Kingdom during April and May.[4] Roughly a third of the deaths that were directly attributed to coronavirus occurred in care homes. This was no unlucky accident. It was a direct consequence of government policy, which in turn was fuelled by casual ageism.

The government of the United Kingdom's initial coronavirus 'strategy' seemed to have consisted of two main strands:

1. Strand one: Hope the virus was not much worse than the flu, and

2. Strand two: Protect hospitals from becoming overwhelmed if it turned out that the virus was actually as bad as China, Italy and Iran were reporting.

Strand one didn't work out too well. It turns out the virus was much worse than the flu – especially for the elderly. The first British death attributed to COVID-19 was reported on 2 March 2020. Over the following three months, the official death toll of those who had tested positive for the virus in England and Wales alone reached forty-six thousand, although the Office of National Statistics' 'excess deaths' figure of 63,629 may be a more accurate picture of the carnage across the United Kingdom during March, April and May of 2020.

The countries that managed to keep death rates from the virus relatively low typically shut their borders to non-citizens in March 2020 and, at the time of writing more than twelve months later, don't look like re-opening their borders until mid 2022. They placed returning citizens into strict, hotel-based quarantine and instigated detailed testing and tracing programmes that worked. In contrast, the UK kept its borders wide open and only began a limited hotel quarantine programme on 15 February 2021. It even abandoned its nascent mass testing and tracing programme in March of 2020 for six weeks, leaving the virus free to roam the country without detection. As I write this in May 2021, the UK's test and trace system is on track to cost the taxpayer an unfathomable £37bn (unfortunately that is not a typo) and it still doesn't seem to work properly. The intensive care units have been full of COVID-19 patients

[4] https://www.theguardian.com/society/2020/jun/09/excess-deaths-in-uk-under-coronavirus-lockdown-pass-63000

once again and the government's official death toll from the virus has exceeded 127,000. The number of deaths where COVID-19 was registered on the death certificate is even higher. The government has presided over one of the worst, if not the worst, death rate in the world[5] and the worst economic retraction of the G7 group of nations, despite borrowing more than any major country apart from Canada. That is quite a set of achievements.

But it is strand two of the strategy that I want to focus on here, as it demonstrated just how rife and deadly casual ageism can be. The objective of strand two was achieved during the first wave of COVID-19: hospitals weren't overwhelmed, even in spite of a decade of under-investment. But this short-lived, pyrrhic victory was only attained because the majority of COVID-19 victims during the first wave in March, April and May of 2020 died at home or in care homes, untested and without appropriate equipment or professional care.

To free up hospital beds for the potential onslaught, 25,000 old people, many of whom were suspected to have the virus, were despatched from hospital and sent back to their care homes between 17 March and 15 April alone. Not only were very few returning patients tested for the virus, government guidance was to send them back even if they were known to be infected. 'Negative tests are not required prior to transfers or admissions into the care home' was the official government advice to hospitals prior to 15 April.[6] The government didn't care whether or not returning patients had the coronavirus, a disease that was already known to be highly contagious and deadly to old people*, they were heading back.

> ** And the danger to the elderly was already well known. As early as February 2020, China reported a fatality rate of 20 per cent among eighty-year-olds, 10 per cent among seventy-year-olds and 5 per cent among those in their sixties, compared to 0.4 per cent for people in their forties, 0.2 per cent for those in their thirties and 0.1 per cent for*

---

[5] https://www.independent.co.uk/news/health/uk-covid-death-rate-coronavirus-b1788817.html
[6] https://fullfact.org/health/coronavirus-care-homes-discharge/

twenty-somethings. On 4 March 2020, Italy reported that the average age of the first 105 Italians to die was eighty-one.[7]

With minimal Personal Protective Equipment and no tests available for care home residents or staff, the virus spread like wildfire, killing an estimated twenty-nine thousand elderly residents across Britain between 2 March and 12 June, according to the Office of National Statistics,[8] and more than a hundred younger carers as well. To be blunt, care home residents simply didn't feature on the government's list of priorities. Even if the decision to send elderly people back into their care homes had been made after weighing up all of the pros and cons rather than in a state of panic or unthinking complacency, it remains a stark reminder of the degree to which casual ageism has infected our society.

If you close your eyes, you can hear that awful phrase; a phrase that is no less awful for being true: 'I mean, let's face it, they've had a pretty good innings ...'

AGEISM IN THE WORKPLACE

Our population is ageing. Our workforces are ageing. Across much of the West and China, the number of people aged between twenty and forty-nine is set to remain relatively flat over the next decade while the number of those of us over fifty will continue to rise. If they can, people are remaining in work for longer. There are now more older workers in Britain than younger workers. A third of workers in Britain and the US were aged fifty and above as of early 2020, while fewer than a quarter of workers were aged between twenty-five and thirty-four. The percentage of over-seventies in either full- or part-time employment has almost doubled in the last decade.

An older workforce is the workforce of the future. And yet, more than two-thirds of companies consider older age a competitive *dis*advantage, according to a recent HBR and Deloitte survey of over ten thousand companies. This floored me! No wonder 41 per cent of workers

---

[7] https://www.vox.com/2020/3/12/21173783/coronavirus-death-age-COVID-19-elderly-seniors
[8] https://www.bbc.co.uk/news/uk-53280011

in their fifties believe that 'age discrimination in the workplace is a serious issue'.[9] It is!

I simply don't understand why employers are not taking full advantage of their more experienced employees. *HR Magazine* reports that almost three-quarters of workers in their fifties and sixties believe they share valuable skills, experience and knowledge with their colleagues, but only 16 per cent said this was valued by their employers.[10] Which is not only bad for business but utterly hypocritical given that the average age of a Fortune 500 CEO at the time they are hired is fifty-seven according to recent research by *Business Insider*.

Employers need to get a grip. They are missing out on a wealth of knowledge, experience and energy. They need to confront this issue head-on and treat their experienced employees as valued mentors. They need to design age-diverse teams as we hinted earlier. Some have begun to do just this. According to an HBR article, companies including Boeing, Bank of America, Walgreens and General Motors have created 'return-ships'; inviting older workers to come back, through specific programmes tailored to the older and wiser employee. That's more like it!

Companies also need to make sure that their recruiters do not discriminate against age – perhaps even training them how to do this. They need to teach younger leaders how to manage older colleagues. They also need to train their older employees. They need to realise that age can be a competitive *ad*vantage.

Yet we have a long way to go. More than a million people aged fifty and over were unemployed in the UK before COVID-19 struck and many of these had been locked out of work due to age discrimination and outdated employment practices. A 2018 report by MPs on the Women and Equalities Committee officially blamed 'prejudice, unconscious bias and casual ageism in the workplace' – despite all of this being unlawful under the UK's 2010 Equality Act.

Maria Miller, MP, who chaired the committee, said:

'Age discrimination in the workplace is a serious problem, as many older people have discovered. Yet despite it being

[9] 'Age as a Barrier to opportunity'. Aviva. 2019.
[10] https://www.hrmagazine.co.uk/article-details/older-employees-feel-undervalued

unlawful for more than a decade, the scale and lack of enforcement uncovered by our inquiry is both alarming and totally unacceptable. Until we tackle discrimination against the growing number of over-fifties, they will continue to be consigned to the "too old" pile instead of being part of the solution.'[11]

'The workforce is changing, and employers need to catch up,' declared Patrick Thomson, a spokesperson for The Centre for Ageing Better. 'Improving policy and practice, tackling age bias and creating an age-friendly workplace culture is vital to ensuring that people can work for as long as they want to.'

And it starts with recruitment. According to one recruitment professional writing on the Encore Personnel site: 'At the coalface of recruitment, there's evidence to suggest a concerning bias against candidates aged fifty and over with employers opting to hire the younger candidate if both CVs cross their desk. Age discrimination in the job market is rife and needs to be treated on a par with gender and ethnic discrimination, or we stand to face huge economic and societal issues.'[12]

We all have tales of implicit and systemic age bias when it comes to recruiting. A close friend of mine returned to Australia aged fifty-seven after a few years in the States as a senior global partner at one of the world's largest strategy firms. Before that, he was an executive director of a major listed Australian property firm. He is one of the cleverest people I have ever met, and he has found it ridiculously difficult to find a job. In a land that, until COVID-19, hadn't had a recession for almost thirty years and whose population is rapidly ageing, he was continually bypassed for younger executives.

Discrimination based on age is real, ubiquitous and can cause long-lasting damage. Ageism is a constant, low-level background noise in much of the West, and when subjected to such a pervasive and insidious form of prejudice, too many people can gradually come to convince themselves that they are not up to the task, which inevitably affects their

---

[11] 'More than a million people aged over 50 are being locked out of the workplace, according to MPs.' Caitlin Morrison, *Independent* 17 July 2018.
[12] Pete Taylor Encorepersonnel.co.uk 24 September 2018.

confidence, their mental health and their performance in a downward spiral of self-fulfilling prophecies. Internal perceptions within older workers can end up contributing to the ageism itself. They start to reflect the very stereotype that is holding them back.

The power to overcome ageism lies within every single one of us: it is all about attitude.

CHAPTER 4:

Attitude

'If you don't like something, change it.
If you can't change it, change your attitude.'
Maya Angelou[1]

Ageing is inevitable; growing old isn't. We can age without growing old if we stay mentally well and physically fit, accept our limitations, appreciate our vast talents and advantages, and adopt a mindset that helps us to embrace the challenges ahead and look for the opportunities. So much is about attitude. The right attitude can both prolong your life and make it even more worth living.

The human mind is one of the most incredible things in existence and we are yet to understand even a fraction of what it can do. We can't see it, we can't touch it and yet it powers, enables or disables everything we do. The brain is a different beast; it is the hardware of the computer inside our heads. The mind is the software. The app. Actually, it is a library of apps – and to a large extent, we can select the app we want.

We don't need to choose the negative app or the grumpy app or the 'victim of ageism' app. We can choose to bypass the 'I can't do this' app and reject the 'I'm not good enough' and the 'But I don't have the skills to do that' apps. They are of no use to us whatsoever.

We need to select the 'choose your attitude' app.

For the wrong attitude can kill you. I mean that quite literally. A study of 660 people aged fifty and older in Ohio published by the American Psychological Association concluded that that those with more

<hr>

[1] American poet, singer, memoirist and civil rights activist (1928–2014).

positive self-perceptions regarding ageing live an average of seven and a half years longer than those with negative self-perceptions.[2] Seven and a half years more!

A later study by the same researchers found that positive beliefs about age are also associated with a lower risk of developing dementia – even for those who were deemed to be at a high risk of the condition.[3] It has also been proven by many studies that a positive attitude to ageing helps with memory retention, recovery from heart attacks and stroke, physical health and, of course, mental health.

Attitude is that important.

'Unfortunately, there are many social barriers that prevent seniors from accomplishing their goals. People's attitudes towards the ageing population can be a mental barrier for many,' says Dr Catherine Barrett, founder of Australia's 'Celebrate Ageing', a national programme aimed at challenging ageism and encouraging respect for older people. 'If we can change the attitude of the community, we can empower the older generation. We need others to believe in them, so that they find it easier to believe in themselves.'

But more importantly, she went on to say:

'Even though ageing is inevitable, we shouldn't let ageism shape our experiences nor be a barrier that stops us from pursuing our dreams. Internalised ageism can stop you living your life to the full. Ageing can be a time of knowing who you are, knowing what you want and going out and getting it. It can be a time of living life authentically. It can be what you want it to be.'[4]

I like that.

If we think we deserve to be slow, unwell, unfit and depressed as we age – then these things will almost surely come to pass. Alternatively,

[2] B. Levy, Martin D. Slade, S. V. Kasl & S. R. Kunkel (2002). 'Longevity increased by positive self-perceptions of ageing', *Journal of Personality and Social Psychology*.
[3] B. Levy, Martin D. Slade, Robert H. Pietrzak & Luigi Ferrucci (2018). 'Positive age beliefs protect against dementia even among elders with high-risk gene', PLoS ONE 13(2): e0191004. https://doi.org/10.1371/journal.pone.0191004
[4] www.agedcareguide.com.au

if we adopt a positive attitude towards ageing and look for the benefits and the opportunities, we will have a far higher chance of living longer and living well. We will also enjoy it more.

Now, don't get me wrong: I am not talking about a happy-clappy, away-with-the-pixies, reality-is-but-a-concept, new-age, crystal-energy style of ingratiatingly and ceaselessly joyous, head-in-the-clouds denial of the realities of life. Although the more I read that sentence, the more attractive that option becomes . . .

I am not advocating pretending that life is always fabulous or fair and that bad things don't happen to the best of us. Life is full of pitfalls. It is littered with pain and anguish. There will be gut-wrenchingly awful times ahead as well as moments of utter bliss – and we will have to cope with them all. We will have to embrace all of them.

That is what Part Two of this book is about – how to cope with and embrace change of all shapes and sizes – good change, bad change and all the shades of grey in between.

We may not be able to change their attitudes, but we can change our own

It isn't always easy for people to adopt a positive attitude when it comes to ageing, for ageism seems to be everywhere. But we must.

We cannot, and must not, wait for society to change. The tragedy is not that this 'pervasive ageism affects our physical and mental health'. The tragedy is that we let it!

We have very little influence over what others think. That's up to them. But we can change what we think. That is entirely up to us.

Older members of our society could rail against the fact that a quarter of eighteen- to thirty-four-year-olds think that 'it is normal to be unhappy and depressed when you are old.'[5] What the Dickens would they know?!

We second halfers could bemoan the stupidity of the fact that experienced older people are the ones who are inevitably made redundant in times of financial hardship to make way for cheaper youngsters. We could all join together in moaning about the ubiquity of casual ageism in

[5] https://www.rsph.org.uk/our-work/policy/older-people/that-age-old-question.html

society – but it won't do us any good nor, in all likelihood, will it change any of it.

Alternatively, we could focus our energies on how we think, what we feel and what we do – and let the daft beliefs of others wash over us. We could laugh at the advertising images we see of second halfers and make a note of the companies who are being ageist, whether intentionally or otherwise – and simply boycott them.

We could take the redundancy cheque and start something new – preferably in competition to the short-sighted company that has mistakenly under-appreciated our worth and stupidly misunderstood the value we have added to their clients. We could turn to our younger friends and point out that older people are actually happier and more optimistic than their generation, and that far from being *over the hill*, 'people in their fifties, sixties and seventies are feeling fit, healthy and sharp.'[6]

'But how?' I hear you ask.

The secret to adopting the attitude that we want also lies within. It begins with self-belief, and one of the best ways to develop this invaluable quality is to identify the positives in our lives and be grateful for them; to identify and appreciate our strengths, and to recognise the value of our experience. Taking these steps will help us to acknowledge the value of what lies within.

Once this solid foundation has been built, we need to fan the flames of our desire to change our attitude, because as we will explore in Part Two, we only change if we want to. Change is 80 per cent emotion, so we need to identify our emotional triggers. You need to identify what gets you fired up – for you know yourself better than anyone.

With all that in place, we will be ready to define and adopt the attitude we want, for we will know that it is based on something real. Like my taxi-driver friend we met earlier, we will then be ready to flick a switch and adopt a new, positive and proactive mindset. Our world will look and feel completely new.

With this renewed vigour, we will be able to ignore the ageist numpties and live longer, healthier lives into the bargain.

---

[6] Ian Atkinson, Marketing Director, SunLife UK, discussing 'Over 50's Regret Retiring'. www.sunlife.co.uk

CHAPTER 5

Extending our prime

'If I'd known how old I was going to be I'd have
taken better care of myself.'
Adolph Zukor, on his 100th birthday[1]

Our aim is not just to live longer, it is to live well for longer.

We all know that if we wish to increase our chances of both we need to exercise regularly, eat a diet that is low in sugar and high in fibre, fruit, vegetables and oily fish, consume less alcohol, eat less red meat, devour sensible portion sizes, exercise our brains, adopt a positive mental attitude and enhance our ability to accept life and embrace change.

Losing weight and stopping smoking are the two best things a *Homo sapien* can do to lengthen its lifespan. Most of the world's population now lives in countries where more people die from obesity than malnutrition – and far too many people die needlessly from smoking. Obesity kills around 325,000 Americans a year[2] and tobacco kills a further 480,000.[3] Members of the latter group can suffer long and painful deaths into the bargain. Smoking and obesity are significant contributing factors to the four biggest causes of premature deaths in the West – diabetes, cardiovascular diseases, cancer and chronic respiratory diseases. If we multiply the US figures above by around sixteen, we will arrive at a good estimate of the global picture. Smoking kills eight million people every year. It will have killed around thirty people by the time you reach the end of this chapter. And on average it takes ten years off your life. The good news is that quitting works, even late in life. The risk of premature death

---

[1] Austro-Hungarian-born US film producer and the founder of Paramount Pictures (1873–1976).
[2] https://www.wvdhhr.org/bph/oehp/obesity/mortality.htm
[3] https://www.cdc.gov/tobacco/data_statistics/fact_sheets/fast_facts/index.htm

decreases by 50 per cent when people stop smoking between the ages of sixty and seventy-five, according to WHO's 'Global recommendations for physical activity and health'. And, of course, slimming down to a healthy weight can also add several healthy years to your life.

But we know all this. We may choose to ignore it and suffer the consequences, we may find it incredibly hard to put into practice, but we know it. So let's take a look at some of the other things we can do to extend our prime, apart from the obvious two above.

I have compiled a list of tips for extending our prime that I find both quirky and insightful, inspired by a fascinating article I read on Prevention.com.[4] I hope you do, too.

Laugh

Laugh as though your life depends upon it. Outgoing people are 50 per cent less likely to develop dementia, according to a study of more than five hundred men and women aged seventy-eight and older from the Karolinska Institute in Sweden. And a fifteen-year study of over fifty-three thousand people in Norway found that for women, 'high scores on humor's cognitive component' (i.e., women who laughed a lot) were associated with 48 per cent less risk of death from all causes, a 73 per cent lower risk of death from heart disease and an 83 per cent lower risk of death from infection. Weirdly, the results were slightly different for men – no correlation was found between humour and heart disease (perhaps because when men laugh heartily, they are usually drinking alcohol at the time, while women are generally laughing about men, according to Jane), but they did find that laughter decreases a man's risk of dying from an infection by 74 per cent.

Drink tea

A Japanese study of more than four thousand men and women found that those who drank five or more cups of green tea every day had the lowest risk of dying from heart disease and stroke. One or two cups of black tea (without milk) a day also releases 'catechins' that help blood vessels relax and protect your heart.

---

[4] https://www.prevention.com/life/g23008201/live-to-100

Don't drink cola

Two comprehensive Nurses' Health Studies in the US in 2005 that followed 155,000 women over twelve years found that drinking even one cola (regular or diet) a day can increase blood pressure, and of course any sugary drink elevates insulin levels. Drinking just one or two cans of any sugary soft drink a day increases your chance of heart disease and diabetes by 26 per cent.[5]

Eat more purple food (including red wine!)

The polyphenols that give purple foods their colour also reduce the risk of heart disease, reduce inflammation and may even offer some protection against Alzheimer's. Aubergines/eggplants, figs, blackberries, purple cauliflower (I didn't know such a thing existed), purple carrots (ditto!), purple sweet potatoes (they're making this up), forbidden rice (this is just getting silly now), purple asparagus (really?!), redbor kale (sigh), passionfruit, elderberries – washed down with a glass of red.

Do the housekeeping

'The exercise is good for you,' says Prevention.com. Alternatively, go for a jog when the cleaner arrives.

Achieve stuff

People who set themselves goals and consider themselves to be self-disciplined and organised achievers live longer and have up to an 89 per cent lower risk of developing Alzheimer's, according to Robert S. Wilson, PhD, professor of neurological sciences and psychology at Rush University Medical Center in Chicago.

Have friends

We are social beings and we need to belong. We need to care for other people and we need people who care for us. Knowing you have people who will be there for you without judgement reduces stress and strengthens the immune system.

---

[5] http://www.diabetesincontrol.com/what-a-can-of-coca-cola-really-does-to-your-body

Get married

A detailed study by the National Center for Health Statistics of the age-adjusted death rate across the US between 2010 and 2017 seems to have debunked the myth that heterosexual marriage is better for men than women.[6] For every one thousand married men who died, 1,840 never-married men passed away. For every one thousand married women who passed away, 2,049 single women died! Maybe marriage is good for women after all...

Preferably marry someone clever

Men who married more educated women enjoy a lower death rate than men married to less educated women, according to a study conducted by Drs. Robert Erikson and Jenny Torssander of the Swedish Institute for Social Research in Stockholm. Strangely, for women the key factor was their husband's occupation. Women married to unskilled manual and routine non-manual labourers were 1.25 times more likely to die than women whose partners were in higher managerial and professional occupations.[7]

Lower your resting pulse rate

Our resting heart rate should ideally be 60 beats per minute or even lower. This is partly genetic, but it is well known that people who are fit or less stressed have lower resting pulses. De-stressing, yoga and exercise obviously help.

But don't push your heart too much!

According to the American Heart Association, our heart rate should remain within a 'target heart zone' during exercise that is between 50 per cent and 85 per cent of our maximum heart rate. Our max heart rate is calculated by subtracting our age from 220. For a fifty-year-old person: 220 – 50 = 170. Therefore, the target heart zone for a fifty-year-old is 80 to 144 bpm. As I am writing this, I am fifty-seven, which means that I really should not let my heart go above 138 for sustained periods when

---

[6] https://www.webmd.com/a-to-z-guides/news/20191010/marriage-tied-to-longer-life-span-new-data-shows#1

[7] *Journal of Epidemiology and Community Health,* online 6 October 2009.

exercising. For some reason it doesn't seem to get anywhere near this milestone. Maybe the pace at which I run has something to do with it.

Be an older mum

According to Prevention.com, it seems that if you get pregnant naturally after forty-four, you are about 15 per cent more likely to live longer than your friends who had their babies in their thirties. Not sure how on earth they would calculate that. Or what you can do with this startling information.

But have a young mum yourself

There is even less you can do about this, I admit, but if your mother was twenty-five or younger when she had you, it seems you are twice as likely to live to a hundred as someone who was born to a woman in their forties.

Vitamin D

We need Vitamin D to keep our bones, teeth and muscles healthy and to help our immune system fight infections – and so many people simply do not have enough. The respected Endocrine Society issued a report in 2011 declaring that we needed at least 30 nanograms of vitamin D per ml of blood, which meant nearly 80 per cent of Americans were Vitamin D deficient. While other teams of experts put the minimum level at 20 ng/ml or even lower, they all agree that we need it to ward off osteoporosis and reduce risk of cancer, heart disease and infection. There may even be a correlation between Vitamin D deficiency and death from coronavirus. On 21 December 2020, 120 health, science and medical experts from the UK, US and Europe signed an open letter to world governments claiming clear scientific evidence that Vitamin D reduces COVID-19 infections, hospitalisations and deaths.[8] During 2020, Britain's NHS began providing free daily vitamin D supplements for people at high risk from coronavirus. You can get Vitamin D from oily fish, mushrooms, fortified dairy and non-dairy products and a small amount from eggs, but mainly it is made in the skin after exposure to sun. Ironically, the same UVB rays that cause sunburn also make vitamin D. So, it seems that while we have been understandably obsessing about skin

[8] https://vitamindforall.org/letter.html

cancer all these years, what we need to do is get out in the sun and perhaps occasionally leave the sunscreen behind – and get down to our local fishmongers and health food store.

Breathe clean air – and avoid traffic

Being in traffic can actually trigger heart attacks, according to Harvard research.[9] Traffic and air pollution account for 12 per cent of heart attacks worldwide. More than four million people die prematurely every year as a result of air pollution, according to the World Health Organization. America's CDC estimate the number could be twice as many. So while COVID-19 killed around 400,000 people in the first five months of 2020, the global lockdown during March, April and May of that year may have prevented a million people from dying prematurely, perhaps two million. I am sure there are lessons we should be learning from that.

Be spiritual

A study of 92,000 women by Yeshiva University and Albert Einstein College of Medicine found a 20 per cent reduced risk of death for those who attend religious services once a week, citing emotional support and respite from stress.

Be a good grandparent

Now this may be a little premature for many of us, but it's worth keeping in mind for later. People who spend time playing with or looking after their grandchildren live longer than those who don't. Those who care for others outside of the family through charity work also live longer.

Flourish

What a great word. *American Psychologist* reports that 'flourishers' (people who have a positive outlook on life, a sense of purpose and community) are far healthier than 'languishers' (people who don't feel good about themselves). It seems we need to be a lot more like Tigger and a lot less like Eeyore. 'In Sardinia and Okinawa, where people live the

---

[9] https://www.hsph.harvard.edu/news/hsph-in-the-news/pollution-heart-attacks/#:~:text=But%20a%20new%20study%20finds,the%20most%20of%20any%20factor

longest, hard work is important, but not more so than spending time with family, nurturing spirituality, and doing for others,' says Corey Keyes, PhD, a professor of sociology at Emory University.

Use it or lose it

If we don't use our muscles, they deteriorate, and this causes our bones to deteriorate as well. Upper body strength, lower back muscles and the 'bandhas', as they are called in yoga (especially the 'mula-bandha' pelvic floor muscles and the 'uddiyana-bandha' abdominals), are critical for a healthy, strong spine and back. Nothing ages us humans quicker than a bad back, and the only way to keep it good is to keep the muscles that support and protect it in good shape.

Obviously 'use it or lose it' applies to the brain as well. Frequent mental stimulation builds up a functional reserve of brain cells. Reading, learning new things, puzzles and activities that require manual dexterity all help sharpen the mind. Exercise also increases the connections between brain cells. So does diet, sleep and building or maintaining social networks. Weird – it's as though the body and mind are connected. Who would have thought . . .

Be sociable

Loneliness, social isolation and social exclusion are important determinants and risk factors of ill health among older people, affecting all aspects of health and well-being, including mental health and the risk of emergency admission to hospital for avoidable conditions, such as severe dehydration or malnutrition. 'Loneliness acts as a fertilizer for other diseases and promotes several different types of wear and tear on the body,' says Dr Steve Cole, a director of the Social Genomics Core Laboratory at UCLA. 'The biology of loneliness can accelerate the build-up of plaque in arteries, help cancer cells grow and spread, and promote inflammation in the brain leading to Alzheimer's disease.'[10]

[10] https://www.nia.nih.gov/news/social-isolation-loneliness-older-people-pose-health-risks

Try intermittent fasting

The 5:2 and other intermittent fasting diets have been shown to extend healthy lifespans in mammals. Reducing food consumption without malnutrition extends the lifespan of rodents by up to 50 per cent.[11] Researchers believe this may be due to the activation of a family of proteins that regulate cellular health called sirtuins, specifically SIRT3, which acts as a shield against mitochondrial meltdown, ageing and neurodegeneration.[12] Numerous studies on humans have also found that intermittent fasting raises the production of SIRT3. It also increases your metabolic rate, helps to reduce inflammation in the body, reduces insulin resistance, lowers blood sugar levels and initiates a cellular waste removal process called autophagy. Studies have also shown that it is good for brain health and may even help to prevent cancer and Alzheimer's.[13]

Eat like a southern European

The Mediterranean diet is high in vegetables, fruits, whole grains, beans and the healthy fats that come from nuts, seeds, olive oil and fatty fish. It includes moderate intake of dairy products and eggs, and very limited intake of poultry and red meat. But it is more than food: other critically important components of the Mediterranean diet are sharing meals with family and friends, enjoying a glass of red wine and being physically active.

Move to Hawaii

A bit drastic perhaps but then the average sixty-five-year-old Hawaiian will live for a further 16.2 years compared to just 10.6 years for your average sixty-five-year-old Mississippian, according to data from CDC.[14] Actually, anywhere warm with great seafood, fresh fruit, fresh vegetables, a slower pace of life and vitalising natural surroundings will do. Grass skirts are optional.

[11] R. Weindruch, R. L. Walford, S. Fligiel & D. Guthrie (1986). 'The retardation of aging in mice by dietary restriction: longevity, cancer, immunity and lifetime energy intake.' *Journal of Nutrition*, 116, 641–654.
[12] https://www.frontiersin.org/articles/10.3389/fnagi.2013.00048/full?utm_source=newsletter&utm_medium=email&utm_campaign=Neurology-w40-2013#B123
[13] https://www.healthline.com/nutrition/10-health-benefits-of-intermittent-fasting#section6
[14] Huffington Post. 'What Hawaii Can Teach The Rest of America About Living Better' by Carolyn Gregoire 4 August 2013; updated 7 December 2017.

Give your brain a rest

Research from Harvard Medical School, published in *Nature* magazine in 2019,[15] strongly suggests that a calm brain could lead to a longer life. After analysing brain tissue from people who died at ages from sixty to more than one hundred, HMS researchers found that those who lived longest generally had lower levels of genes related to neural activity. 'This study shows that daily periods of slowed activity, whether spent in meditation, uni-tasking, or simply being still or sleeping are as important for brain health and longevity as activity and exercise,' said Gayatri Devi, MD, a neurologist and psychiatrist at Northwell Health in New York.[16] The brain consumes almost a third of our energy and occasionally it needs a break.

Volunteer

Volunteers are not only happier, numerous studies have also found that volunteering can help reduce the symptoms of chronic pain, decrease hypertension, improve our ability to manage stress and stave off disease, and enhance our brain fitness. A 2018 study by *The Journal of Economics and Ageing*[17] of more than sixty-four thousand subjects aged sixty and older, found that volunteering slows the cognitive decline associated with ageing. Individuals who volunteered for just a hundred hours a year scored, on average, almost 6 per cent higher in cognitive testing than non-volunteers.

But here's a fascinating caveat – volunteering only helps us to live better for longer if our motives are selfless. A 2012 study for the journal *Health Psychology*[18] concluded that longevity will not be affected if you are only volunteering to make yourself feel better or to post it on your Facebook feed. You will only live longer if you are genuinely doing it to help others. This 'path of unselfish action' is also known as karma yoga. And as Mahatma Gandhi said: 'The best way to find yourself is to lose yourself in the service of others.'

[15] https://www.nature.com/articles/s41586-019-1647-8
[16] https://www.healthline.com/health-news/tips-on-how-to-quiet-your-brain-and-live-longer
[17] https://www.sciencedirect.com/science/article/pii/S2212828X17300646#///?mod=article_inline
[18] https://psycnet.apa.org/record/2011-17888-001

De-stress

Stress is an even bigger killer than lack of exercise, according to a Finnish Institute for Health and Welfare study reported in *Science Daily* in 2020.[19] Being under heavy stress shortens the life expectancy of the average thirty-year-old Finn by 2.8 years whereas lack of exercise shortens their lives by 2.4 years. Women suffering from stress or anxiety are reportedly up to two times more likely to die from heart disease, stroke, or lung cancer. For men, the risk of premature death is up to three times higher.[20]

Practise yoga

One of the best ways to strengthen your upper body and lower back, firm up your core, increase your energy, help you to fall back in love with your body and your self, unclutter your mind, cope with stress, embrace change and live a longer and healthier life – is yoga. Yoga is quite miraculous. Even doing a class once a week can have incredible health benefits, but two to three times or more is recommended by my co-author.

Yoga helps us to become more aware of our bodies, to value them more and to preserve and strengthen us physically. It helps us to be in the moment, to live mindfully, to quieten our frenzied mind and calm our racing heart.

It helps us to realise that the body and the mind are not only connected, but that they are one. The poses enable us to increase our physical flexibility and strength, which in turn helps us to be still and quiet our mind. Yoga is more than its life-changing physical benefits. It is mindfulness, meditation and the ability to detach ourselves from our whirling worries and negative thoughts. It is about helping us to find our true self – and like what we find.

Work

Highly motivated, successful, career-oriented people tend to live longer, according to Dr. Howard Friedman, co-author of *The Longevity Project*,[21] the result of an eight-decade study into health and longevity. 'They didn't work themselves to death. They worked themselves to life.'

---

[19] https://www.sciencedaily.com/releases/2020/03/200311100857.htm
[20] https://www.healthline.com/nutrition/13-habits-linked-to-a-long-life#section9
[21] *The Longevity Project: Surprising Discoveries for Health and Long Life from the Landmark Eight Decade Study*, Hudson Street Press 2011.

Working later in life is good for our souls and our health as well as our bank balances. It can keep us vital. It can lengthen our lives and it can increase our quality of life. It can keep us relevant. It can even give us Purpose. And as we will discuss in the very last chapter, Purpose and Relevance are perhaps the most valuable aspirations of all.

THIS IS OUR TIME

Act One is over. It is now firmly in the past where it belongs. Now is our time to take the learnings from our first half and move confidently into our second. Your Part Two is yours to discover. But before we do that, let's take a moment to pause to take stock. Yes, our physical capabilities may not be at their freshest and our synapses may be firing at a slightly lower speed than they once were, but our years of experience more than makes up for both.

In this first part of the book, we discovered that age is in the mind of the beholder. If we feel old, we will be. We discussed how ageism, casual or otherwise, is everywhere we look – in the media, at work, in government policy even – but it needn't exist in the most important place of all, between our ears. We have the ability to laugh off any ageism we may encounter and adopt the attitude we need to thrive in our Part Two.

Knowing how much our lifestyle can affect both our vitality and our longevity, we can influence how well and how long we live with some simple adjustments to how we live: regular exercise, throwing away the cigarettes, moderating alcohol intake, eating like a southern European, giving up cola, eating more purple food, being social, volunteering, developing a positive outlook on life and practising yoga. It also helps to develop a clear sense of purpose, whatever that purpose may be.

But no matter what lies ahead for you in your Part Two, planned or not, we can guarantee one thing: it will involve change.

PART TWO:

It's all about change

'Everything is impermanent and changing.'
Buddha

Part Two is all about change. Our bodies are changing, our minds are changing, our hormones are changing, our relationships are changing, our identities are changing, our lives are changing, our livelihoods are changing. Or they are about to.

Change should be nothing to fear; it is an inevitable part of life. However, major change can be tough, even when we know it is coming.

In these next chapters, we not only discuss some of the major changes that lie ahead in your Part Two but more importantly, we explore how the emotions we experience during times of significant change are entirely normal, how to overcome the barriers that each of us naturally erects to change and finally how to learn to accept it, embrace it and look for the opportunities.

CHAPTER 6:

Menopause vs MenoPorsche

Fifty-one per cent of the adult population
will go through the menopause.
The other 49 per cent will think they are.

Let me be crystal clear right up front: there is no comparison between menopause and the male midlife crisis we have labelled 'MenoPorsche'. One is a profound hormonal transformation full of significant and life-altering physical and emotional changes. The other is an attempt to disguise waning virility in the andropausal male with the acquisition of a red convertible.

And with that pithy comment, I think it is best that I hand the keyboard over to Jane.

MENOPAUSE: FREE AT LAST!

To paraphrase Ruby Wax's quotation from the front cover of one of the most insightful books I have ever read on this subject, *The Second Half of Your Life*, by Jill Shaw Ruddock:[1] 'Menopause is the start of the best years of your life – no longer a slave to your hormones. Free at last! Free at last!'

Menopause is all about change. In fact, the label that our mothers and grandmothers gave it was precisely that – 'the change'. To be accurate, perimenopause, menopause and post-menopause are all about change. Menopause is a fleeting point in time that occurs exactly twelve months after our last period. Before that day, we are perimenopausal. The

---

[1] Vermilion 2011.

day after, we are post-menopausal. The medical fraternity loves their labels.

And the changes can be profound. While some women sail through menopause, so many others find it to be the most difficult time of their lives. Most menopausal women struggle at work, with 63 per cent reporting that their working life has been negatively affected, according to a 2019 study of one thousand menopausal women in the UK.[2] Menopause specialist Newson Health puts the figure at 94 per cent and states that as many as 20 per cent of menopausal women have had to give up their job due to the severity of their symptoms.

We are also more prone to suffering from anxiety and depression at this time in our lives. The highest suicide rate for women is in the age group forty-five to forty-nine (10 deaths per 100,000), according to the Australian Bureau of Statistics. The second highest rate is in women aged fifty to fifty-four.[3]

Every significant change comes with its own roller coaster of emotions, and none more so than menopause. The 'change curve' we will meet in Chapter 8 (p.80) is just as relevant here, as we traverse a terrain of heightened emotions full of shock, denial, anger, fear, melancholy and depression, until our heads can start to plan a route forward and finally our hearts are able to embrace the changes that are happening to us. The emotions that we experience throughout 'the change' are entirely normal. They are a by-product of the natural hormonal changes that are happening to our bodies.

But even given that it is entirely natural, completely normal and the number of people going through the menopause is approaching a billion worldwide, 75 per cent of women aged between thirty-five and sixty still feel that it is something of a taboo subject, according to recent research conducted by menopause support group and specialist resource hub, Generation Menopause (www.gen-m.com). Two out of three women were taken by surprise by the perimenopause, a fact that certainly surprised me, and 36 per cent agreed with the statement 'it made me feel invisible'.

---

[2] https://www.forthwithlife.co.uk/blog/menopause-in-the-workplace
[3] Australian Bureau of Statistics. 3303.0 - Causes of Death, Australia, 2015. Canberra: Australian Bureau of Statistics; 28 September 2016.

It doesn't have to be like that.

We can look at menopause in one of two ways – either as something to regret or as something to accept; as the end of something precious or as the start of something new. And it is both. Yes, it marks the end of our fertile years and it is entirely natural that we may pause to mourn the loss of that fertility. But it can also be a life-changing, life-affirming experience. It can be the opportunity to free ourselves from the mundanity of menstruation, the pain, the mood swings and the energy-sapping exhaustion of the monthly cycle. After so many false dawns, I am on the home stretch and I can't wait!

In this chapter, I will be discussing my personal experiences with perimenopause and just some of the things that I have learnt from helping other perimenopausal and post-menopausal women to cope with, accept and embrace the transition. I will talk about traditional hormone replacement therapy (HRT), bioidentical HRT and, of course, yoga. I will also share the mindset I have tried to adopt when it comes to menopause; what perimenopause means to me and why I am looking forward to a post-menopausal life.

Then Campbell will return and talk about bonobos and rams.

Menopause can be an extraordinarily exciting time for a woman

It is a wonderful opportunity for women to go from being the nurturers to looking after themselves for a change. It is an opportunity to make a real shift in the way we look at ourselves, our bodies, our emotions and our minds. One of the things I encourage my yoga therapy clients to do is to 'feel the way they're feeling' and to embrace these feelings. At this time in our lives, we are undergoing a whirlwind of different and often conflicting emotions, all of which are entirely natural. It's okay to be feeling the way we feel. We give teenagers plenty of space as they navigate their changing hormonal journey; surely we can do the same for ourselves!

I help my perimenopausal clients to divert their inner gaze to what is working well with them right now. What do they like about themselves right now? What do they love about themselves? We also work on what they would like to change if they could and to identify those things that they can actually change. It could 'simply' be changing the way they think about themselves or how they think about menopause. Or it may be even more substantial than that: some women decide that they want to change where they live or change their job. Some even want to change their partner. A recent study by the American Association of Retired Persons (now there's an uplifting acronym if ever I have heard one!) found that 66 per cent of all divorces are initiated by women in their forties, fifties and sixties.[4]

During this phase of our lives, we experience a reduction in both oestrogen and progesterone, and our testosterone can increase a little, which means that we may find ourselves becoming a little bit more 'bolshie' as I like to say; a little more strident perhaps. I know I am, much to Campbell's distress at times, but then he knows what he bought into – I think. To me, the fact that we may become a little more opinionated, disgruntled and confident is a really positive thing. And, dare I say, more 'male-like'.

Talking openly about menopause is a new and welcome development in our society. I agree wholeheartedly with Jill Shaw Ruddock, who, in her life-changing book that I mentioned before, *The Second Half of Your Life*, described menopause as being an element of the 'fourth wave of the feminism movement'. The first wave began in the nineteenth century – 19 July 1848 to be precise – with the world's first women's rights convention at Seneca Falls in New York State, and continued into the twentieth century with the suffragette movement. The second wave kicked off in the 1960s with the pill and sexual liberation and a drive for equality. 'Equal Pay Acts' were introduced in the US in 1963 and in the UK in 1970 (a year before Swiss women were finally allowed to vote!). Putting aside the sad fact that equal pay still remains an ambition fifty years on, the third wave of feminism started in the 1990s and took on a very different form. Germaine Greer, Gloria Steinem and Simone de Beauvoir gave way to Madonna, The Spice Girls and, later, Pussy Riot. To many of the vanguards of the second wave, this new wave seemed to be selling out; throwing away their mothers' hard-fought gains as they adopted high-heels, push-up bras and low-cut necklines that the likes of Germaine and Gloria would have identified with male repression.

[4] https://www.aarp.org/research/topics/life/info-2014/divorce.html

A video game called 'The Power Babes' captured the zeitgeist with the tag line 'It's possible to have a push-up bra and a brain at the same time'.

So, is embracing menopause part of the fourth wave? I'd like to think it is. Our mothers' generation didn't really talk about the subject. I know my mother went through a really tough time in her forties and fifties. Mind you, which part of that was due to menopause and which part was due to my father dying so suddenly, I am not sure. She didn't take anti-depressants, nor did she take HRT. She just 'got on with it'. These days, we have access to so much support for both bereavement and menopause. I think we are enormously lucky.

Menopause can be a liberating time in a woman's life. It is indeed a time of change, but it needn't only be change that is done *to* us. We can also place ourselves in the driver's seat and instigate changes of our own – changes in our attitude, our situations, our careers, our finances – whatever they might be. If we look after ourselves and treat ourselves with kindness and compassion, we can channel all this energy into moving forward with a sense of exhilaration and optimism. I think it is a really exciting time.

Some women breeze through menopause. Their hormone changes don't seem to affect them at all. In one sense, that must be bliss. And yet, a part of me wonders if they are missing out on something profound. Mind you, if you are reading this in the middle of a hot flush and thinking even semi-seriously about 'sticking a knife into your husband', to quote one of my clients, perhaps the word 'profound' doesn't quite do it for you at this point in time. But I definitely feel that the menopause is a 'one door closing and another door opening', life-defining moment.

While some women only have to take the occasional painkiller to get through it, for most of us, 'the change' is very challenging indeed.

Quite a few of my clients have come to me in a near state of despair, suffering from any number of symptoms – hot flushes, panic attacks, sadness, bouts of anxiety, depression, joint pain, headaches – sometimes the whole lot. Their despair stems not only from their symptoms, but also from the fact that society doesn't seem to respect, empathise with or understand what they are going through. Too many times, the response from their doctor has been: 'Well, you can take an anti-depressant, or I can put you on HRT.'

Yes, the hormonal imbalance of perimenopause can cause symptoms that mirror those caused by depression: apathy, futility, anxiety, fatigue, low confidence, poor concentration, low libido, insomnia ... but that doesn't necessarily mean we are 'depressed'; it may just mean we are perimenopausal! Many of us don't want the pharmaceutical sticking plaster of anti-depressants; we want to take back a little bit more control – of our physical health and our mental health; our sense of well-being – and we would prefer not to rely on medication to achieve this.

I am not saying that we shouldn't take medication. Anti-depressants definitely have their place, as does HRT, which we will discuss in some detail later. But pharmaceuticals are not the only or the total solution, either. Yoga can be an incredibly powerful treatment for perimenopause and post-menopause (and depression and anxiety, no matter what the cause). As a fully trained yoga therapist, I have successfully treated a large number of people experiencing all four. Some of my clients have been able to come off their medication as a result of their specialist yoga therapy sessions, some have been able to reduce their reliance on anti-depressants, some have found it to be a valuable complementary therapy that has worked alongside their medication. We are all different.

By the time this book is published, I sincerely hope that England's NHS will have started to prescribe yoga therapy as a recognised treatment for anxiety and depression. There are signs that they might. Numerous studies have renewed calls for precisely such a change. One such study from the Grossman School of Medicine at New York University[5] treated people who were diagnosed with anxiety in three separate ways and compared the results. One group was treated with cognitive behaviour therapy (CBT), another with stress-management education and the third with kundalini yoga. The CBT group fared the best with 71 per cent of people reporting improved symptoms, but 54 per cent of the yoga group reported improved symptoms compared to only 33 per cent of the stress-management group. The NHS website already sings yoga's praises on its website.[6] Seeing that one in five of us suffer

[5] 'Generalized Anxiety - A Treatment Evaluation'
https://clinicaltrials.gov/ct2/show/NCT01912287?term=NCT01912287&draw=2&rank=1
[6] https://www.nhs.uk/live-well/exercise/guide-to-yoga

from 'generalised anxiety disorder' (GAD),[7] prescribing yoga would be a wonderful step towards helping millions of people cope with this debilitating condition.

Menopause and yoga

Yoga has a powerful role to play in helping us experience and embrace both peri- and post-menopause. It not only helps us to be physically healthier but more importantly, it gives us the tools, the techniques and the approach to gain a degree of control over what is happening to us. It helps us to clear the mind and accept what we cannot change – and identify what we can. That alone can be incredibly empowering.

However, first let's address a common misperception about what yoga is and what it is not. Some of you may be thinking that yoga is not for you. The thought of squeezing into skin-tight leggings and sitting in a hot room surrounded by ultra-bendy thirty-somethings doing pretzel impersonations is about the last thing you want to do. This is not what yoga is about. It saddens and frustrates me when I see yoga reduced to images of young, toned, acrobatic, hyper-mobile young women modelling the latest Lululemon gear. It merely serves to reinforce the Western infatuation with youth and image. It does little more than sow more seeds of self-judgement and self-criticism: *'I couldn't possibly do yoga as I am not thin/young/pretty/bendy/photogenic enough'*. This couldn't be further from the true essence and meaning of yoga. Yoga is not about youth. It is not about image. It is not about posing. 'Yoga' means union: the joining together of mind and body. The postures help us become stronger, more flexible and help us release tension. When we connect with our physical bodies and our breathing, we find our busy, chattering minds fall quiet. We feel calmer and present, less reactive, less judgemental.

I didn't start seriously practising yoga until after my daughter was born. I was in my thirties. I didn't start training as a yoga teacher until I was in my forties. I was fortunate to be taught by a very special teacher, Ruth White, who had been trained by Iyengar himself. She was older and she taught me what yoga was actually all about.

Yoga isn't about youth. It isn't about fashion. It has nothing to do

[7] https://www.ncbi.nlm.nih.gov/books/NBK441870

with how you look. It is all about connecting our bodies, breathing and minds to bring us to a calm place to help us embrace change and live life.

I have been asked so many times how can yoga help us cope with the symptoms of menopause; how can we stay calm in the middle of a hot flush or anxiety attack?

My reply is that it is difficult, but it can be done. Yogic breathing techniques and meditation don't require you to sit in the lotus position on top of a Himalayan mountain. We can do them anywhere. And sometimes it helps to move. I do a lot of breathing-moving meditation. When someone is very anxious – their mind churning rapidly with worry about their children, their parents, the house, their partner, finances, or just churning for no logical reason (because anxiety often has very little to do with logic) – getting them to sit down, cross their legs, close their eyes and meditate is pretty much impossible. So, I get them moving.

Movement helps people to become aware of their body. They start to notice how their body is moving and then they start to notice how the breathing is synchronised with the movement of the body. This has the effect of bringing them 'into their body', into the present moment – and that is what yoga is all about. As Patanjali, the author of one of the definitive yoga texts, *The Yoga Sutras of Patanjali*, said, the purpose of yoga is to calm the chattering of the mind.

'But what if it's the three in the morning and you are not in the room with us?' I know that for a lot of women it is the middle of the night when we can find ourselves bolt upright in bed with a hot flush. It may be the heat that woke us but now we are awake, our heart is racing and then our mind is also racing. We can become quite panicky and often not even sure why! How can we incorporate movement-breathing techniques at this time of night?

In the middle of the night when it is dark and quiet, negative thoughts and negative feelings become heightened. My advice is, as you find yourself sitting up in bed anyway, you might as well check in with how your body is feeling. This alone will act like a circuit breaker. Notice your heart rate, notice your breathing, notice your thoughts – but do all of these in a non-judgemental way. Remind yourself that what you are experiencing is normal and that these experiences are not you nor do they define you. They are simply natural symptoms of menopause. And, as I suggest for insomnia sufferers, you may want to ease yourself out of bed and make a nice cup of herbal tea. You may want to do some simple restorative yoga poses while the tea is brewing or cooling. All the while staying in the present. Make the tea mindfully, do some poses mindfully, savour and enjoy the tea. That is far more restful than lying awake in bed, tossing and turning, watching your mind ruminating about things that you can do nothing about.

And while we are on the subject of sleep, I suggest to my clients not to worry if you wake up in the middle of the night. That's just what happens. The whole idea that you go to sleep and should sleep a solid eight hours – it's a myth.

Just accept that you may be feeling a little tired today and if you can, find a time in your day where you take some rest. Just because you're not asleep doesn't mean you can't rest. It can be incredibly restful simply lying down with your legs up the wall or lying back on some cushions with a lovely eye pillow on your eyes – focusing on your breathing, focusing on where there may be some tension in your body and just letting all that go. On the days when I feel tired, usually about 3 or 4 pm, I'll take twenty minutes. That's it, twenty minutes. I just lie down and focus on my breathing. And that's enough for a quick recharge. But I could only do that once I overcame that inbuilt guilt that I should always be on the go.

Yoga to help with your monthly cycle

Our cycles can go crazy during perimenopause – one month heavy; one month light; one month nothing; one month a veritable deluge. We can go several months without a period and then they come every three weeks. Often when your cycle changes so rapidly, your energy levels hit rock bottom and the last thing you feel like doing is exercising. Yoga can help in this situation, too.

The first thing to do is to recognise that your energy is low, which is what yoga helps you do – be aware of the present. This is called 'santosa', and it means the ability to positively accept what is going on. But sometimes acceptance can be really tough. The perimenopause heralds that the time when we are not able to have children anymore is approaching. This realisation can have a profound effect on us emotionally and psychologically. Again – these reactions are completely understandable and entirely normal. Accepting that this is happening is the first, and perhaps the most important, step. We need to come to terms with the fact that these feelings are both natural and normal; and that it is okay to be feeling them.

The second thing I recommend is to listen to your body. If you are having heavy flows, the last thing you are going to feel like doing is a strong ashtanga yoga practice or an aerobic vinyasa, a strong power flow of yoga postures. I would stay away from hot yoga in this situation, too. In my view perimenopausal women should stay away from hot yoga, period (pardon the pun). Why would you want to make yourself hotter? But then, I am not a big fan of hot yoga anyway. To me, it's akin to doing Step Reebok in a sauna – and why would anyone want to do that?

If you are experiencing a heavy cycle, there are poses you should avoid: strong twists, for example. When you come out of a yoga twist, there's a release of energy that could increase the blood flow. I would also advise you to avoid strong inversions, head stands and shoulder stands, which can cause flooding. Central to yogic philosophy is the concept of 'life force', which in Sanskrit is called *'prana'*. A subset of this life force is *'apana'*, the downward and outward flow of energy in the body. Among other things, *apana* drives excretion, urination and menstruation. According to yogic philosophy, when *apana* is weak, we can become susceptible to illness, fear, doubt, confusion, insecurity and, interestingly, a loss of purpose. Think about this for a second and it makes sense, for it also works in reverse – fear, doubt, anxiety and depression can cause constipation, as your GP will attest. During a heavy cycle, your prana is very active – everything is flowing out. So, doing inversions would be trying to force your body to do the opposite of what it wants to do.

What I would recommend is a restorative yoga practice. It's very calming and highly effective. The breathing techniques, postures and meditation within a restorative practice stimulate the para-sympathetic nervous system. The sympathetic nervous system prepares the body for the 'fight or flight' response during any potential danger. The parasympathetic nervous system inhibits the body from overworking, regulates the stress response mechanism and restores the body to a calm and composed state. Restorative yoga not only calms the mind, it also produces a physiological change, reducing heart rate and blood pressure.

If you're getting cramps, what really helps is to lie down on your mat and place a weight on your lower belly in between your tummy button and your pubic bone; a nice heavy pillow or a warm hot water bottle. Then breathe into that weight, which will help to soften all the muscles around the diaphragm and all the muscles in the abdominal area. Just lying on your back, taking your hands on to your tummy, and breathing into your hands means you're bringing that breath down into the lower part of the body.

Lower backache is another common symptom because everything is linked to the uterus and to cramping. Ideally, find someone who can help you go into a child's pose and place the pillow or weight or hot water bottle on your lower back. And then breathe into it. The diaphragm is linked to your lower ribs, which are in turn linked to your lower back. As you breathe in and out using your diaphragm, you will feel your lower back relax and release.

Yoga for energy

But yoga is helpful when you want to boost your energy levels, too. Sometimes we just feel, well, sluggish is perhaps the best way to describe it. That voice inside our heads tells us, 'I can't be bothered. I'm going to sit on that sofa, open a packet of chocolate biscuits and just collapse.' In these situations, getting on your mat and practising some poses to build your energy up can be a good thing. Just doing a couple of triangle poses or warrior poses can give you more energy at a time when you need it.

It's all about being connected with how you are feeling.

Menopause can play havoc with our energy levels. They change all the time. When I was training to be a yoga therapist, I had a wonderful teacher and I remember her making a big circle out of ribbon on the floor of the studio. She then divided it into four and wrote one season in each quarter: 'summer', 'winter', 'spring', and 'autumn'. Then she said to us, 'Okay, where are you in your cycle? I'd like you to stand in the quadrant that best reflects where you are.' Some people were at the beginning of their cycle so they went and stood in 'spring'. Mid-cycle women went and stood in 'summer' and so on. It was a fascinating way to look at it.

Then she said, 'Okay, all you women who are experiencing perimenopause, where do you think society insists you stay?' And, of course, we all then went and stood in the summer quadrant, the season when our energy is sky-high and we're feeling sexy and bright eyed. But when we are perimenopausal, that is often the exact opposite of how we are feeling. It was a clear lesson that we shouldn't listen to the expectations of others, we should listen to our bodies and accept the fact that we go through different 'seasons' in our cycle and we feel differently during each one.

When we are in winter and want to curl up in a little ball and wrap ourselves up – that's okay. But as perimenopausal women, we often feel we are not allowed to stay in bed until midday. We've got to keep performing. We've got to keep doing what we do. This expectation can place an enormous strain on us, because sometimes we simply need to take some time out for ourselves. And we should. After all, we are going through the same sort of hormonal turmoil that teenagers go through – and, as I mentioned earlier, we all know how much we tiptoe around them!

This is the opportunity that the perimenopause offers us: the opportunity to think about what we may want as individuals, as women, rather than as partners or mothers. It provides us with the opportunity to say, 'We are going through this really exciting time in our lives and for the majority of us, our children have started to lead their own lives (we hope!). We don't need to nurture them as much.' I am not proposing abandoning our loved ones at all, just acknowledging that our individual needs are also important.

Menopause can be a real turning point. A lot of women go back to university, some decide that they have always wanted to explore their creative side or return to something they used to love doing when they were in their twenties. Some start new businesses. Some even decide that the relationship they are in is not where they want to be.

I think the whole thing is very liberating. It is feminism in a new form.

It is our time.

HRT and me

One of the most disturbing things about menopause is the feeling that you are out of control; that all this change is being done *to* you. Our hormones are buffeting us around as though we were a little boat on a raging sea. They affect everything – our body temperature, digestion, libido, moods, emotions – they can even cause inflammation in our bodies. They affect the way that the neural pathways work to and from the brain. And yes, yoga can definitely help in almost magical ways.

But sometimes we need more.

Accepting this truth was difficult for me. I was determined that I was going to be able to cope with the perimenopause without any kind of hormone replacement therapy. I saw myself as a rational, educated, fully informed woman and imagined that I would use my knowledge of yoga, health and nutrition to sail through the perimenopausal years, coping with whatever was thrown at me with a knowing smile from the knowledge that I 'had the menopause all sorted'.

How wrong I was.

I often introduce my yoga therapy clients to three fundamental yogic philosophical principles:

- Positive acceptance and contentment (*santosa*): the ability to accept what it happening;
- Recognising that there are obstacles (*kleshas*) that shape our intentions and seeing how these are the driving forces behind our actions, and;
- Knowing that one of these obstacles is *asmita* – i.e., our tendency to over identify with our ego.

And yet I found myself not following any of these when it came to the issue of HRT.

As the perimenopause started, I read all the literature I could find – and there are some great books around written by some great women. I felt well-armed and ready to cope with the sensations I was feeling in my body and the challenging thoughts that were swirling around in my mind. Yes, I felt tired – but I was teaching yoga every day plus dealing with two young adults with their own angst and worries about exams and life. With the tiredness, I felt at times angry, at times weepy, but most of the time just determined to carry on regardless. I was one of the lucky ones – a loving husband, great kids, a beautiful life in the Cotswolds, lots of friends and a wonderful family. And I was doing something I love: teaching yoga and helping others through my training as a yoga therapist.

For goodness sake, I had no right to feel down! I had no right to be self-indulgent. I had no right to whinge. I just needed to get through it and hopefully emerge quickly from this unfortunate 'phase' that I was going through.

But then the nightly hot flushes began in earnest and I was existing on not much more than three hours sleep a night. I became even more fatigued and felt continually exhausted. I was doing all the things I had read about – good diet, exercising, reducing alcohol and caffeine. I tried a litany of herbal remedies. I switched to cotton pyjamas, swiftly followed by no pyjamas, even in winter. And of course, I was practising my yoga and meditation. So why wasn't it all working?

I came to realise from my personal yoga practice that it was an ego thing. To me, my identity as a yoga teacher made me determined to exclusively seek 'natural' solutions to coping with perimenopause rather than resorting to pharmaceuticals. I shy away from painkillers and anything that is not 'natural'. I am mainly vegetarian – well, a pescatarian really as I do love seafood. I sought advice from an Ayurvedic doctor in India, twice. After a lengthy consultation in his clinic within an Ayurvedic hospital in the Western Ghats in Southern India, he prescribed a bespoke cocktail of herbs and natural ingredients; a thick, brown liquid that I was able to drink if I held my nose at the same time. And it was a miracle cure for a good year. But as I approached my mid-fifties, the symptoms returned in spite of my daily dose of the good doctor's natural remedies. I was still having periods and I was now getting hotter than ever. And even more fatigued.

My ego was telling me that I shouldn't need to resort to pills and that I should be able to cope with these 'temporary symptoms', that they would pass. But my body was begging me to do something now so I could get on with enjoying this exciting second half of my life.

I finally had to accept that I needed HRT. And perversely, for someone who teaches 'acceptance', this wasn't an easy thing for me to do.

I had many friends who raved about HRT, but I was also aware that it came with a small increased risk of breast cancer. Of course, nothing is clear cut. In discussion with Louise Newson, menopause GP, she told me that HRT can deliver other surprising benefits, such as reducing the risk of developing cardiovascular disease by 50 per cent. She also asserts that women taking HRT for more than eighteen years have a lower increased risk of developing heart disease, type II diabetes, osteoporosis, depression and dementia.[8]

However, I must admit that one of the things that has always put me off traditional hormone replacement therapy is that the most common oestrogen-based HRT, and the biggest selling drug in the US for many decades, Premarin, was manufactured from the urine of a pregnant mare. But I appreciated that it and other forms of HRT were working for many of my friends and for millions of women around the world.

And I needed help.

So, I threw myself into further research and learnt about different forms of HRT, 'Body-identical' HRT and 'Bioidentical' HRT. These forms of HRT, I understand, are still manufactured in a laboratory, but are not synthetic, derived from diosgenin, a substance sourced from Mexican yams. They are identical in chemical structure to our own hormones, and their effects and benefits replicate them closely. Yes, it is still medication, but it sounded far more attractive to me than the other options.

A pioneer in the field of Bioidentical HRT is Dr Marion Gluck, who founded her eponymous clinic way back in 2007. She explains all about it in her book, *It's Not My Head, It's My Hormones.*[9]

The compound her clinic prescribed was uniquely formulated for me as a result of comprehensive blood tests and one-to-one consultations. 'Everyone is unique, which is why off-the-shelf medicine has a different effect on everyone. You have to be incredibly gentle when you're prescribing hormones, which as every woman knows are very powerful things. That is where experience really comes in,' Dr Gluck explained in an interview with the *Daily Mail.*[10]

However, BHRT has not been universally accepted by the medical establishment. The British Menopause Society commented in the same article that 'compounded HRT isn't regulated, doesn't necessarily work and might even carry additional risks'. Dr Gluck's response was that the

---

[8] https://www.menopausedoctor.co.uk/news/stop-the-scaremongering-very-low-breast-cancer-risks-for-women-taking-hrt
[9] Orion Spring 2019.
[10] https://www.dailymail.co.uk/femail/article-7769703/Why-happy-pills-instead-HRT.html

critics simply fail to understand BHRT and how her practice operates. 'The compounding element is basically old-fashioned pharmacy, the kind of work doctors used to do in the past.'

I now take a quarter of a specially formulated lozenge twice a day and it has certainly worked for me! After only a week on Dr Gluck's BHRT treatment, I was sleeping soundly with no hot flushes and I felt as though a fog had been lifted inside my head. I turned to Campbell one morning and asked him, 'Have I been really hard to live with?' It was an unfair question, I know, and the nervous look on his face as he stumbled and struggled in vain to find a coherent answer told me all I needed to know.

I now realise that I was being both arrogant and naive to think that I didn't need any help. Body-identical, bio-identical and new forms of HRT seem to be coming to the market at an ever-increasing rate. With the particular solution I am currently on, I have to pay for the consultations and blood tests and scans and compounds out of my own pocket. However, I calculate that the total cost is around £3 a day. Not bad for feeling energised, well and able to continue with getting on with my life. There are cheaper alternatives now available which is all good news.

My strongest recommendation is to find out what works for you. Knowledge is power. Do your research. Talk to a well-informed GP or medical specialist. Do what you feel is right for you.

MENOPORSCHE

Okay. After Jane's eloquent insight on the complex and vexed subject of menopause, I feel a little like a tribute band that has been booked to follow the real thing. I am 'Bjorn Again' to Jane's ABBA, I'm 'Proxy Music', 'Fake That'. For it is now my turn to talk about the male menopause.

The first question that springs to mind is, 'Is the male menopause real?' And the quick response is, 'Yes'. The more considered answer is, 'Yes-ish'.

The male menopause is real, as all psychological conditions are real. But it is not chemical; it is not even hormonal, which surprised me. But whether you call it the midlife crisis or the male menopause, something is definitely going on – and not just between the ears of so many males over the age of forty-five.

We have all seen the evidence. A man turns forty and buys a

motorbike, even though he has no idea how to ride one. Mine was a Vespa scooter with a mighty 49cc of raw power and I was thirty-nine. Another turns fifty and develops a penchant for vintage cars and petite blondes. Luckily, I have never been into vintage cars. These are stereotypes obviously, but like all stereotypes, they are based on at least a soupçon of reality.

Often the cause can be tracked back to unrealised expectations. 'The Midlife Crisis is something we invented after discovering that life didn't unfold exactly as we would have wished.'[11] By forty, I was going to be rich, famous and successful. When the day dawned, I was none of the above. By fifty, I was going to be set for life and a doyen in my chosen field. Hmmm.

Cue another Mars–Venus moment. Most men define 'success' to be work-related and money-related. On the occasions over the years when, in the odd fit of self-indulgence, I have lamented to Jane about my apparent lack of relative 'success', she would turn to me with more than a hint of exasperation and proclaim, 'Are you mad? Look at us, look at the kids, look at our families. Just look around you. If that doesn't add up to "success", what does?!' Of course, she was right. Yet, to the male mind, we see all sorts of friends and peers climbing higher on the corporate ladder or building valuable businesses and we cannot help but compare and contrast. We don't seem to focus on the ones without a job or the ones with messy divorces or with troubled children. We only see the 'successful' ones. It isn't logical. It is entirely ego-driven, but these mad and pointless comparisons are so common.

A key reason for this is that work and career assume a disproportionate degree of importance in the minds of men. This is the inescapable conclusion of research conducted by Dr John Barry, Honorary Lecturer at University College London and co-founder of the Male Psychology Section of the British Psychological Society, who conducted a comprehensive survey of five thousand men across the US aged between eighteen and ninety-five in 2018.[12] Dr Barry concluded that 'the number-one thing that matters most in men's lives, far more than whether they're healthy or have good relationships with family or friends,

---

[11] 'As I See It: Midlife With Crisis', Victor Rozek, ITjungle.com 7 July 2014.
[12] Harry's Masculinity Report, 2017 and 2018. https://qz.com/work/1474562/what-makes-men-happy-a-study-by-harrys-says-job-satisfaction/

is whether they find satisfaction at work.' Sad, in a way, but true.

And yet, something else is also happening.

Another comprehensive well-being study published in *The Conversation*[13] back in 2013 found evidence of a clearly defined U-curve dip in happiness among men, with the trough of dissatisfaction occurring in our forties. Around sixty, we bounce back to being as happy as we were in our twenties and by the time we get to seventy, we are at our happiest. (Incidentally, the research also found that the dip was not only more pronounced for women, but they never regained the 'happiness' they once had in their twenties!)

It seems that we men look at our lives in our forties and wonder '*Is this all I have accomplished?*' Then fifteen years or so later, irrespective of whether we have achieved anything whatsoever, we look at our life and think, 'Actually, things are pretty good!' So many studies have found a similar pattern, and no one quite knows why.

Curiously, it is the same for apes.

The same U-shaped pattern of male midlife dissatisfaction was also found among a study of 508 great apes as reported by the National Academy of Sciences in the US.[14] It seems that the well-being curve is not uniquely human, which implies that the origins of the midlife slump may be biological, hidden somewhere in the DNA we share with our primate cousins.

But rams?!

A study of Soay sheep in 2002 by Lincoln A. Gerald found that once rams have stopped mating, their testosterone levels fall and they become withdrawn and grumpy, 'striking out irrationally'.[15] Lincoln gave this phenomenon the fabulous title of 'Irritable Male Syndrome':

'Males of many, and perhaps the majority, of long-lived species, express periodic changes in testicular activity and behaviour during their normal life cycle. In the most extreme examples, as illustrated by the Soay ram, males continually cycle between the sexually active/fertile state

[13] https://theconversation.com/hard-evidence-is-the-midlife-crisis-real-17909

[14] https://www.pnas.org/content/109/49/19949

[15] Gerald A. Lincoln (8 February 2002), 'The irritable male syndrome', *Reproduction, Fertility and Development*, 13 (8): 567–576, doi:10.1071/RD01077, PMID 11999307

and the sexually inactive/infertile state, often on an annual or long-term basis. In individuals, testicular activity may vary with changes in social status, nutrition, health, age and other factors. This also applies to man.'

'Testicular activity may vary with changes in social status.' That made me laugh. In other words, the higher 'rank' a man is, or believes himself to be, the greater his testicular activity is likely to become. Why do the names Clinton, Murdoch and Johnson suddenly spring to mind?

However, unlike rams, our testosterone levels don't fall off a cliff. They decrease fairly gradually at roughly 2 per cent a year from some date in our thirties, according to Britain's NHS.[16] This explains why some seventy-year-olds can still father children. Whether they should or not is an entirely different question.

So, testosterone cannot be the reason for the recognised dip in the life satisfaction of human males, a dip so profound that a 2008 study by Blanchflower and Oswald[17] described its effect as being equivalent to 'a third of the effect of being made redundant' – and being made redundant can feel like a blow to the solar plexus, trust me. They also analysed large data sets from twenty-seven European countries and found that the use of anti-depressants peaked in men (and women, to be fair) in their late forties. 'Being middle-aged nearly doubles a person's likelihood of using anti-depressants.'[18]

But again, I wondered – why?

One theory often spouted is that unhappy people tend to die earlier than others, therefore affecting the statistics. Even though this makes some sense and, as we have already seen earlier in the book, a positive attitude to ageing could add as many as seven years to your life, there must be more to it.

It could be that as we get older and therefore closer to death, many of us re-evaluate what is important and what is not. We work out that life is not about competition, it is about relationships. We realise that 'the bucket list', a concept much favoured among men, is not important, and

[16] https://www.nhs.uk/conditions/male-menopause
[17] http://andrewoswald.com/docs/2008ushapeblanoswald.pdf
[18] https://www.theatlantic.com/magazine/archive/2014/12/the-real-roots-of-midlife-crisis/382235

as we get even older, it starts to dawn on us that, perhaps, it never was.

One of my closest and dearest friends, the irreplaceable Will Fetherston, was diagnosed with advanced pancreatic cancer at the age of forty-seven. The diagnosis was a death sentence and even though he was to undergo some awful radiotherapy and chemotherapy to prolong his life as much as possible, the moment his doctor first broke the news to him, we all knew there was only going to be one outcome. It was just a matter of how long. When he rang me to tell me the news, I immediately asked him what he planned to do with the time he had left. 'What are you going to do? What's on your bucket list? Are you going to take the kids out of school and travel the world? See the pyramids? The Northern Lights? Dance naked in the snowfields of Sweden?' His reply was so damn perfect that it instantly exposed the utter superficiality of my line of questioning. I could almost hear his crooked smile at the other end of the phone, 'Cam, I am going to take the boys to school and pick them up at the end of each day. I am going to watch them play cricket and rugby. I am going to be home with Lizzie and savour every single moment with all of them. Everything I will miss is right here.'

Will, Liz, Sam, Jake and Joe all came to stay with us in Portugal in August of 2011 for what was obviously going to be Will's last holiday. At the end of this unforgettable week – a week full of yogic breathing, good food, good wine, lots of laughs and dragging himself out of bed to watch his talented sons play golf – Will took a decided turn for the worse but, fortified by Oramorph liquid morphine, he was determined to board the flight back to England. He did and he was admitted to hospital the next day. He died a few months later.

To be asked to be one of the pall bearers at his funeral was one of the proudest and saddest moments of my life. The cavernous church was standing room only. As was The Hurlingham Club afterwards for his wake. He was an immensely popular man with the rare gift of somehow making you feel that you were the only person in the room whenever and wherever he was talking to you. At the wake, one of the other pall bearers and I were standing alone in the middle of the noisy and bustling throng, numbly consoling one another with a beer. Adrian looked around at the packed venue and marvelled at the sheer volume of people. 'I'll be lucky to fill our front room for my funeral,' he remarked.

'Don't worry,' I reassured him. 'I'll be there.'

MENOPAUSE OR MENOPORSCHE – 'THE CHANGE' CAN BE AN EXCITING AND REWARDING TIME

As long as we adopt the right attitude and work at it.

Coping with menopause is not easy for so many women. The hot flushes, the mood swings, the body changes, the feelings of irrelevance and despair can be overwhelming. But it doesn't need to be this way. We can cope with peri- and post-menopause with the knowledge that it is a normal and natural part of life, however challenging it may be.

Seek assistance from medical professionals – and help the same professionals to see the menopause as a condition in its own right rather than simply masking anxiety or depression. Get on your mat, not only to enjoy the immense physical benefits of yoga but also to practise listening to your body, to help yourself reach a state of tranquillity, to calm your mind with your body, and to give yourself energy when your body craves it.

We need the ability to accept what is happening, to acknowledge the obstacles in our way and to realise that one of these obstacles will be our ego. But it is well worth the effort. The world after menopause is our chance to shine. It can be a world of renewed energy and renewed purpose. A new Part Two.

For men, 'the change' is less defined but real, nonetheless. To overcome the biologically programmed midlife dip in satisfaction we need to review our sources of identity and purpose. We need to throw away our bucket list and focus on what is truly important – which, more often than not, will be standing right in front of us.

CHAPTER 7:

Changing relationships

All relationships change – or stagnate.

This is the time in our lives when almost all of our relationships are changing: the relationships we have with our children, our parents, our partners and even ourselves.

FAMILY TIES

Our kids are growing up

Some of them are even becoming adults in their own right. The day you start turning to your son for advice is simultaneously magnificent and weirdly unsettling. He was only five yesterday!

Mind you, they aren't called the boomerang generation for nothing. The offspring you thought had left home to go off to university have a habit of turning up on your doorstep three or four years later with a car full of rarely washed clothes, battered kitchen pans, chipped supermarket crockery and bags bursting at the seams with fancy dress costumes. Just as you had begun to cherish the tidiness and peace of the empty nest, it's full again with twenty-somethings whose circadian rhythms would be far better suited to life on the other side of the planet.

Nearly a million more young adults in the UK are living with their parents than was the case two decades ago, according to a study by the thinktank Civitas. Whereas the majority of our generation fledged at seventeen or eighteen, a 2019 survey of American millennials, sponsored by TD Ameritrade, reported that the age at which they regard it to be embarrassing if you still live with your parents has increased to twenty-eight! None of this is surprising given the meteoric rise of student debt, the infestation of unsavoury unpaid internships and zero-hour employment contracts combined with a lack of affordable housing and sky-high rents. And COVID-19.

But the situation is rarely healthy for either party. While co-resident adult children 'can be a source of emotional and practical support for parents', according to research that the London School of Economics conducted across seventeen European countries between 2007 and 2015, returning children can also be the cause of significant conflict and stress, 'violating an exciting stage in their parents' lives and causing a substantial impact on well-being similar to what might be seen when someone develops an age-related disability.'[1] I assumed that returning offspring would ramp up the tension in the household for a while, but I had no idea they could prematurely age us!

Our relationship with our parents starts to change

During Part Two, the well-established parent–child relationship can start to turn. Little by little, you seem to be the one helping to make, or even sometimes making, key decisions, which will always seem a little strange as to some extent you will always be their little girl; their little boy.

Relationships with partners can also start to change

For so many couples, Part Two can be a watershed time. As we mentioned in the previous chapter, it is the time when quite a few couples break up, and quite a few more think about it. Sometimes this is planned as they had only been 'staying together for the kids'. But often it is unplanned. The empty nest phase prompts many of us to pause, take a look around, assess where we have got to in life and start to think about what we want from our Part Two – and with whom we wish to share it.

It can be the moment to look back on the time you have been together and evaluate how it has gone, where it has got to and where it is going; to ponder on what each of you wants from the relationship, or any relationship, in the future.

Some of us, women especially it seems, come to the realisation that the person they have been with for all these years is not the person they want to spend the rest of their life with after all. While divorce is still far

[1] https://www.theguardian.com/society/2018/mar/07/boomerang-offspring-damage-parents-wellbeing-study-finds

more prevalent among 'first halfers', the rate at which younger adults divorce has been decreasing while the divorce rate for people over fifty has been on the increase. In the US, the over-fifty divorce rate has doubled since the 1990s. For those over sixty-five, the divorce rate has tripled.[2] And 69 per cent of all divorces are instigated by women.[3]

But even if it doesn't end in divorce, and let's face it, the majority of marriages don't, it makes sense that the relationship with our partner will change to some degree. Is this the same person that I met all those years ago? How have they changed? How have I changed? What do we still have in common? Do we still share the same values? What did I want out of the relationship back then? What do I want out of one now?

Women no longer need a partner for procreation, so what are the needs that this partnership serves? Sexual fulfilment? Mutual financial support? Friendship? Love? Someone to share Part Two with who will actively support your aspirations for the second half, and someone whose aspirations you can support? And for men...?

What role do you want your partner to play in your Part Two?

A TIME FOR RE-EVALUATING FRIENDSHIPS

People can crudely be lumped into two camps: radiators or drains; people who give you energy and people who drain your energy. Part Two is the time to make sure we hang out with more radiators. We change. Our friends change. It's okay to let go of drains.

It takes courage to change our lives in meaningful and permanent ways. Don't be surprised if you discover that some 'friends' aren't as supportive as you would wish. The people who really know and understand you, and what's going on in your life, will be accepting, delighted and will support you all the way.

Good friends – true, long-lasting friendships – are interdependent: you need them as much as they need you. Good friends see you for who you are – and like you anyway! They are not friends because of your title or your status or your identity. They are friends because they enjoy your company, share similar values and respect any differing interests,

[2] https://www.pewresearch.org/fact-tank/2017/03/09/led-by-baby-boomers-divorce-rates-climb-for-americas-50-population
[3] https://www.asanet.org/press-center/press-releases/women-more-likely-men-initiate-divorces-not-non-marital-breakups

opinions and beliefs. Good friends understand that everyone has their off days. They bring light, not heat, to problems. They bring truth, too – wrapped in a way that helps you to best absorb it in that particular moment. Good friends make you feel good about yourself. Simply being in their company makes life a little sunnier. They help you to find that place within you that is full of warmth and forgiveness.

We are a social species. We need to belong. Friends are important. Good friends are life-affirming and essential.

Are you a good friend?

THE RELATIONSHIP WE HAVE WITH OURSELVES

All relationships need nurturing – even the one we have with ourselves. In fact, nurturing the relationship we have with our self lies at the core of yogic philosophy. For only through establishing a genuine, supporting and loving relationship with our self can we hope to establish a genuine, supporting and loving relationship with others.

The philosophy at the heart of yoga contains some simple and yet profound 'moral codes' known as *yamas*. They are universally relevant, no matter what upbringing we may have had or the religion or beliefs we may ascribe to. Some texts describe the *yamas* as abstinences or restraints, but I, Jane, prefer to think of them as principles that can help us to be at peace with ourselves and those around us. And as you will see, they are interconnected with one another.

The five main *yamas* are:

1. *Ahimsa*: non-violence or non-harming – in words and thoughts as well as deeds. Not harming others is obvious, but *ahimsa* is also about not harming ourselves. It involves genuinely understanding ourselves, being kind to ourselves and not letting our ego get in our way. For example, some of my friends have injured themselves doing High Intensity Training classes, perhaps because they were listening to their egos rather than their bodies. While for others, HIIT classes are a key part of their exercise routine, and their bodies thrive on it. We are all different.

I have seen students complain of a sore back but

refuse to use a prop to assist them with the pose. I try to help them practise *ahimsa* – to be kind to themselves, listen to their body and use a block or a belt or allow me to help them make the adaptation they need to make the pose work for them. If we adopt the principle of *ahimsa*, we can start to listen to our body and accept the truth that it is telling us.

2. *Satya*: truthfulness – staying true to ourselves. *Satya* is about being honest with yourself, honest with others, and refraining from judgement of both. It is recognising that we bend the truth constantly, even to ourselves, and that there is a freedom in being able to be who we really are, rather than hiding behind a mask of what we think others expect us to be. It is realising that the voice inside our head saying that we are not good enough is not the truth. It is our fear speaking and fear is too often *false evidence appearing real*.

Accepting the truth of things on the outside will, over time, help us to accept the truth on the inside. Levels of falsehood will start to fall away and we will be able to recognise our own essence and reality. There is a great calm and peace to be found in admitting and accepting the truth.

3. *Asteya*: non-stealing. This *yama* is so much more than not taking someone else's property. It is also not stealing their love, their ideas, their time, their self-respect. For instance, people who habitually arrive late, to meetings or yoga classes, are not only stealing time and respect from the others, they are also stealing the same from themselves. One of my students was routinely late for group classes – depriving herself of time to settle into the class, of that magical time in her day when she could be present and calm. Sometimes she would even leave the class before *savasana*, depriving herself of arguably the most important part of any yoga class, the moment when we completely let ourselves go.

The practice of *asteya* reminds us of the non-material richness of our lives. It helps us to engage with the perfectly imperfect reality of the moment. Practising *asteya* on your mat helps you to explore the small ways you withhold care and respect from yourself. It helps us to let go of wanting.

4. *Brahmacharya*: moderation, using energy wisely, conserving, nurturing. The modern world is all about *more* – more money, more cars, better holidays, bigger houses, more clothes, more muscle tone, more weight loss – and even when we get what we wanted, we still want more. All of which inevitably brings us more stress and more pain. Let's stop comparing ourselves and judging ourselves. Accepting who we are and appreciating what we have doesn't diminish us, it frees us.

5. *Aparigraha*: non-possessiveness or non-attachment. The joy of letting go. This *yama* is more than reducing our reliance on, and attachment to, material things. More profoundly, it is the joy of letting go of *non*-material baggage – negative thoughts, ego-driven identities, old grudges. It is letting go of thoughts and fears, of entrenched ideas, thoughts and beliefs about others and ourselves. When our son moved back home after university, Campbell and I suddenly found ourselves looking at life through the eyes of a caring twenty-something with a passion for treating everyone with respect and kindness, and very different ways of looking at the world, which sometimes rubbed up against our ingrained perspectives. It was a chance to re-evaluate several of our biases and beliefs – and let go of some of them.

One of my clients is a successful corporate executive who was experiencing back pain, headaches and insomnia. Gradually over time he came to the realisation that it was his need to be seen to be 'successful' that was the real cause of his pain – especially now that his time as a high-flying merchant banker was coming to an end. The pending loss of this identity was causing him to drink more and was having a drastic effect on his relationships, his work and his finances. He was in a constant state of anxiety with an unhealthy dose of self-loathing. Through his yoga practice, he was eventually able to realise that this long-held identity was superficial, and to let it go – bringing freedom, ease and lightness back into his life.

The *yamas* can lead us back to ourselves. They are 'the fundamental renunciation of a life based on fear. They are the change.'[4]

Imagine if everyone put these five *yamas* into practice. Imagine if our politicians and world leaders lived by them. What a glorious, safe and mutually prosperous world we would create.

This time in our lives is a wonderful opportunity to enhance the relationship we have with ourselves – after all we are the one person with whom we are present every second of our entire lives – 24/7, 365.25 days a year. This relationship is critical to a successful Part Two. How can we hope to 'thrive' if we don't like, respect or value ourselves?

Yoga teaches us to love and accept who we are. It also helps us to appreciate that we are more than a physical body; that we are a breathing, thinking, emotional, intuitive, spiritual entity that deserves to be content. We shall talk more about contentment in Chapter 10 (p.99).

Learning to live with and nourish others begins with learning to live with and nourish ourselves.

[4] Rolf Gates, *Meditations from the Mat* (Bantam Books 2002).

CHAPTER 8:

How we react to change

'Change is not something that we should fear. Rather, it is something that we should welcome. For without change, nothing in this world would ever grow or blossom, and no one in this world would ever move forward to become the person they're meant to be.'

BKS Iyengar[1]

There is a poignant, short scene at the end of *Harry Potter and the Goblet of Fire*. After yet another harrowing year at Hogwarts, Hermione turns to Harry and, with a sense of nervous trepidation in her voice, tinged with a fear of what the future may hold, she asks, 'Does this mean that everything is going to change forever?' Harry turns to her and delivers a simply perfect one-word response, infused with inevitability, acceptance and reassurance. 'Yes,' he replies.

Change is inevitable, but that does not mean it is easy. Coping with change can be tough. Embracing change can be even tougher, but it can also be incredibly liberating.

Our ability to embrace the inevitable and innumerable changes that lie ahead is the most important factor in determining our ability to thrive in the second half of our lives, and it is a skill that can be learnt and honed. Yes, some of us are naturally more resilient when it comes to change, the way that some people are better at drawing or running or sudoku. But every one of us can improve our resilience immeasurably. And we must if we wish to thrive in our second half.

This chapter is a condensed and updated version of the content I have been using in my 'Leading Change' and 'Embracing Change'

---

[1] Bellur Krishnamachar Sundararaja Iyengar (1918–2014) was the founder of the style of modern yoga known as 'Iyengar Yoga' and is considered one of the foremost yoga teachers in the world.

workshops for many years, adapted ever so slightly for the particular changes that we are likely to experience in our Part Two. For a more detailed exploration of the subject, may I suggest turning to *The Power to Change* (Kogan Page 2020).

Let's face it, Part Two will throw curve balls in our direction and some of these potential changes will be nasty ones – parents becoming ill and needing looking after, parents dying, partners dying, accidents, illnesses (some annoying, some serious), financial mishaps or even calamities – the future will come at us from all directions. We may be able to anticipate and prepare for some of these events, but so many are likely to strike us completely out of the blue. Even expected changes can be life-altering, no matter how clearly they were foreseen. The death of a parent for example, however inevitable it may be, can affect us in ways we hadn't imagined. And no matter how 'successful' or resilient we may consider ourselves to be, large changes can throw us sideways.

We need to accept that we will not be in full control of so many of the changes that will be coming our way. We won't be in control of when they will arrive, the size of their impact or even some of the consequences.

What we will have control over, however, is how we react to them.

HOW WE REACT TO CHANGE

I would like to share five key truths I have learnt about change over the decades of helping leaders to lead change and people to embrace change. Keep yourself in mind as we step through the list.

1. All change is inevitable. Change is not a phase that we can sit out. It is a part of life. Admitting this is the first step towards embracing it.

2. All change is personal. Even the most comprehensive organisational or social change is the culmination of a myriad of personal, individual changes.

3. Each of us erects our own personal barriers to change. It is an instinctive, evolutionary response. Some barriers will be small and last a few seconds, others will be large and may last a lifetime. But no matter how large the barriers appear to be, we can overcome them.

4. All change is emotional. The roller coaster of emotions we experience during times of major change is completely normal – and necessary. Emotion is four times more powerful than logic when it comes to change.

5. We only change if we want to. No one changes because they are told to; we only change if, and when, we want to. Therefore, if we wish to change, we must help ourselves to *want* to change. This will require finding the emotional triggers within us; the motivation we will need to embrace the change and seek out the opportunities. A key role of leadership in today's fast-changing world is helping your people to want to change. We can be our own change leader.

HOW WE REACT WHEN SIGNIFICANT CHANGE IS DONE TO US

How we react to major change that is forced upon us is both highly emotional and highly predictable.

One of the most profound and useful pieces of analysis concerning the emotions we experience during moments of dramatic change was conducted over fifty years ago by a Swiss psychiatrist, Dr Elisabeth Kübler-Ross, and published in her book, *On Death and Dying* (Macmillan 1969). After observing people who were dying of terminal illnesses, Dr Kübler-Ross observed that they experienced a common roller coaster of emotions and that these emotions occurred in a predictable sequence. But it wasn't only the patients who experienced this 'grief curve', as she called it; their loved ones did too. Change practitioners, psychiatrists and psychologists have since taken Kübler-Ross's curve and put it to use in their respective disciplines. I am no exception.

The 'Burning Platform' Change Curve

The 'Burning Platform' Change Curve is my modified version of Kübler-Ross's grief curve and I have been using it, and refining it, for decades. It outlines the sequence of emotions we experience when big change is done to us. Dramatic changes such as a diagnosis of a serious illness, being made redundant, an accident, divorce, the menopause, a sudden financial loss, or, yes, the death of a loved one.

I am continually reminded how simple and yet how powerful this curve is. During one memorable session in one of my workshops, I couldn't help but notice that one of the delegates was discreetly wiping away tears the entire time. She came up to me in the break and thanked me. Her father had died only a few weeks before and when this curve was presented on the screen she gasped, as it described the very emotional roller coaster ride she had been on. Her tears were not only from grief. Yes, she was re-living every single emotion as I stepped the group through the curve, but they were also tears of joy. 'I can't tell you how much of a relief it is to know that the emotions I have been experiencing are normal,' she revealed.

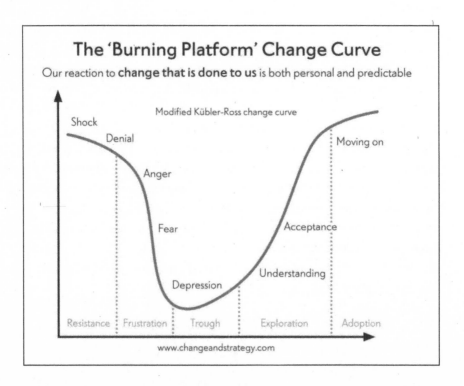

The 'Burning Platform' Change Curve

Our reaction to **change that is done to us** is both personal and predictable

Modified Kübler-Ross change curve

Shock
Denial
Anger
Fear
Depression
Acceptance
Understanding
Moving on

Resistance | Frustration | Trough | Exploration | Adoption

www.changeandstrategy.com

Let's take a canter through the curve. As we do, make it real and personal to you. Either think of a significant change that was forced upon you in the past or think of a significant change that you are likely to experience in the future.

Are you thinking of one? Good. Let's crack on.

Shock

When significant change is done to us, the first emotion we experience is shock. We don't say anything – well, nothing we would like to be remembered or recorded anyway! We don't hear anything either, and our thoughts are not particularly coherent. We are in a state of shock. If you have ever been made redundant, you will identify with this. The moment the words 'at risk of redundancy' leave the lips of the manager or the HR representative seated on the other side of the desk, you instantly cease to hear anything else they are saying. Receiving a phone call about a death of a close family member elicits an even more profound experience of shock: time stands still.

Denial

Hot on the heels of shock comes denial. Depending upon the situation and the size of the change, denial can appear in a variety of forms from mild ('This can't be happening') to strong ('This is not happening!'). Sometimes, in the most extreme circumstances, a little denial can be good for us. As Dr Kübler-Ross said, *'Denial helps us to pace our feelings of grief. There is a grace in denial. It is nature's way of letting in only as much as we can handle.'* But clinging on too long is unhealthy, for we would only be kidding ourselves. One day, we will have to face up to reality – and the sooner we do this the better, for denial can be insidious: the longer it continues, the harder it is to address.

Anger

When denial does begin to subside, it invariably gives way to anger. We rage at the universe, at our God or gods in general. We get angry at the unfairness of it all. We get angry at whoever we think is responsible for this change. We get angry at ourselves. The injustice and unfairness of the situation enrages us, and, in our fury, we will invariably say or do things that we may live to regret. When you find yourself in this situation, be kind to yourself and understand two things: first, the anger is a normal reaction to big change that is forced upon you, and second, the anger isn't you, it is simply you letting off steam.

Fear

Anger often conceals a deeper set of emotions – most noticeably, fear. Fear of failure, fear of losing our identity or status, fear of looking like a fool or a 'loser', fear of the consequences of the change. Again, this is a normal reaction to dramatic change that is done to us. By far the best thing to do is to voice your fears and concerns; get them out on the table. If we keep them bottled up, they take on a size, an importance and a severity that is often completely out of proportion. Our fears often shrink once we air them, so write them down, talk about them. With these simple acts, you will find that they may not be as scary or as daunting as they appeared to be when they were trapped inside your head.

What are your fears or concerns about your Part Two?

The trough

The 'trough of depression', as I lovingly refer to this next emotional state, is a necessary evil, for this is when we grieve. Grief isn't a sign of weakness; it is an essential part of the healing process. This is the time for us to feel sorry for ourselves, to wish that this change hadn't happened and to mourn the loss, whatever that loss may be. Allow yourself this essential step but, again, be careful not to linger too long, for 'the trough' is where victims dwell.

Victimhood is an insidious and oddly seductive enemy, one that can ruin our lives, sometimes without us fully realising that we are allowing it to happen. When major change happens to us, we feel a loss of control. We didn't ask for the change and yet here it is. But even though we may indeed be a victim of this change, we must be careful not to let victimhood define who we are. We must treat the feeling of victimhood as transitory; as a stage we are going through, rather than a destination. We must shrug off the sinister cloak of victimhood as soon as we can, for the longer we wear it, the more comfortable it can become.

We all know people for whom victimhood has become a core part of their identity. They received one large shock, or perhaps one shock too many, and have succumbed to the world that seemed to be out to get them. Their feeling of powerlessness is so overwhelming that they give in to it. They can start to wonder whether they did something to cause it, perhaps even convincing themselves that, in some way, they deserve it. Some people even begin to believe that 'victim' is the role that they were always destined to play and that they are powerless to do anything about it. They are wrong – on all counts. Don't allow yourself to descend into this downward spiral.

Realising that all of the emotions that we outlined above – shock, denial, anger, fear, and a feeling of hopelessness – are normal is the first, significant step out of the trough. The second and even more powerful step is to ask yourself the magic question: 'So, what am I going to do about it?'

Understanding

Understanding is when our head kicks in, we acknowledge that the change has happened and that it is up to us to do something about it. We still may not like it, but we at least acknowledge what has happened and why it has happened. We start to make plans and explore options.

Acceptance

Acceptance is a step further. A big step. It is when our heart finally accepts what our head has been trying to tell us. We have explored options and, perhaps tentatively, have made some of the changes that we need to make. We may have slipped back down into the trough once or twice, but we have persevered and now know that we can cope with this change, that we can make this change work. We have accepted it.

Acceptance allows us to move on.

Case Study: Accepting the inevitable changes that come with age

Innumerable significant changes lie ahead of us as we get older and our ability to accept them will be one of the most important determinants of our future happiness. Fighting against changes that are inevitable expends a great deal of energy, makes us miserable and wastes both time and energy. It is ultimately pointless.

We can see this more clearly by observing people who are currently in their seventies, eighties or older. We will inevitably see people who have been hit with strokes, heart attacks, heart operations, hip operations, arthritis, cognitive decline, bereavement, cancers, this list could go on for a while. Whoever first coined the phrase *'old age sure ain't for sissies'* hit the nail right on the head.

Those who are able to accept these conditions with minimal regret and zero self-judgement, and adapt their lives accordingly, are far happier and far more content than those who fight inevitable changes every step of the way. They accept they now need an afternoon nap rather than seeing it as a form of weakness. They accept when their eyesight is no longer good enough for them to drive at night, so they don't. Perhaps they even make a decision not to proceed with chemotherapy and are content with the decision. None of these decisions is giving up. It is acceptance. Giving up is giving in. Acceptance is admitting reality – and accepting it with grace and a sense of positive calmness.

A mantra that Jane often uses in her private practice and with her clients as well is 'I do enough. I have enough. I am enough.'

We will return to this key topic in more detail in Chapter 10 (p.99).

HOW WE REACT WHEN WE INSTIGATE SIGNIFICANT CHANGE

Surprisingly, we also experience a roller coaster of emotions when we instigate the change. The emotions may not always be as powerful, but they are just as real. And this is a change curve that very few people talk about.

The 'Quantum Leap' Change Curve

I call it the 'Quantum Leap' Change Curve and it outlines the sequence of emotions that we experience when we instigate significant change ourselves – quitting a job, starting a new job, getting married, leaving a relationship, starting a new relationship, starting a business, embarking on a new chapter of our lives.

Again, as we step through each of the emotions on this curve, think of a big change you have initiated in the past or one that you may be initiating in the future.

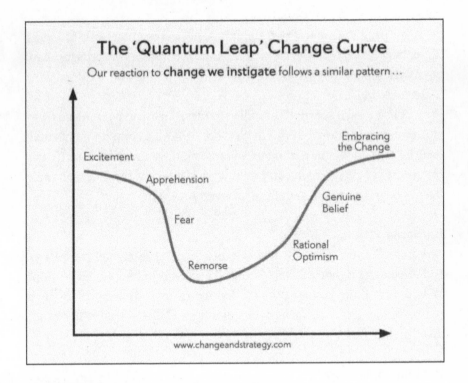

Excitement

Inevitably, we are excited when we embark upon something new that we have instigated. This excitement can be intoxicating.

Apprehension

But we wouldn't be human if doubts didn't start to creep in – even when it is 'good' change that we have chosen. *'Do I have what it takes to succeed?'* All of the things we don't know can bubble to the surface. All of the things that could possibly go wrong can start to reveal themselves. A small voice inside our heads begins to ask, *'What have I done?'*

Fear

Our evolutionary protection mechanism is never far below the surface. Doubts can grow into fears and fear of failure again can come to the fore. Or to be more accurate, fear of the consequences of failure. At least in the last curve, someone else was forcing us to change, so if it all went pear-shaped, we would at least have someone else to blame. Not this time. This one is our doing. We have chosen this path and the consequences will be on us, entirely. We are worried about how not succeeding could affect us financially, how our self-esteem or reputation could take a battering, how our relationships may be affected. We fear we may be fully exposed with nowhere to hide.

The intensity of this fear will vary from person to person and from situation to situation, but it will be there. It is also completely normal, healthy even, if we turn it to our advantage; if we use it to identify the things that could go wrong and then work to prevent them, lessen their likelihood or impact, or get ready to overcome them.

Remorse
This curve has a different trough. Rather than depression, it is remorse. Did I make the right decision? Should I have stayed in the relationship? Why did I sell the house? Why did I start my own business? Feeling a twinge of remorse about a big decision is normal. Let's observe it, but not dwell on it.

Rational optimism
Rather than 'understanding', I have called this stage 'rational optimism'. We have looked at what could possibly go wrong, spurred on by our doubts, fears and a dose of remorse, and our brains have established that despite the risks, success is indeed possible. It may take longer than we originally thought. It may be a different shape than we originally planned, but we can do it.

Genuine belief
And then, just as with the 'Burning Platform' Change Curve, our heart kicks in and we genuinely believe that we can succeed; that we can make a go of this big change that we have set in motion. We get our mojo back.

We can proceed with embracing the change we have instigated and making the most of it.

Case Study: Gaele Lalaly – climbing Mount Olympus
Gaele Lalaly has, by her own admission, recently completed her Part One and made a giant leap into Part Two, instigating a massive career change for no reason other than life is simply too short not to.

After twenty years with Japanese electronics giant, Panasonic, Gaele left her prized job as 'UK head of marketing communications, Olympic strategy and digital innovations' only a few months before the 2020 Tokyo Games were originally due to begin. It was a job that she had coveted and then made her own after seizing the initiative to channel a large swathe of Panasonic's global Olympic marketing budget into online for the 2012 London Olympics.

With the success of Panasonic's 2012 Olympics campaign, Gaele was promoted to head of marketing communications in 2014. Fast forward to 2020, she was invited to join the company's 'high potential talent pool'. Her career was in the fast lane, heading for a head of business role in the not-too-distant future.

And then she quit.

Why? She admits that two things she simply adores are the Olympics and Japan. So, here she was, the UK head of Olympics for a major Japanese sponsor and her career was on an upward trajectory. Most people fight to cling on to their corporate jobs for decades longer than they really wish they had. Proactively changing when you are at the top of your game is very brave and extremely rare. So, I asked her what was her impetus for making such a courageous move?

'I'm going to say fear. The fear of becoming what I didn't want to become gave me the courage to jump.

'I joined Panasonic because they were a global Japanese company and they were sponsoring the Olympic Games. My ambition was to run Panasonic's Olympic marketing and to visit Japan as much as possible. That kept me focused and driven. And then, quite early on in my career, I had the biggest opportunity on earth for a marketing professional, to be involved in a Home Olympic Games. I was talking to friends at Adidas who thought the same: "London 2012 will be the highlight of our career," they said. I was only thirty-seven. I am now forty-five and London 2012 has indeed been the highlight of my career.

'Once I realised that fact, I had to leave. I have so many more highlights left within me. I've got another twenty years. I want another three or four careers. Panasonic has been amazing to me. It is a great company with values that so fundamentally fit my own, I have had so many wonderful and diverse opportunities. But I needed to go. So, with a great deal of self-reflection, courage and support, I gave myself permission to leave Panasonic and start anew.'

Gaele's experience on the Quantum Leap Change Curve

'I love this version of the change curve!' declared Gaele. 'I can absolutely relate to it.

'But even before I got to the curve, I needed to prepare as much as possible for the change ahead. I needed to be completely clear why I was doing it, so that I didn't spend the next few months and years asking myself the question over and over again. In my moments of doubt, I have been able to remind myself of why I made the decision to change, a reason that was fully matured before I made the leap. This gives me a much greater feeling of control as well. I know the road ahead will have its tough moments and my self-confidence will be tested. But I am prepared for it, because I will never forget why I have made the decision.

'Panasonic being such a wonderful employer, it was very difficult for me to leave. But I needed to be free – free in my mind to start to explore my next phase and to start to look at other opportunities, and I didn't want to do this part-time. I really needed to be in the emptiness in order to discover those little sparkles of gold. I knew that I wouldn't have been able to discover them until I was properly in the void.'

As you can probably tell by the colour and the drama of her prose, Gaele is gloriously French.

With a great deal of guidance from her intuitive, empathetic and insightful coach, Sharon Hall of River Deep Coaching, Gaele is now ascending the right-hand slope of her Quantum Leap Change Curve, oscillating between 'rational optimism' and 'genuine belief'. She is networking as only she can and has the rescheduled 2021 Tokyo Olympics and the 2024 Paris Olympics in her sights. She dreams of working at the heart of the Olympic and Paralympic movement itself and enjoying several different careers, from start-ups to academia. She has the passion, drive, commitment, focus, attitude and support that she needs to succeed.

If anyone can make their dream come true, it is Gaele.

CHAPTER 9:

Overcoming our barriers to change and building resilience

'Resilience is accepting your new reality, even if it's less good
than the one you had before. You can fight it, you can do nothing
but scream about what you've lost, or you can accept that
and try to put together something that's good.'
Elizabeth Edwards[1]

Each of us erects our own personal barriers to change. No matter how high our natural resilience may be, every one of us has our own particular change hurdles that we need to overcome. And almost every single one of these hurdles is emotional.

In our years of experience helping people to cope with, embrace or instigate change, we have seen and experienced a host of obstacles that get in the way: how we see ourselves, our ego, a fear of failing, fear of the unknown, fear of others, fear of blame, difficulties with our past, physical challenges, our biases, our beliefs – and every single one of them resides between our ears.

Negative thoughts are so powerful that they can make us ill through the release of cortisol, the 'stress hormone', which weakens our immune system. Too much cortisol 'can derail your body's most important functions. It can also lead to a number of health problems, including anxiety, depression, headaches, heart disease, memory and concentration problems, problems with digestion, insomnia and weight gain.'[2]

---

[1] American attorney, best-selling author and healthcare activist (1949–2010).
[2] www.webmd.com

Our mind is the most powerful organ in our body. It can prevent us from functioning, and it can help us to soar. And while it erects barriers to successful change, we can also harness its power to disassemble those barriers or to diminish them to such a size that we are able to step over them with ease.

And this process starts with the simple act of observation.

THE POWER OF OBSERVATION

Tackling our negative thoughts and our innate fears requires more than adopting a positive mental attitude. 'The power of positive thinking' is all well and good but it must be supported by substance if it is to have any effect. Reality needs to be accepted. It can't be magicked away with mantras, however well-meaning they may be. More importantly, no positive thought has any chance of taking root in a cluttered, busy mind.

The first step to adopting a more helpful, positive attitude is to declutter the mind and the best way to do that is through observation. Jane explains how she does this with her students:

'When my students arrive at their evening yoga class, they are buzzing. Their minds are busy; full of whatever they have done during the day, thinking about what they are going to do this evening and thinking about tomorrow – all at once. They are wondering whether they should have done something differently, whether it will matter that they couldn't get a project finished, worrying if their colleague had taken offence at that off-the-cuff remark. They are wondering about dinner and what mayhem will be waiting for them when they get home. They are wondering about what their agenda looks like tomorrow. I can almost hear their internal wheels spinning as everyone bursts into the studio.

'The first thing I do is to ask people to lie down, close their eyes and "arrive on their mats". Then I ask them to take a deep breath and simply watch their busy thoughts race around inside their heads. I say to them, "Don't interact with these thoughts. Don't judge them. Just observe them. And breathe."

'Within a couple of minutes, the entire energy in the room starts to calm. It's as though someone has turned a dial somewhere. I can almost hear the buzzing slow to a stop as every single person starts to relax, as every person starts to observe and detach from their thoughts.'

The human mind has many tens of thousands of negative thoughts every day, a strange evolutionary hangover from our earliest ancestors' 'fight or flight' survival instincts. That may have been fine for early *Homo sapiens*, who were lucky if they lived a couple of decades, but we twenty-first century versions have to endure all this negativity for eighty years or more. If we are not careful, it can be exhausting!

With minds that are programmed to be constantly on the lookout for dangers, both real and imagined, we can easily come to identify with some of these negative thoughts and emotions. We can come to believe a mind that is continuously warning us that we may not be able to do something, that we have never done it before, that the odds of failure are high. A mind that is continually ruminating about something we said or something we did or something that might happen can blow things out of all proportion. When our mind is constantly berating us and judging us for getting angry, for being angry, for being too emotional, for reacting, for not reacting, for being depressed – we can begin to believe that we are these negative thoughts and emotions. We can allow them to define us.

But we are not 'depression'. We are not 'anger'. We are not 'regret'. We cannot be defined by our negative thoughts for the simple reason that they are not us. They are simple thoughts – ephemeral, transient and ultimately irrelevant.

As Jane says:

'The simple act of observing our thoughts; of stepping back and simply watching them, without any judgement whatsoever, instantly helps us to realise they are not us; they are something completely separate. I advise my clients not to interact with them. Don't try to fight them as they feed and grow on attention. But don't try to shut them out either. They thrive on that sort of energy too. To rob them of their energy, of their power, we have to ignore them. Like unwelcome guests, by all means let them in the front door, but sweep through the house to open the back door for them and watch them leave.

'The same thing goes with emotions, too. Simply observing the fact that you were upset or angry or distraught or hurt helps to diminish the hold that strong emotions can have on us. But again, we must observe them without judgement. There is nothing wrong with strong emotions at all; they are part of being human. But don't cling on to them, and certainly don't let them define you in any way. The simple act of observing that "I was angry then" or "I was really upset by that" doesn't make the anger or the hurt any less profound or any less meaningful; it just puts some space between you and the emotion.'

When you start to detach yourself and your emotions or negative thoughts, you can start to do something about them.

Non-attachment

Once observed, negative thoughts can be diminished, perhaps even ignored, through the practice of non-attachment.

The concept of non-attachment, or *aparigraha*, is central to yoga and like anything worthwhile, it can take some time to comprehend fully, a lifetime to master and comes with its own inbuilt paradox. But it is critical to our ability to embrace change.

Non-attachment is not being aloof or distant. It is not 'not caring'. It is not chilling out and being oblivious to the world. In many ways, it is actually the polar opposite of all of those. It is being so alive and so connected to the core of your body that you are completely aware of what is unfolding around you and yet you remain unphased by it. Not untouched: unphased.

Once we can let go of how we look or how we think others think of how we look, of what we think about ourselves and what we think others may be thinking about us; once we start listening to our bodies rather than our egos; once we stop comparing ourselves to other people; once we let go of the urge to rush to the end of the yoga pose but instead savour every stage of each *asana* (posture), then we have started to practise 'non-attachment'. And of course, what works on the mat works just as well when we are off it too.

The easiest form of non-attachment to understand is detaching ourselves from physical things. After all, a car is just a car. A house is just a house. A boat is, well, let's just say that the best boat is one you return to the owner at the end of the day.

Non-attachment becomes especially relevant when we are able to apply it to those key intangibles that drive our behaviours and actions: our ego, our identity, our thoughts, our beliefs, our emotions, our fears. It means separating you from your ego; separating you from your negative thoughts or beliefs; separating you from your fears. A simple statement such as 'That's my ego talking' is non-attachment. It shows you recognise that while your ego is part of you, it isn't all of you; it doesn't define you. There is no need to feel guilty because of something your ego said or did. Observing it then enables you to do something about it.

People who stay rigidly attached to their egos are unable to do this. If their pride has caused them to lash out at someone, they will find it impossible to apologise because their pride is who they are. Admitting a mistake is not something their ego will do, therefore it is not something they will do. However, if that person was able to detach themselves from their pride, they could realise that their ego had hurt someone. They would be able to take responsibility and apologise – because they are more than their pride; they are more than their ego.

Overcoming fear of failure

'I've missed more than nine thousand shots in my career. I've lost almost three hundred games. Twenty-six times, I've been trusted to take the game winning shot and missed. I've failed over and over and over again in my life. And that is why I succeed.' — Michael Jordan

Fear of failure is the most common fear when it comes to change at any time of life, but it seems to be heightened when it comes to Part Two.

The default settings for the human mind when change happens are doubt and fear. Our minds become full of doubts about our ability to succeed, full of fears of failing. In some situations, the fear of failure can be so strong that it can cause us to sabotage our own efforts, thereby fulfilling our own prophecy of doom. Sometimes, the fear of failure can be so great that we decide it is better not to try at all, thereby condemning ourselves to a constant background hum of inadequacy rather than face the potential of trying and possibly being found wanting.

In these moments, we forget that every single success is actually the end result of numerous 'failures', numerous setbacks along the way. As Nelson Mandela put it: 'Do not judge me by my success. Judge me by how many times I fell down and got back up again.'

Falling is not failing. It is the only real way to learn. We learn very little if we succeed first time. Let me give you a trivial example: I was a whiz at maths when I was thirteen. I didn't understand what the fuss was about. In fact, during the whole of the eighth grade, I got one exam question wrong. What did I learn from grade eight maths? Naff-all. Except that I could take the subject for granted. Fast forward to the second year of university and oh my goodness, maths was impenetrable! I learnt how little I actually knew and how much I still had to learn. I had to dig deeper than I have ever had to dig just to pass the year. I finished the year with 99 questions wrong out of 200 and it was so much more valuable as an experience than the 199 I answered correctly six years before.

We learn very little from the things we are naturally good at, unless we pause to look closer and work out how we could have been even better – which we rarely do. We learn a great deal from those things that we need to work at. We learn very little from our successes. We have the opportunity to learn so much from our 'failures'.

I hate the word 'failure'. I hate the word 'hate' too, but that's for another time. Ritz Carlton, the world-famous hotel operator, once banned the word 'failure' from their corporate lexicon. Instead, they suggested everyone use 'glitch'. Why? Because 'failure' is hard to stomach and incredibly difficult to bounce back from. 'Failure' feels terminal.

'Glitches' on the other hand – anyone can recover from glitches. Glitches are simply bumps in the road. Failure is the end of the road. Try something and you don't succeed first time? That's just a glitch. Not succeeding the second time? A glitch. Third? Um, maybe there's a pattern here that needs a little closer inspection. We need to learn from our glitches, not just repeat the same process and expect a different result as if by magic. But it's still not a failure. Thomas Edison famously experienced ninety-nine glitches before, on his one hundredth attempt, he finally succeeded in getting his electric light globe to work.

Actually, he labelled his first ninety-nine attempts as 'failures' which I think is simply not helpful. Bad Thomas.

ENHANCING OUR RESILIENCE

Resilience is most often used to describe stoicism. The D-Day Veterans were hailed in the British press as 'The Resilient Generation' during the seventy-fifth anniversary celebrations in 2019. But resilience is more than being stoic in the face of adversity.

Put simply, resilience is the ability to embrace change; to roll with punches, accept what has happened and move forward in whatever sized steps you can.

The American Psychological Association lists four key attributes to resilience:

a) The capacity to make realistic plans and take steps to carry them out;
b) a positive view of yourself and confidence in your strengths and abilities;
c) skills in communication and problem solving, and;
d) the capacity to manage strong feelings and impulses.[3]

Or, in our language:

• Achieve things – don't be a bystander to your own life or a victim of someone else's;
• Like yourself and trust yourself;
• Communicate and solve problems calmly, and;
• Stay as non-attached, as objective, as possible.

These four concise bullets are clear, self-explanatory and a great place to start, but they gloss over a few important details that are buried

---

[3] https://www.apa.org/helpcenter/road-resilience

in the layer beneath. Let's take a few moments to delve a little deeper into some of the other things we also could look at doing to enhance our resilience.

Letting go of the past

You can't change what has happened. Good or bad, let it remain in the past. If it was good, feel free to look back on it fondly, but without wishing to return to it, because you can't. If it wasn't so good, let it go. Don't keep dragging it into the present and don't let it affect your future. By all means, learn from it, but look forwards. A close friend of ours describes this as 'the joy of ex': the delight of being an ex-first-husband, ex-first-wife, ex-parent-of-small-children, ex-employee, ex-owner-of-a-large-house, ex-runner, ex-rugby player, ex-anxiety sufferer. It really is the joy of letting go and not only accepting, but perhaps even revelling in, the situation you find yourself in at this point in your life. It is about embracing the present, living in the moment.

Social connections

We humans are a social species. Relationships are critically important. Helping others, accepting help from others, being part of a community – these are all life-enhancing, life-saving and life-expanding, and each one builds our resilience.

Accepting that change is part of life

Accept that stuff happens – bad stuff happens, good stuff happens, and the one thing we have control of is how we react. This is the foundation upon which resilience is built. Certain goals may simply no longer be attainable as a result of adverse situations. Accepting the elements that you cannot change can help you focus on those elements that you can.

Keep things in perspective

Being able to see the bigger picture is a key skill that also enhances our resilience. When something bad happens, find the good things in your life to gain some broader perspective. Of course, this is not always easy. Another friend of ours lost his father while we were writing this book. His father was in his late eighties with heart and lung conditions.

COVID-19 was the last straw. Even though he knew that his father was not immortal, and that this day would inevitably arrive, our friend was staggered at how much it affected him. He was now the eldest in his family and felt, in some strange way, he was no longer a 'son'. This sudden change of status bowled him over. Something profound had changed in his life, forever. 'But then I thought: *One of the worst things that I have feared and dreaded has now happened,*' he explained. '*So, I no longer have that fear to worry about.* This thought put it all into perspective somehow. That and how lucky I am to have a lovely wife and a lovely life.'

Move forward – even in baby steps

No matter how traumatic the change may be, take action – no matter how small your initial actions may seem to be. Forward momentum is evidence of acceptance, and acceptance is the first stage of resilience; of your ability to accept and embrace change.

Be kind to yourself

Our favourite in the concise four-point list earlier is 'Like yourself and trust yourself'. But while doing both of those, don't expect infallibility. You aren't perfect, don't expect yourself to be. Not every step you take will be a good one. Not every decision will be the right one. So, please, give yourself a break. The last thing you need is someone berating you for perceived underachievements – especially if that someone is you!

Optimism

With an optimistic outlook, we can embrace the future with confidence. With a pessimistic outlook, we will fear it. When something bad happens, the last thing we need is a little voice telling us *'If you think that is bad, wait until what's coming next'.* We need a little voice that tells us that we can rebuild and recover; that due to inherent nature, skills and talents, our future can be a success.

Transform hope into confidence with action

The bedrock of resilience, the engine that drives resilience, is hope. A belief, a faith, a confidence that we can take the knocks, embrace the changes that come our way and thrive. This confidence is strongest when it comes from a place of strength. Wishes alone will never be sufficient; hope based on wishes alone is hollow. Hope needs to be based on a confidence built on reality; on an acknowledgment of our strengths, our skills and that the power to cope with change that lies within. It also must be based on action. Simply wishing to lose weight or become healthier doesn't work without action. Wishing for a better job or a new career doesn't work either. They too require action; action based on a confidence that you can make the changes you need in full knowledge that obstacles will invariably be thrown at you and you will be able to work out how to overcome them.

You may also find that what worked for you at one time in your life no longer works so well now. That's entirely normal. Work to accept that change is inevitable and that leaving behind our old ways of doing things is entirely healthy.

Change is nothing to fear. It is something to be embraced – with confidence.

CHAPTER 10:

Radical acceptance and the holy grail of contentment

'He who is not contented with what he has,
would not be contented with what he would like to have.'
Socrates [1]

RADICAL ACCEPTANCE

What a brilliant phrase. I wish I had invented it, but unfortunately, I didn't. I received it second hand from our daughter who in turn heard it from a rheumatologist in Sydney. It is so much more powerful than mere 'acceptance'.

What I love about 'Radical Acceptance' is that it is active. Mere 'acceptance' can sometimes, incorrectly, be regarded as passive. Passive acceptance could even tip over into victimhood if we are not careful. Radical acceptance is dynamic. It reeks of momentum, of action, perhaps even of destiny. It is not just accepting the way things are, it is proactively embracing reality, so that we can then do something about it.

In Chapter 8 (p.80) we saw that 'acceptance' is the last critical stage of the change curve – a mandatory step that enables us to move on. I would now like to take this concept one step further. 'Radical acceptance' is acceptance with purpose. It isn't only accepting things as they are; it is accepting them, embracing them and incorporating them into your life.

[1] Ancient Greek philosopher (c.470–399BC).

Santosa

Hi. Jane here. We couldn't have a chapter on acceptance without talking about *santosa* (also spelt *santosha*), the practice of proactive, whole-hearted acceptance that is a central tenet of yoga. The word is derived from two Sanskrit words: *san* meaning 'completely' or 'altogether', and *tosha* meaning 'contentment', 'satisfaction', 'acceptance'.

In other words, complete contentment through acceptance.

Santosa is one of the five *niyamas*, practices that require us to observe our inner selves:

1. *Saucha*: recognising and removing bad habits.

2. *Tapas*: which translates into a combination of 'self-discipline' and 'burning enthusiasm'. Ekhart Yoga describes *tapas* as 'our inner wisdom that we sometimes ignore and the fiery passion that feeds our sense of purpose.'[2]

3. *Svadhyaya*: self-reflection to bring us in closer contact with our true self.

4. *Isvara Pranidhana*: often translated as 'contemplation of, or even surrendering to, a higher power'. As we will discuss in Chapter 25 (p.217), this higher power can be God, gods or the divine that lies within.

5. *Santosa*: Complete contentment through acceptance.

Santosa is a lack of desire for what you perceive others to have. It is the ability to appreciate what we have right now, accept reality, embrace it and move forward with contentment. Through practising *santosa*, we can be free from cravings, pointless jealousies and ego-driven desires; free to follow our own path without fear. Free to embrace the present and the future with positivity.

The concept and practice of *santosa* is central to yoga therapy. When a client is able to wholeheartedly accept where they are in their lives physically, mentally and emotionally, they become open to change and I am then able to help them to help themselves with hope, courage and confidence.

---

[2] https://www.ekhartyoga.com/articles/practice/an-introduction-to-the-5-niyamas

But acceptance is not always an easy thing to achieve. Denial can be such a powerful emotion – denying the reality of a relationship that is bad news, a job that is bad for us, or denying that we may be addicted to something. We can be so terrified of changing that we cling on to our unhealthy, perhaps even dangerous, status quo for as long as we can. Often, it isn't until we hit rock bottom that we finally accept reality and decide to do something about it.

One wonderful woman I know is simply too frightened to come off her anti-depressants. When I talked to her about yoga therapy and how so many of my clients have been able to reduce their reliance on these drugs and that some have even come off them altogether, she just doesn't want to know. When I suggested that perhaps she could have a chat to a psychologist or a cognitive behavioural therapist, her alarmed response was, 'but they will only tell me to come off my anti-depressants!'

Another bright and equally brave young woman came to see me when a break-up had thrust her into a desperate bout of depression. She stopped eating and started loathing herself. She especially hated to be on her own, especially at night, when there was nothing to fill her head but her negative thoughts. She would lie in bed, sleepless, picturing her ex out partying and perhaps even sleeping with other people. She began drinking to block out her constantly ruminating thoughts, which, she said, 'only made things ten times worse the next morning'. She had fallen into a vortex of depression. We practised yogic breathing techniques which, enabled her to watch her thoughts and feelings from an anchored and present place. I gave her permission and the space to feel the way she was feeling. That it was okay to feel sad. That it was normal. It was okay to feel angry or jealous. And that none of these emotions were her. They were just emotions. After the ninety-minute session, she bounced into her home declaring, 'I feel liberated!' Her mother shed a tear at her next line: 'And I'm starving!'

How to practise *santosa*

The practice of *santosa* is conceptually straightforward. It is learning to see things as they are and accept how or why they have happened. But while theoretically simple, it can be difficult in practice, sometimes even painfully so. It starts with being calm, bringing your attention into your body, watching your breath and then calming your breath. Calming the breath calms the body and begins to calm the mind. When we are calm, we can then start to detach ourselves from our thoughts and feelings. It can be a very profound moment. Sometimes the release can be overwhelming.

Over time and with the help of guided meditation, we can start to feel or reveal our true self. Your true self is anchored. Like a boat on a swirling sea, it is safely anchored to the seabed. The winds may buffet it. The swirling seas may throw it around. But it is safe and secure. Whenever you feel as though you are being tossed about by outside forces or inner thoughts, come back to your anchor: come back to your breath, to your body, to your true self. That is where you will find inner peace and strength.

Your true self is not someone who is psychologically addicted to anti-depressants. It is not someone who is depressed. It is not someone who is physically addicted to alcohol or cocaine or heroin or tobacco. It is not someone who is anxious or fretful or negative about themselves. It is not a victim. It is much more profound and universal than all of that.

It is you.

CONTENTMENT

What is 'contentment'?

Let's start with what it is not. It is not ticking off everything on some great to-do list of life. It is not smugness, either. Nor is it complacency. Genuine contentment is not possible without humility and constant change.

Contentment is both a sense of inner peace and an ambition to continually strive to maintain that feeling – and this requires acceptance of change.

Genuine contentment is not an easy thing to achieve, as we have seen already and will continue to explore in many places throughout the rest of this book. Gurus, teachers, prophets and philosophers alike have been discussing it and striving to achieve it throughout the ages. It is a common theme, often with only subtle differences, across pretty much every religion.

To devout Christians, genuine faith in The Lord is the path to contentment. It lies in 'belonging to the living God for that will lead to true happiness'.[3] 'I have learned, in whatsoever state I am, therewith to be content,' wrote Paul from prison in his letter to the congregation he had established in Macedonia.[4]

Islam adopts a similar attitude to contentment. It also concurs with Plato[5] and Christianity that contentment does not lie in the pursuit of worldly goods. Plato said, 'The greatest wealth is to live content with little'. The Islamic equivalent is: 'Look at the person who is inferior to you; and do not look at one who is superior to you. Thereby you would be able to better appreciate the blessings that God bestowed upon you.'[6]

However, in both Islam and Christianity, contentment comes with one rather important caveat – it is available only to the believer. 'As for him who disbelieves, I shall leave him in contentment for a while, then I shall compel him to the torment of the Fire, and worst indeed is that destination!' proclaims The Quran.[7] The Biblical view is of a similar ilk: 'That word of Christ, "He that believes not shall be damned", will judge all unbelievers to eternal ruin; and there are many such words.'[8]

I must admit, I prefer the Jewish ode to contentment: 'A joyful heart makes a cheerful face; a sad heart makes a despondent mood. All the days of a poor person are wretched, but contentment is a feast without end.'[9]

Buddhists concur. 'Contentment is the greatest wealth,' proclaimed Buddha. But he also believed that genuine contentment is not possible without accepting and embracing change: 'A person who wants all things in the world to be just as he wishes is as foolish as a person who builds a house in sand and believes he will live there for thousands of years.'[10]

Aristotle[11] had a slightly different take on contentment: 'Knowing yourself is the beginning of all wisdom.' Yes, it comes from acceptance but also from realising one's full potential.

---

[3] https://www.evangelical-times.org/25346/christian-contentment
[4] Philippians 4:11.
[5] Ancient Greek philosopher (428–348BC)
[6] Sahih Muslim.
[7] Al-Baqara, Chapter 2, Verse 126.
[8] John Chapter 12.
[9] The Book of Proverbs.
[10] The Scriptures of Won Buddhism, p.211.
[11] Ancient Greek philosopher (384–322BC).

Contentment comes from accepting things the way they are, but this does not mean capitulation or inaction. You can still be content but retain a drive, a purpose, an energy. Contentment with how things are today does not mean subjugating yourself to victimhood, nor does it negate a willingness to instigate change.

You can be utterly content but still follow the simple and yet profound wisdom of The Serenity Prayer: 'Grant me the serenity to accept the things I cannot change, courage to change the things I can, and the wisdom to know the difference.'[12]

Both contentment and radical acceptance are impossible demands of a busy, cluttered mind. If your mind is full of negative thoughts, of unrealistic expectations, of fears about the future, of regrets for past mistakes; if your mind is continually replaying past scenes over and over again, judging every wrong step and wishing different things had been said and different things had been done – your mind will never be able to pause, accept and move on.

But if we can calm the mind, accept the present and embrace the future, whatever it may bring, the holy grail of contentment can indeed be within our grasp.

LIFE IS CHANGE

Change is the invisible watermark embossed upon every page of this book, for it will be the ever-present theme throughout your Part Two. If we are to thrive in our second half, we will not only have to cope with a countless number of changes: some good, some bad, some trivial, some devastating – we will need to embrace them all.

The strongest barriers to contentment, acceptance and change lie between our ears. They lie in our beliefs, our thoughts, our attitudes, our identities, our egos. They lie in how we see ourselves, how we think others see us, what we think others think of us, our need for the approval of others, the limits we place upon ourselves and the expectations we set for ourselves.

To embrace change successfully, we must first acknowledge the existence of these barriers, without judgement. We need to appreciate

---

[12] Karl Paul Reinhold Niebuhr (1892–1971), an American theologian.

that all change is emotional and that the emotions we experience during times of major change are both normal and inevitable. Once we have observed these emotions, and the negative thoughts that so often accompany them, we can start to put them into perspective. Then we can find the positive emotional triggers that will enable us to adopt the attitude we need to embrace the change and make the most of our new reality.

We must work continually to enhance our resilience, our ability to embrace change, and we have explored a number of ways to do this throughout these chapters. We need to be proactive – moving forward, even if it means small steps to begin with, in the direction in which we wish to travel. We need to like ourselves, believe in ourselves and go easy on ourselves. We need to stay calm and be as objective as possible. We must throw off the insidious cloak of victimhood the moment we realise that we have wrapped ourselves in it. We need to build confidence in our ability to thrive in a world of change.

PART THREE

Rethinking the 'R word'

It is high time we redefined the anachronistic concept of 'retirement'.
There is so much more to Part Two than fading away.

WE NEED TO REDEFINE 'RETIREMENT'

The very mention of the 'R Word' strikes fear deep into my soul. It is a word designed for someone whose battery is running out of charge, whose vitality is fading away, whose usefulness is diminishing – rapidly. It is a word signifying that the end may indeed be nigh.

It is a word that has been banned in our house for years.

To me, the concept is a relic from a bygone era, from an age when men dominated the workforce and commuted into work every day for forty-plus years, retired on their sixty-fifth birthday and dutifully died soon after, leaving a bewildered wife to live off a pre-determined percentage of her husband's pension. And don't get me started on the even more depressing 'p' word that conjures up images of sensible shoes, cheap clothes, cheap soap, park benches, bus passes and cutting out supermarket coupons from the newspaper.

For many of us, those days are gone.

The 'job for life' days are gone, too. The 'career for life' days are also over. Today, we change employers, change industries, change careers, more than ever before. We take career breaks. We are made redundant, dust ourselves off and move on. We flit between employment and self-employment – and back again. We travel. We move. We live longer, much longer.

Fewer and fewer of us will follow the paths of our parents or grandparents: attending our sending-off party, donning a gold watch, cutting our living expenses to match our reduced salary and spending more time on our allotment.

And for good reason – traditional retirement can be bad for your health! A recent report from the Stanford Center on Longevity found that 'compared to those who are retired, adults of the same age who work have higher levels of cognitive functioning.' The MacArthur Foundation Research Network study on successful ageing found that people who felt useful in their seventies were significantly less likely to develop health problems and at least one French study indicated that working longer can lower the risk of developing dementia.

This could be one reason why 61 per cent of people over sixty-five do not feel ready to retire[1] and almost nine in ten retired people over fifty

---

[1] 'Age as a Barrier to Opportunity'. Aviva. 2019.

think they retired too early, according to SunLife UK's 'Big 50' survey. A record number of people are now 'unretiring', having called time on their career too early (25 per cent of Brits and 40 per cent of Americans are 'unretiring', according to a recent article in the *Financial Times*[2]).

We don't want to tend our gardens; we want to start a market garden business. We want to write a book, lecture, mentor, write a blog, record podcasts, consult, volunteer, work part-time for a number of companies, start our own business, give something back, help the kids, or even continue to work full-time – because we can.

Women understand this far better than men. They always have. 'Retirement' has always been a very male-oriented concept, steeped in the tradition of man-as-breadwinner. Far fewer women would label themselves as 'retired'. The current generation of female second halfers were living 'portfolio careers' well before men even thought about defining it as a career option.

They have been full-time career women, full-time mothers and carers, part-time career women and full-time career women again. They have been the main breadwinner, the joint breadwinner, the secondary breadwinner and the bread-maker at different times in their lives. They have been the rock upon which their family is built. They have changed direction career-wise, several times: started their own businesses, given back to society and built loving families along the way. And that's just Jane!

They are increasingly financially independent, financially savvy and find it difficult to conceive of a day that they would suddenly stop and don the traditional faded and worn-out costume of the 'retired', for the simple reason that for most women, identity is not solely wrapped up in work. They also know that 'work' doesn't stop when you leave a full-time job. Far from it.

Women are also acutely aware that pay inequality is still rife in our societies despite the Equal Pay Acts that were passed into law more than fifty years ago in many parts of the world. In the year to April 2018, the average annual salary for a British woman in her fifties was £32,052 compared with £44,561 for men, according to the UK's Office of National Statistics. Whether intentionally or otherwise, age amplifies existing biases against women.

[2] 'The "unretired": coming back to work in droves', *Financial Times*, 4 December 2017.

Our options for Part Two

There are far more options for Part Two than winding down. An increasing number of us want more, much more. Traditional 'retirement' is just one of a host of paths that lie ahead, and it is one which fewer and fewer of us are following. Either through necessity or choice, or perhaps a little of both, we are choosing to:

- Stay at work longer – because we can
- Change careers, perhaps multiple times throughout our Part Two
- Start our own business (after all, older entrepreneurs are more successful)
- And yes, transition from full-time employment

Obviously, we may not always be in complete control of if and when we get to choose from the above list.

Some of us will have no choice but to stay at our current work longer for financial reasons, while others will choose to stay at work simply because we love the challenge, the camaraderie, the self-esteem and yes, the financial rewards.

Some of us will change careers of our own volition while others will be forced to jump ship.

A significant and increasing number of us 'second halfers' are deciding to start our own business, either compelled to do so because of redundancy or proactively making the leap ourselves. The numbers of 'second halfers' becoming entrepreneurs are large enough but the number who want to but don't know where to start is even larger. So large that the subject demanded its own chapter.

Some of us will choose to make the transition from full-time employment to start working part-time and/or volunteering. If we are incredibly fortunate, some of us will have the financial security to be able to follow our heart – using our vitality, knowledge and experience to do those things we have always wanted to do.

CHAPTER 11:

Working in the second half

'Retirement, we understand, is great if you are busy, rich and healthy.
But then, under those conditions, work is great too!'
Bill Vaughan[1]

A 2019 study by Fidelity International described 'an emerging "No Desire
to Retire" generation with 45 per cent expecting to work into their
seventies, and almost one in ten into their eighties or beyond.'[2]

So many people in their sixties and seventies are leaving their
pension pots untouched. Why? Because they are still working.[3]

And financial pressure isn't the only reason we are staying in work
so much later in life. Those with higher incomes are even more likely to
want to continue working. Maike Currie, Director for Workplace Investing
at Fidelity International, said, 'Today's so-called retirees are healthier,
living longer and retiring at different ages. So, it is unsurprising that people
have no desire to retire and are defying traditional expectations.'

And yet, as we saw earlier, unemployment among the over-fifties
is already high and rising. 'There is a wealth of untapped over-fifties
talent in the UK,' declares Natasha Oppenheim, the CEO of specialist
over-fifties recruitment and employment business aptly named No
Desire to Retire.

The business Natasha runs was formed back in 2012 with the dual
purpose of helping those of us aged fifty and over to find employment and
helping organisations to hire workers aged fifty and over. More than

[1] American journalist (1915–1977).
[2] https://www.yourmoney.com/retirement/half-of-uk-adults-plan-to-continue-working-in-retirement/
[3] https://www.pensionsage.com/pa/Almost-1-in-3-over-60s-pension-pots-remain-untouched.php

thirty thousand members now use their service, and they have relationships with more than three hundred employers. You can find out more about them from www.you-part-two.com.

The benefits of older workers should be obvious to employers: experience, reliability, well-developed soft skills, higher productivity and greater loyalty than their younger peers. Experienced workers are also more flexible – not just in terms of type of employment (full-time, part-time, contractor), but also in terms of the varied types of roles that experienced people can fulfil. Older workers make the best mentors as they carry a wealth of experience with them wherever they go.

The benefits of a diverse workforce are also well-known. Countless studies have shown that teams of men and women significantly outperform male-only teams, and that adding a mix of ethnicities into teams enhances performance and decision-making even further. But the greatest uplift in decision-making and performance comes from including a mix of ages in that team, according to Mary Bright of The Phoenix Group, who we quoted earlier.

While the majority of corporations may need Natasha's help to 'realise the value of experience', some employers are leading the way themselves.

Aviva's lightbulb moment

Aviva is a major international general insurer, life insurer, pensions provider, asset manager and institutional investor with annual profits in excess of £3 billion, more than 30 million customers worldwide and total assets of around £460 billion.

And while there is a great deal to admire about the breadth and quality of the solutions they provide and the way they run their vast business, perhaps the thing I admire most about them is the fact this UK-based international financial services giant recently had what I can only call a 'lightbulb moment': they realised that their second half employees are their most valuable, and yet under-rated, assets. So, they decided to do something about it.

Like every financial services firm, Aviva already knew that we second halfers are their most important clients. After all, something like 75 per cent of total personal wealth is held by people aged forty-five and over. But it wasn't until Lindsey Rix became MD (and then CEO) of Aviva's UK Savings & Retirement business mid-way through 2017 that it began to dawn on them that the government, the financial services industry and the entire corporate world had all only been focused on just one half of the solution that is required to fill our generation's massive savings gap.

'There are two levers most people can pull to take financial control of their later lives,' says Lindsey. 'They can try to save more, or they can work longer. We had all only been focused on the former. We now need to expand our horizons to support the second lever, particularly the opportunity to think more flexibly about retirement. We must ensure that those who would like to work longer have the opportunity to do so – and lead a fuller working life in the process.'

And Aviva is now leading by example.

Five thousand of their 15,000 UK-based employees are aged forty-five and over. This group is the fastest growing segment of their workforce and its members have been with the company the longest. However, they had started to leave the business at an increasing rate, taking an abundance of irreplaceable knowledge and experience with them. While researching why this was happening, Aviva uncovered an unconscious bias against older workers that the leadership simply never knew existed. This bias manifested itself in numerous subtle ways including the fact that the business was not investing to a great degree in the career and personal development of its older employees. Annual appraisals for experienced employees would often begin with, 'This won't take too long, will it?'

The same thing is happening in countless organisations across the Western world – older workers, often the largest and most loyal group with the most knowledge and experience, are being underserved or ignored. This is bad for employers and bad for society, because older workers need to keep working longer to fund their retirement. The alternative for many is old age poverty and increased reliance on state aid. Besides, the way the age demographics works in so many parts of the world, for every ten older workers that are likely to leave the workforce in the next decade, only seven younger workers are set to join it. The business world needs its older workers.

Aviva decided to begin changing their work practices to better support their valuable, experienced employees, and one of the many ways they did this was to roll out a 'Midlife MOT' programme across the business, a concept first touted in 2017 by John Cridland in his review of the UK state pension age. Aviva's version is a simple, once-a-year, two-hour session led by experts that enables their 'midlife' employees to pause to consider their wealth, work and well-being needs. Ultimately, the company's leaders want to ensure that 'age does not become a barrier to opportunity', to quote Lindsey Rix.

'The workshops have been oversubscribed,' said Alistair McQueen, Aviva's Head of Savings & Retirement. 'It was telling that the first cohort arrived asking whether this was a workshop to prepare them for retirement, when its purpose was actually the complete opposite. We told them that we wouldn't be mentioning the "R Word" once in the next two hours.'

The workshops cover fundamental financial planning topics such as state and private pensions, debt, mortgages, wills and funding long-term care. Delegates discuss the rise of older workers and the sense of purpose work provides so many of us. They discuss training, personal development, support for older workers, employment rights and career support. They also talk about well-being: health checks, exercise, nutrition, mental health, sleep and the importance of volunteering.

The workshops have started to challenge and change cultural misconceptions about age in the workplace at Aviva, plus they have increased employee confidence, engagement, participation, retention and productivity while reducing absenteeism. It has also increased personal saving among their employees.

The company has since taken their 'Midlife MOT' workshops out to five different client organisations at the time of writing and the results have been the same.

An interesting footnote to this story is that Lindsey Rix was headhunted by Canada Life to be their new UK CEO in 2021, which demonstrates two things: firstly, it pays to look after valuable Second Half customers and employees; and secondly, that sometimes in order to change career, you have to change companies, even when working for the most enlightened of employers – a theme we explore in more detail in the next chapter.

Does your employer offer a Midlife MOT? Maybe they should.

The 'You: Part Two' Online Programme that we provide organisations based on this book incorporates all of the subjects covered in Aviva's 'Mid Life MOT' and more – for it also explores all of the insights contained within the pages of *You: Part Two* – including pragmatic techniques for embracing change, finding your purpose and planning your Part Two.

You and your employer can preview the programme at www.you-part-two.com.

CHAPTER 12:

Changing careers

Why settle for just one career?

When you are on top of your game, change your game

Successful sports teams and organisations alike know that the best time to change is when you are on top, when you are in your prime. This is why the New Zealand All Blacks are the most successful sports team in history, and probably always will be. It is why Microsoft continues to be one of the world's largest companies after more than forty years in arguably the most competitive industry of them all.

The same goes for us. If we wish to remain relevant, vital and content, we will need to change – including when we are at the top of our game. Right now, we are in our prime; in the sweet spot where experience and capability combine. And our prime is often the best time to look at our current career and decide whether a change may be needed. It may be the time for something new. Because if we don't change, we stagnate. Stagnation inevitably leads to irrelevance.

A change of career does not necessarily mean changing employers. If your employer is enlightened, they will have realised the value of your experience and will be helping you to develop your skills even further and will be looking for new ways to leverage them for the benefit of you and the business. So many people I have known have had numerous careers while working for the same employer the whole time.

Enlightened employers invest in helping their employees develop their careers even if they end up leaving to ply their trade elsewhere, for the simple reason that they outperform while they are with the organisation. They also become advocates for the firm once they move on.

But sometimes even the most progressive employer can fail to see your ability to thrive in a new role. Sometimes familiarity breeds blindness. I have seen many people passed up for promotion over external candidates. One particular head of sales springs to mind. As an external consultant, it was clear to me that he was the obvious candidate for promotion to sales director, and yet even though he and his team were responsible for bringing in the entirety of the company's new business revenue, he was continually overlooked for the board-level role in favour of external applicants. If he wishes to become sales director, he will have to leave. When he does, he will take years of experience and a host of incredibly valuable client relationships with him. This is a common phenomenon, as we will see below.

Sometimes, if we wish to grow, we must take the matter into our own hands.

CAREER NOMADS

Global recruiter, Korn Ferry, has uncovered a new and expanding category of workers, which they have labelled 'career nomads': high-performing, talented professionals who are switching jobs, organisations and even careers at a faster rate than others. When asked about why they had moved employers, respondents in the 2019 Korn Ferry study listed three main reasons:

1. They felt that their skills weren't being utilised fully by their previous employer;

2. They believed their values were no longer aligned to the organisation, or;

3. They were leaving to 'find appreciation and recognition'.[1]

We all need to be appreciated and recognised.

But sometimes, as we have seen in 2020 and 2021, employers have no choice but to lay people off. When they find themselves in this situation, enlightened employers activate well-defined career outplacement programmes to help their departing employees transition

---

[1] https://www.kornferry.com/insights/perspectives/perspective-career-nomads

successfully. Why? Because every single remaining employee is watching how their departing colleagues are being treated, fearing that they may be next. Korn Ferry reports a 20 per cent decline in job performance from survivors after a round of lay-offs and a 36 per cent decrease in commitment to the organisation. Poorly managed redundancy programmes cost a great deal of money in decreased productivity and increased staff turnover.

Enlightened employers help their people make the transition and give remainers and leavers alike the greatest gift of all – the ability to embrace change.

Moving on

Changing careers is rarely easy, particularly if we are unsure of what our next step should be. Trust me on this: I have changed my career more than a dozen times throughout my life. It pays to do some self-analysis and some research. I suggest that you:

- Consider your timing. Now may not be the ideal time for a variety of valid reasons – perhaps you are in the middle of studying or need to look after ageing parents. But don't put off planning. Recruiters suggest it can take six months or more to change careers.
- Document what you like and dislike about your current job.
- Identify and document your transferrable skills. It is easier to build your next career upon something you have already done.
- Consider industries that are expanding. Your skills will be transferrable across industries. Be brave.

There is one particular group of people we could observe and learn from, as every single one of them changes career at least once and often at a very young age – sportspeople.

SPORTSPEOPLE DON'T 'RETIRE'; THEY CHANGE CAREERS

Sportspeople bandy the word 'retirement' about from a very young age. They 'retire' really early. Most footballers stop playing in their thirties, rugby players even younger and gymnasts in their early twenties, if not earlier.

But of course, hardly any of them actually 'retire'. They change careers.

While I am not sure how much we could learn from how the likes of Michael Jordan, Greg Norman, Wayne Gretzsky, David Beckham, Maria Sharapova and Steffi Graf are spending their money now that their first career has come to its glorious conclusion, we can certainly learn a thing or two from how the vast majority of 'normal' professional sportspeople go about preparing for and embarking on their inevitable career changes.

Their lives are only a quarter or a third of the way through when they are suddenly forced to take stock and plan for their Part Two and the majority of their life that is yet to come. These are people we can learn from.

To understand how professional sportspeople prepare for their inevitable change of career, I had a lengthy and fascinating conversation with Simon Taylor, the CEO of the UK's Professional Players Federation (PPF), the organisation that sits across and coordinates the efforts of thirteen key professional players associations (unions) representing 17,500 professional sportspeople from the worlds of football, golf, netball, cricket, darts, horseracing, billiards and snooker and rugby. And at this point, let's not bother debating whether darts, billiards or snooker should be defined as sport, as even darts players reach that day when they have to put down their pints and look for a 'real job'.

Contrary to popular myth, 90 per cent of professional sportspeople need to work after 'retiring' from their sporting career and most are in what we might call 'normal' jobs.[2]

However, many find it incredibly hard to adapt to their Part Two. Their sport is all that they have known from a young age. More than half of professional sportspeople are concerned about their mental and emotional health once they have moved on from their chosen sport, yet only four in ten seek help. Fourteen per cent admit to high levels of anxiety/stress or a loss of self-esteem and confidence. A similar percentage admit to feelings of depression and despair. As we know from Part Two, these are all normal reactions to significant change.

---

[2] 'Initial Career Transition Research Findings'. PPF. 5 February 2018. 'Findings from a study of the mental, physical and financial wellbeing of retired professional sportsmen'. PPF 2014.

A significant number of players struggle financially in the first few years after their playing days come to an end. The vast majority are forced to accept a drop in earnings once they stop playing, with just over half reporting financial difficulties in the five years immediately after their sporting career had come to an end.

Only 29 per cent of retired players are able to choose when they stop playing professional sport and 78 per cent wish they had taken more financial advice when they were playing.

In other words, they are just like the rest of us!

But unlike the rest of us, professional sportspeople are well supported by their players associations, who provide a range of services to help their members prepare for life after sport.

Examples abound of players making a successful transition from their playing career to their next career: rugby player to entrepreneur, cricketer to motorsport engineer, jockey to plumber, and one of my favourites, cricketer to barista.

Tim Linley, a Surrey seam bowler who ended his career with two hundred first-class dismissals, opened Coffee on the Crescent near Headingley Stadium after retiring from playing. But thanks to the Professional Cricketers Association, he was able to start planning for life after cricket well before he was forced to hang up his spikes. With the help of the PCA, Tim was able to attend barista and financial accounting courses while he was still playing, plus he received a PCA scholarship of £2,500 towards the costs of setting up his new business venture.

Who am I?

Tim says that one of the things he struggled with most was finding a new identity when he stopped playing. Many of us find this tough. Our identities can be extraordinarily strong barriers to change, and to our happiness as well. How we see ourselves influences how we think and what we do. When such a major part of our identity is ripped away from us, it can be highly unsettling. Our job can be a major source of our identity and once that is removed, we can struggle. We are forced to confront who we are without the smart suit and the title, without the team jersey.

The value of a 'can do' attitude

One of the many things I love about Tim's story is his attitude. 'You've already made a hobby a career, there's absolutely no reason you can't do it again!' he proclaims. Developing his business plan gave him something to focus on away from cricket, which was healthy in and of itself, and he says it removed the anxiety of what he was going to do when his cricket career was over.

What did I take away from Tim's story? Plan, reframe your identity, and adopt a positive, proactive attitude.

But the world of sport hasn't always been this advanced. When the Jockeys Education and Training Scheme (JETS) began its operations back in 1995, their sessions about career planning had to be conducted behind closed doors as the prevailing industry view of jockeys was that they would go back to being stable hands once their riding days were over. Those running the horseracing industry at the time were worried that JETS' training was going to lead to jockeys leaving the industry. This short-sighted view was once common in the world of business too: the mistaken belief that helping employees to develop their careers was a waste of money, as employers would be skilling them up to leave and take their new-found skills elsewhere.

This view has proven to be nonsensical. Helping people prepare for their next career actually helps them to be better in their current role, as Aviva also discovered. The Rugby Players Association has observed this phenomenon numerous times; players who have begun to plan for life after sport also tend to perform better on the field. Being less anxious about the future seems to allow them to play more freely and focus all their energies on the moment and the task at hand.

JETS concurs. Most jockeys stay within the racing industry once they stop riding, and a significant proportion of those who do leave the sector return after gaining experience elsewhere. 'We now start talking about career development and transition openly from the very first time we get jockeys together on their licensing course,' JETS CEO, Lisa Delaney, was proud to tell me over the phone.

The Personal Development Plan (PDP) that JETS has designed is frankly better than any I have seen in the world of business these last four decades, which too often tend to focus only on business-related skills, ignoring equally important aspects of mental health, well-being and attitude. The JETS version is so much more holistic. As Lisa told me, 'We treat our jockeys as human beings, not just athletes.'

I think we could all learn something from it. Just look at the sections they cover:

- **My support team:** The jockey is asked to list their employer, their coach, their agent, their strength and conditioning trainer, their physio, family, peers and partner. No development plan I have ever seen has had a section like this, yet it makes so much sense. What does your support team look like?
- **Well-being:** A great title but even better when you see the detailed areas they cover – confidence, physical well-being, financial well-being, social well-being, concentration, relaxation and community. How would you fare at each one of those?
- **Psychology:** Positive attitude, goal setting and resilience. We have already discussed the critical role of each of these. The three of them act as a virtuous circle: a positive attitude enables us to set, and achieve ambitious goals, which both help to build resilience, which in turn engenders a positive attitude.
- **Personality/traits:** Self-awareness is key. Knowing our own default settings for how we process information and how we react lay the foundations of any future plan.
- **Career:** Visualising and planning where we want to go and what we will have to do to get there.
- **Nutrition:** We all need knowledge about nutrition. As we have seen, what we consume is one of the key levers we can control to affect the quality and duration of our second half.
- **Strength and conditioning:** Again, not only relevant to jockeys. If we don't use it, we lose it.
- **Communication and media:** A key skill for so many sportspeople to develop for their Part Two. What skills will you need to thrive in yours?
- **Managing finances:** We all need this and we will speak more of this in Part Five.
- **Interests and hobbies outside of riding:** Jane keeps telling me

I need an interest outside of working, writing, her and family.

• **Performance goals:** What gets measured, gets done.

• **Actions:** What is the point of a plan without action? One of my favourite sayings comes to mind: 'Strategy without action is a daydream. Action without strategy is a nightmare.'

• **Pay it forward:** What are your plans to give back to the community or support network? I love that.

Now that's what I call a Personal Development Plan!

If you would like to find out more about the JETS PDP, and personal development in general, head to www.you-part-two.com.

'All I can do is ride race-horses'

Another thing that we could learn from is how Lisa's team helps jockeys to identify those skills that they can put to good use in their next career.

Many jockeys find it difficult to appreciate the valuable skills and talents that they have developed during their riding carer; skills that employers desperately desire in their employees, but rarely find. Skills such as time management (you can't be late for the start of a race), organisation (jockeys travel all over the country, sometimes riding in two separate meets in a day), self-discipline (diet, physical strength, mental strength, focus), dedication, loyalty and, of course, bravery.

I don't know how jockeys do what they do. Yet many can struggle to appreciate how skilled and brave they actually are. When one asked Lisa what she had done before coming to run JETS, she explained that she had been a competitive equestrian. He replied, 'I couldn't do that. That's so dangerous!' The man had just ridden in the Grand National, one of the most dangerous feats in the world of sport. On average, jump jockeys fall off their horse one in every twelve races. It's not only falling from a couple of metres in the air while travelling at speed, but also having to dodge a dozen or more sets of thundering hooves once you have hit the ground.

Sometimes we all need a little help to appreciate our own skills and talents; skills that others can often see clearer than we can, and value more than we do; talents that we could use to open new doors and forge new careers.

Now is the perfect time for you to conduct a stock-take of the skills and talents you have developed throughout your Part One. Write them down. Be sure to include the softer skills you have honed over the years – the way you work with people, your skills of persuasion and communication, for example. When listing your skills, I suggest you go beyond the bullet points and note down stories about how you used them. This will spark some ideas about how you may be able to use these very same skills in different situations in the future.

Now move your mind away from the workplace and examine the skills you have demonstrated in other settings – with friends or at home. What has your experience as a friend or partner revealed about yourself – how you negotiate, how you plan, how you communicate? What has parenting taught you? I have always thought that being a parent is the best form of leadership and management training of them all.

Once you have analysed your own skills, consult others. Ask friends, relatives and partners for their view of your skills and talents. Add their views to your notes. The document you will have created will be an invaluable list of skills that you can put to use in future careers. They may even open your mind to a host of possible career paths that you may not have considered.

For the final words of advice on changing careers, I would like to turn to the Professional Players Federation.

ADVICE FROM PROFESSIONAL SPORTSPEOPLE ON CHANGING YOUR CAREER

The following is a summary of the recommendations from 1,200 retired sportspeople surveyed by the Professional Players Federation on changing careers, and they are equally as relevant to the likes of you and me:

- Think ahead, plan and prepare: It's never too early to start planning for the next phase;
- Gain experience and qualifications as early as possible: It's never too late to start doing this;
- Appreciate your playing days: Come away from your sport with no regrets;
- Make contacts and take advice: Networking is one of the most

important things you can possibly do when looking to change your career and there is never any shame in asking for help;

• Treat people well: You never know when you might need their help;

• Make as much of your second career as your first;

• Use your experience: Recognise the value of the skills that your sport has given you;

• Look after your money: It won't last for ever, and;

• Broaden your horizons beyond sport: it helps bring perspective.

Substitute 'sport' for 'current career' or 'current job' and every single one of the above is applicable to any of us.

CHAPTER 13:

Starting your own business

'If you don't try something, you'll always wonder.
What could that have been like?
What if...?'
Maria Shriver[1]

Are you thinking of starting your own business? You are not alone. It is now an aspiration shared by so many of us that we decided to dedicate a whole chapter to it. The age of the experienced entrepreneur has arrived.

More Part Two-ers are self-employed than ever before and the numbers are growing every year. Of the 5 million self-employed in the UK in 2019, 2.3 million were aged fifty and over, a million of whom were sixty or older. We have been the fastest growing segment of entrepreneurs in the last decade, according to restless.co.uk, and the trend looks set to continue. It is a similar tale across the rest of the Western world.

Some of this growth has been fuelled by increased redundancies among second halfers in the decade that followed the 2008 recession, when almost twice as many over-fifties were made redundant than those aged between twenty-five and thirty-four.[2] History then decided to repeat itself in 2020 as the number of newly unemployed over-fifties increased by 33 per cent – faster than any other age group – and 2021 looks set to increase the numbers of experienced entrepreneurs even further.

Of course, not all new entrepreneurs are forced into starting their own businesses; an increasing number eagerly choose it of their own volition.

---

[1] American journalist, author, former First Lady of California, and the founder of the non-profit organisation The Women's Alzheimer's Movement (1955–).
[2] 'UK percentage share of redundancies per age group 2008–2017'. ONS.

The great news is that older entrepreneurs are more successful. This was the empirical finding of a detailed 2019 study by the prestigious Kellogg School of Management in conjunction with MIT and the US National Bureau of Economic Research titled 'Age and High-Growth Entrepreneurship'.[3]

They discovered that the majority of successful new business creators are middle-aged or older. They found that a fifty-year-old entrepreneur was almost twice as likely to achieve stellar growth than a thirty-year-old founder. Founders in their early twenties had the lowest likelihood of either a successful exit or creating a top growth business.

This startling observation should not come as a surprise. Even though the press is enamoured with stories of fresh-faced Mark Zuckerberg types making it big, these youngsters are the exception, not the rule. Zuckerberg once famously said, 'If you want to found a successful company, you should only hire young people with technical expertise.' Ah, the arrogance of youth, blinded by the fact he is, quite literally, one in a million. Most entrepreneurs in their twenties have limitless energy but very limited experience. While Branson's 'intelligent naivety' has its place, most of the time, not knowing what you don't know is a *dis*advantage. On the other hand, we second halfers have experience, contacts, capital (or hopefully the ability to access it) and credibility.

However, no matter whether you are starting your own business through necessity or choice, it can feel like a leap into the unknown. A plethora of fears and doubts can prevent us from making that leap if we let them. The four most common fears, or objections if you like, that I have witnessed over the years are:

1. Financial concerns;
2. Fear of failure – or fearing you may look like one;
3. 'But I don't have the big idea'; and
4. 'I don't know where to start'.

Let's tackle each of these head-on.

[3] https://www.nber.org/papers/w24489

OBJECTION 1: FINANCIAL CONCERNS

Freshbooks' 2018 annual report on self-employment in America[4] declared that '24 million workers in the US think that working for themselves would be their dream job'. That is almost one in six American workers. However, a year later very few had turned their dream into reality. The two main reasons were financial:

Insecure earnings

Thirty-five per cent were worried about inconsistent income and 27 per cent about earning less money. With good reason: inconsistent income often goes hand-in-hand with being self-employed and it is the norm for new entrepreneurs to earn less as they start their new business, often for some time. But these aren't barriers, they are hurdles. They are facts that require plans to cope with. However, I would argue that wages from full-time employment aren't secure earnings either – as the lengthening unemployment queues during 2020 and 2021 have amply demonstrated.

Lack of capital

Twenty-eight per cent of respondents said they were delaying their leap into self-employment because they didn't have the cash to invest or they needed to pay off debt first. While these reasons will undoubtedly have been true for some, for many they will have been excuses. Starting a business can be a little like having a baby: you may never have enough cash and you may never find the right time.

Starting your own business is almost certain to have financial consequences. You will need to budget. You will need to plan. You will need to be realistic and honest with yourself. You will need contingencies. And you will need to keep costs as low as possible for as long as possible.

OBJECTION 2: FEAR OF FAILURE – OR FEARING YOU MAY LOOK LIKE ONE

When it comes to starting your own business, several of the barriers to change that we discussed in Part Two can all come to the fore at once. The fear of failure, fear that we will look like a fool, fear of a loss of status. Our fears, fuelled by ego and attachment to old identities, are powerful

---

[4] https://www.freshbooks.com/press/annualreport

forces that can do their utmost to dissuade us from taking the plunge.

They are also utterly illogical states of mind made up of strong emotions and a potpourri of falsehoods.

The first step to overcoming fear is to acknowledge it – and give yourself a break; fear is normal. You wouldn't be human if you weren't a little trepidatious about jumping into a brand-new venture or adventure. Doing anything for the first time can be daunting. But you have done lots of things for the first time throughout your life. Trust yourself. Believe in yourself.

What are you afraid of? And I don't mean that pejoratively. I mean that quite literally. Actually ask yourself, *'What am I afraid of?'* Spell out your fears and concerns about starting out on your own – and be honest. Write them down; they are bound to look less fearsome on paper. Then, you can deal with them.

If you are afraid of failing, stop using the word. There is no such thing as failure; there are only learning experiences. And speaking of learning, do your homework – about setting up a business, your intended market, competition, pricing and potential business models. Talk to people. Learn from others.

If you are afraid of losing all of your hard-earned savings, then scale your ambitions back a little. It is always better to start small, anyway.

If you are afraid of looking like a fool; to whom? Who are you picturing when you think this? Your family? I doubt it. Your friends? If true, they are not real friends, so who cares what you think they might think. The person we are afraid of usually ends up being ourselves. We are our own worst critics. More often we are afraid of looking like a fool to some idealised version of ourselves that is an entirely imaginary being, drawn by our ego.

If a loss of status is the thing that concerns you the most, reflect on this a while. Your status as what? The status that was conferred by your old job is over. You are now a *former* CEO, a *former* doctor, a *former* executive, a *former* schoolteacher. But only if you wish to be labelled as such. Why be defined solely by the thing you aren't doing anymore? After some reflection, it may become apparent that the 'status' you had was ephemeral, it was transitory, Furthermore, it wasn't you, it was just a title, it was just a role. The person that lay beneath the status is still there.

Perhaps you just need to coax them out into the open.

This is your opportunity to create a new identity, a new status that is even more exciting and most likely even more genuine.

OBJECTION 3: 'BUT I DON'T HAVE THE BIG IDEA'

You don't need to find 'the big idea' to start your own business. But you will need passion. Running your own business can be all-consuming, and both the highs and the lows can be wild. A barrage of challenges will be thrown in your path, and so many of them will be completely unexpected. But whatever it is that you decide to do, do it with passion and drive. Otherwise, your chances of success will be slim, at best.

Don't let the initial absence of a big idea hold you back. Find a small idea and make it your own.

Try exploring one or more of the following avenues of thinking and see where it takes you:

- What does my current employer not do very well?
- Could I advise or work for my current employer's competitors?
- Could I do what my employer does, but better or cheaper?
- Is there a part of the market that my current employer is currently not interested in (perhaps it is too small) that I could create a solution for?
- What if I 'crossed the floor' and helped our customers get better deals with my current employer and its competitors?
- What skills and contacts do I have that I could leverage, either in the same industry or perhaps in an adjacent industry?
- And then finally, put aside the thorny issue of money for a second and ask yourself, 'What have I always dreamed of doing?'

OBJECTION 4: I DON'T KNOW WHERE TO START

More than a few friends who have spent their careers in full-time employment have asked me over the years: 'How do I start my own business?' The first time I was asked this, I thought the person asking the question was joking. He wasn't. Another colleague, a senior global partner with one of the big consulting firms for whom he had been working for forty-three years, even asked me if he could use my website and business name when he retired from the firm, as he genuinely had no idea where to start. He then moved to Nairobi and became a father again at the tender age of sixty-eight. I do hope he hasn't handed out too many cards.

Obviously, start with a business plan (and we will talk more about this in a minute). But in my experience of having switched from full-time employment to my own business so many times throughout my life, there are two things that I strongly recommend you do before commencing work on your business plan: first, ask yourself 'why?' and second, be flexible.

Ask yourself 'Why?'

There are two types of 'why': the 'real' reason and the 'right' reason. In the context of starting your own business, the 'real' reason is usually self-centred. The 'right' reason needs to be focused on the customer.

Let's get the 'real' reason out of the way. Why are you starting your own business? Is it to be your own boss? Is it because you have just been made redundant and feel as though you might as well give it a go? Is it because you have spotted an opportunity? Is it because you fancy or need a change? Perhaps it is a combination of several of those. This self-centred version of 'why' is important to know. Acknowledge it to yourself and keep referring back to it. Then articulate the 'right' reason, as this is the reason that will drive your business from here on in.

What is the 'right' reason for your business to exist? Imagine that one day you will have employees and that they will need to know the driving customer-centric reason behind everything the business does – and for whom. Write that down. That is your business's purpose. Your purpose must not only be 'right', it must also be genuine. It must be based on what you do, your key skills, what will make your business special, your core ethos and most importantly of all, the needs, wants and aspirations of your target customers.

Be flexible

A business plan is critical, but it isn't a treasure map to be followed to the letter. It is a guide. The moment you take your business to market, your strategy will need to adapt. As German military strategist Helmuth von Moltke (1800–1891) once wrote: *No battle plan survives contact with the enemy.'* Heavyweight boxer, Mike Tyson, was a little less delicate: *'Everyone has a plan until they get punched in the mouth.'*

When I restarted my consultancy in 2017, my business strategy was straightforward. I was going to enable CEOs and leaders to align their teams to a clear strategy and lead successful change. I had written a book on leading change in my spare time during 2016, which I was planning to self-publish and use as a calling card and marketing tool. I had identified two key industries I was going to focus on. I knew their needs and I was confident that I could fulfil them.

But while the core essence of my business didn't change once I actually went to market, just about everything else did. Wiley miraculously decided to publish my book, which opened up opportunities in keynote speaking and lecturing at a business school. One of the customer segments I was sure would be a winner bombed completely. But I designed workshops based on the first book, which opened up a new avenue of services to sell, and when it won the Business Book of the Year, this opened up the opportunity for the second book and subsequently a second stream of workshops. It also made this third book possible: a new direction again. Four years on, my business is a very different beast than the one I had planned, even though the core purpose, and core activities, have remained the same.

Be flexible.

ENTERPRISE NATION

Rather than relying solely on our own experiences for this chapter, we went looking for independent expertise and insight to enhance our own stories – and struck gold in Emma Jones, MBE, the founder and CEO of Enterprise Nation, one of the most impressive resources for small business that I have come across. More information about Emma's business and a link to her services can be found at www.you-part-two.com.

Emma launched Enterprise Nation in 2005 with one purpose: to help people start and grow successful businesses. She and her team do this through connecting start-ups and founders to relevant content, events, training, peers and advisers. In their opinion, informed by decades of experience, if a business accesses support at the earliest stage of its journey, it is far more likely to succeed.

Emma Jones' top tips for budding entrepreneurs

I asked Emma to provide us with her top tips for starting a new business. They are worth their weight in ostrich feathers:

Focus

The more niche, the better. For example, rather than simply starting a business to offer HR services – why not offer HR services to companies in the food and drink sector? Doing so will mean you rapidly become an expert in that area, which will keep customers loyal, and it also means you know where your customers are, keeping marketing costs low.

Do something you love doing

Whatever the idea, base a business on doing what you love as you're going to spend a fair few hours working on it!

Write a business plan

With idea in hand, it's time to write it down. Your business plan will define where you are now, where you want to go, and the broad steps you'll need to take along the way. So many people have asked us what to include in a business plan that we came up with an acronym for it that is very easy to remember – it spells I'M OFF!

- I – what is the Idea for your business
- M – who is the Market you're going to serve
- O – what are the Operations you need to get started? This could be simply an internet connection and a contacts book!
- F – this F is for Financials and involves doing a basic cashflow forecast for your business setting out the sales you expect to make, less the costs to deliver, which equals your projected profit for the time period for which you are writing the plan. Doing this basic calculation will give you faith and confidence that the business can indeed make money. The second element of Finance is to understand if you need to raise any to get started. The cashflow forecast will help you understand if you do need to raise funds and, if so, there are plenty of places to look including friends and family, the bank, StartUp Loans, crowdfunding or angel investors. Each

have their own pros and cons and the advice of an accountant is invaluable to understand the funding option best suited to you.

- F – the final F is for Friends, rather more professionally known as your support network or advisory board. When you start out, it's likely to be just you as founder and sole employee. Surround yourself with experts in the topics that aren't your strong suit. Are you great at making the product but not so strong in marketing it? If so, connect with marketers and bring them into your peer team; you can hire them on a freelance or full-time basis when you have the budget!

Add an Executive Summary to the above and you have a business plan to tuck under your arm and you are off on your business journey! (By the way, you can download the Kindle version of Emma's 'The Startup Kit' from Amazon.co.uk for free.)

Make a sale

One of the first jobs to perfect as a start-up founder is the ability to sell. This will be made easier with a strong understanding of your customers. When pitching, be sure to stay focused on what's in it for the customer. One easy way to check this is before clicking send on a pitch email or printing any sales assets, see how many times you've used the word 'you' versus 'I' or 'we' – in short, the focus should be on 'You'! Make it clear how the product or service will deliver for the customer and if you don't get an immediate response, be persistent.

I would like to add a few pointers here from my own experience as a provider of services to businesses. It pays to appreciate that your potential customers almost never work to your timetable, so be patient as well. I have also learnt that 'less is more' when it comes to pitch documents. I spend so much effort in compiling them and get so close to the subject matter that my pitch documents invariably end up being far too detailed. I forget that they will be seeing this for the first time. It is also worth reminding yourself that sales is a process. The purpose of the first email is simply to secure a phone call, not to give them a lengthy sales pitch that they will never read. The purpose of the first phone call is to pique their interest enough for them to want more information. The purpose of the follow up discussion document can often be to inspire even more detailed discussion and start to define their key areas of interest so that you can return with a proper proposal. I tend to want to go from cold email to detailed proposal and sale in one go, which never works.

Make some noise

Customers are more likely to buy from you if they've heard about you. Get covered in the press and online through knowing your story and getting to know the journalists who reach your ideal customers. Follow them on Twitter, regularly check #journorequest call-outs and send press releases that include stats, quotes, images and a headline that appeals to a busy writer.

Network like your life depends upon it

I am going to interrupt Emma's insights again to add another of my own: network. No one ever won any business sitting in their home office staring at the wall. Join networking groups – like Emma's. Meet people who are interesting and may one day be able to bring business your way – just to chat. Call people for the same reason. Call people to help them. Explore opportunities with like-minded people. Opportunities will come from the most unlikely of places.

Embrace social media

As a start-up, technology is most certainly your friend. Social platforms such as Facebook, Instagram, Twitter and LinkedIn enable small and new businesses to reach and engage with customers and powerful trading marketplaces such as Amazon and Etsy take that a stage further through enabling you to start a business on Monday and be trading with the world by Friday. Embrace these platforms and understand how to best use them – there is an abundance of training and support on how to get this right.

Balance the business

As the business grows, you will feel you are spinning numerous plates. As the boss, your job is to ensure the product is perfect, sales are coming in, customers are happy and, if you have staff, that this is all being delivered by a motivated team. My advice on how to balance the business, and stay sane, is to think about three key parts of the business: Operations, Business Development and Admin; and split your time in these three ways. Operations means getting the product or service right and ensuring the team is happily delivering. Business Development focuses on ensuring existing customers are happy while attracting new ones too and Admin is all about managing the books through ensuring you are getting paid on time and that you're paying suppliers too.

There is much to consider when starting and growing a business, but it is also one of the most fulfilling things you can do in life. Building your own venture to serve a gap in the market you have identified creates value and offers freedom and flexibility that you will struggle to find in a salaried job. Many challenging days lie ahead for sure, but so many gratifying ones too.

ADMIN AND INFRASTRUCTURE

To round this chapter off, we have put together a checklist of the more pedestrian and yet essential elements of starting your own business:

Domain name

Start with the internet. Log on to a domain name provider (lcn, godaddy or any of the multitude of competitors) and search for a name that is available. For the latest reincarnation of my consulting business, I wanted the name to reflect what it is that I was about to do. I help companies with strategy, and I help them with change. So, I typed 'strategyandchange' into lcn.com and discovered it had already been taken. Then I flipped the words around and found that 'changeandstrategy' was available. I immediately snapped up .com, .co.uk and .net.

Jane's process was even easier. 'janemacphersonyoga' was available in both .com and .co.uk versions. Job done.

Company or sole trader?

Talk to your accountant to work out the legal structure of your business and whether you will need to register for VAT or GST. Being a sole trader is less hassle, arguably cheaper but you have to pay income tax on every cent or penny of your profit. The advantage of a limited company is that you don't have to pay yourself every cent you earn – you can store any surplus cash for future years. And your partner can be a shareholder and receive dividends.

If it is a company you need, log on to Companies House or the equivalent wherever you live and check that the company name you would like is available. Then I suggest paying your accountant a few hundred pounds or dollars to set it up. Suddenly, you will have the company name registered, be issued with a company number and reams of paperwork will magically appear such as an 'Articles of Association' and even minutes of Board Meetings that you don't recall ever taking place. You could do it yourself, but life is too short.

Banking

The next step is to open a bank account. The question is, with which bank? There are so many new online business accounts now that are worth considering – and can get you up and running in minutes. If you are using a traditional bank, you may want to ponder whether you want to use the same bank as your personal account, or not. Personally, I like to keep them separate. Banks are notorious for offering you an umbrella when it's sunny and wanting it back from you the moment it starts to rain. They are strange bicephalic beasts, seething with contradictions.

Website

No matter what your business does, you will need a website. Maybe you could get away with building a simple, super cheap one with the tools on offer from your domain name provider. If this is either too daunting or too limiting, ask around and find a cheap but effective website builder and hosting business to help you build a web presence that sums up what you do. You should not have to pay through the nose for this.

Tech

Work out what technology you will need. That, too, no longer has to be expensive. For her online yoga classes and sessions, Jane has a laptop, a good USB webcam, a Bluetooth lapel mike, two LED studio lights and a 20m Ethernet cable. I have a laptop, webcam, podcast mic and printer. We both have Zoom accounts and I use Xero for my accounts. Jane uses Excel. That's it.

Insurance

Seriously consider professional indemnity insurance, no matter what your business is and does.

Support

Here's the support infrastructure Jane and I have in place for our businesses:

- An accounting firm that looks after both of us;
- A local website hosting company (guy) who keeps the websites up and running and does the tricky things in Wordpress – like helping to build Jane's brilliant password-controlled and pay-by-credit card online yoga subscription service, and the You: Part Two Online Programme;
- A graphic designer who works hand-in-hand with the website hosting guy;
- Someone who manages the Google mail servers for our company emails, and;
- On top of that, I have a video guy who edits my videos and an online marketing firm who run marketing and lead-generation campaigns from time to time.

And you're off!

CHAPTER 14:

Stories from second-half entrepreneurs

'If opportunity doesn't knock, build a door.'
Milton Berle[1]

Let's now hear from some people who have been there and done it. Here are three stories from among millions of people who have started their own business later in life. We can learn different things from each one.

Sean is our first entrepreneur. When the bank made him redundant aged forty, he decided to leverage his skills and contacts to start his own business.

Trish is our second. Aged fifty, after thirty years as a secondary school teacher and having never lived outside of Australia, she moved from a sleepy Queensland beachside town to New York City to teach teachers how to teach.

Our third is Bryher. Spurred on by the death of her mother, she became an eCommerce entrepreneur at sixty after a successful career at the BBC.

Each story is different, but you will find that they share some universal themes: leveraging existing skills, talents and contacts; bravery; embracing the change; passion and commitment. None of these three were half-hearted entrepreneurs. No successful entrepreneurs are.

Sean

Sean Russo was made redundant as Managing Director of Rothschilds Treasury aged forty. My kindergarten-level description of his job as one

[1] American comedian and actor (1908–2002).

of the youngest full board directors of one of the world's most prestigious investment banks is that he loaned gold to gold miners. To this day, he swears it was far more complex than that. His redundancy changed his status overnight and his earnings went from a hundred miles an hour to stationary in an instant – and it didn't bother him in the slightest. Sean has an inner resilience to take whatever cards life deals him and crack on with it.

The first thing he did when the axe fell on his career at Rothschilds was to take his kids out of school and travel. The second was to take some time off and get fit. The third thing was to reflect before deciding precisely what his new business was going to do. With a daughter who had recently graduated from high school, he gave himself poor marks as an 'involved' father. He had a list of trips and activities he had talked about doing with her in those formative years and the majority were left undone. Reflecting on his own school years, he realised that most of the involved fathers he knew had been self-employed. If he was going to do a better job with his two younger sons, he reckoned that he too needed to be self-employed. He also figured out that as well paid as he had been, there was never a year where he hadn't sacrificed more family time for his employer than they gave him in annual leave; leave he was often too 'busy' to take. In the next chapter he vowed that time with family and friends would be his most precious commodity.

He knew how investment banks worked when it came to the gold industry, so he decided he was going to jump over to the other side of the desk and use his expertise to help the major gold and base metal producers secure the best financing arrangements from Rothschilds and other banks. Gamekeeper turned poacher.

He was also going to help them hedge currency risk. Gold producers' costs are in their local currency while their revenues are in US dollars. An unfortunate upturn in the currency at the wrong time in the gold price cycle could wipe out their profits – or double them if they were lucky. Sean and his team set about convincing them that they were gold producers not gold-price-gamblers. Noah's Rule now manages the currency hedging strategies of a significant number of companies, and not exclusively mining firms. Cricket Australia is a key client. He and his business partner, who he met at Rothschilds over thirty years ago, now manage a team of nine. 'A seventeen-year overnight success,' as he likes to describe the ride.

Sean also has an innovative way of charging for his services that so many fee-based advice businesses could learn from. Those of us who charge fees for our services continually struggle with how much we should charge – too little and clients won't take us seriously, too much and clients won't hire us. Sean has arrived at an innovative solution – he asks his clients to decide how much to pay once he has finished the work! He sets a base minimum fee and asks the client to pay a discretionary bonus of up to three times that amount once the job is done. Zero extra is absolutely fine. A 300 per cent bonus is fine, too – or anywhere in between. And what is the average bonus his clients pay? Almost 200 per cent. When clients see the value that Sean's team has added, they willingly pay its full worth.

By the way, the term 'Noah's Rule' is attributed to Warren Buffett. The rule is this: 'Predicting rain doesn't count. Building arks does.' Last year Sean and his daughter walked the Kokoda Track in Papua New Guinea together – as promised all those years ago. 'Better late than never,' declared Sean with a grin.

Trish

Trisha Wilcox took the plunge into self-employment soon after turning fifty. After thirty years as a secondary school teacher in a beachside town in Queensland, Australia, and having reached the heights of Department Head and Deputy Head, she not only made the brave decision to join the ranks of the self-employed, but she packed her bags and moved to New York to teach American teachers how to teach. She was divorced with two adult children and had never lived outside of Australia. Now that is what I call change!

Trish was born to be a teacher and she is simply brilliant at it, because she loves it. But she was ready for a new challenge.

I asked Trish to pen something on why and how she made such a momentous change and, because she is such a fine writer, I think her story is best told in her own words . . .

I first heard about the possibility of working in New York in

2006, waiting for a coffee at my local café. Beside me was Bronwyn, the mother of one of my past students. As we waited for our flat whites, she was bursting with the news that she had been offered the opportunity to work as a literacy consultant in New York City. It would mean being self-employed, something that she had never done before, but she was packing up and going. New York could not have been further removed from the scene in which we were standing. Coolum is a sub-tropical town on Queensland's Sunshine Coast with kilometres of off-white sand leading to the warm, pounding Pacific surf. No building is more than two stories high and the pace of life is glacial. Manhattan it was not! I can remember being so happy for her and intrigued by the idea as we stood drinking our coffees, talking about her exciting new career move. 'You should look into it, too,' was her parting comment. A seed had been planted.

But the dream had to be put on hold. I had two kids about to start secondary school, a newly ended marriage and had just finished a disastrous rebound relationship. I had to get serious about making some solid career choices and saving some money, so I threw myself into my teaching career. However, the idea of working and living in New York as a consultant kept calling me.

In 2012, my daughter moved to New York and six months later, another friend called me and asked if I was still interested in working in NYC. I was getting frustrated with a job that seemed to be more about managing student behaviour than innovating curriculum, teaching or learning, so I threw my hat in the ring and somehow, in September 2014, I was on a plane to JFK and on to a whole new chapter.

I have loved it. It has had its ups and downs, all change does, but it has been one of the best things I have ever done. The capacity I have to help educators make their work richer, more engaging and more rewarding for their students is simply a joy. I'm not organising playground duty rosters or calling parents to suspend their children or sitting in meetings where decisions are postponed once again – I'm helping teachers and school leaders to make the world a better place for their students to increase their power as literate thinkers and global citizens.

This city makes my heart beat a little faster every morning and even with all of its challenges: blizzards and heatwaves, trash in the streets and endless noisy nights, it is so much more than I could have imagined that day fourteen years ago chatting with Bronwyn over a coffee, but it has been worth all the hard work and risk it took to get here and make it work.

Bryher

Bryher Scudamore was Editor of *That's Life!*, one of the BBC's signature programmes that ran from 1973 to 1994 with audiences frequently in excess of 20 million viewers an episode. She then went on to be Editor-in-Chief of the fledgling BBC Online before becoming Director of Communications at The Eden Project at the end of 2002.

She then decided to put her successful career behind her to become an eCommerce entrepreneur at the age of sixty. Her decision was inspired by the sudden death of her beloved mother, Peggy, with whom she had enjoyed a long and close relationship; always talking about life and the issues of the day. But it wasn't until her mother's sudden departure that Bryher realised that she knew very little about her history. As she was clearing out her mother's house, she came across boxes of letters and photographs and articles that were a complete mystery to her.

'Why didn't I ask her about all this when she was alive?' she lamented. So, she decided to throw herself into finding out as much of her mother's story as she could and put it all into a book. Not for publication, simply so that it was available for future generations to appreciate and enjoy.

Then a lightbulb lit up inside her brain. 'There must be so many other people who are in the same boat,' I realised. 'Why don't I set up a business to help everyone do this? Not just to capture their parents' story but to capture their own as well. As I like to say, "Your family history starts with you."'

'Autodotbiography.com' was thus conceived – an online service that would make it easy for people to write their own story, with the end result being a beautiful and professionally bound folio-style book for their children, grandchildren and great-grandchildren to cherish. 'I could have simply started a ghost-writing business to do this, but that would have been expensive. I wanted to make this available and affordable to everyone.'

But the birth of the business had to be put on hold. Only a few weeks after leaving full-time employment to start the new venture in 2007, Bryher was diagnosed with breast cancer. 'The following year would be filled with bouts of treatment, interspersed with periods of exhausting recovery,' she explained. 'Planning the business was actually a welcome distraction.'

Her bout of cancer did not blunt her passion for the new venture, so once she came out the other side and her energy returned to its default 'boundless' setting, she threw herself into it. For the next year or so, she took on some consultancy work while designing and redesigning what the customer experience needed to be. She registered autodotbiography as a limited company in October 2010 and soft launched the whole venture at the *Who Do You Think You Are?* live show at Olympia in February 2011. She sold eighteen autodotbiographies in the three days of the show. In the nine years since, many hundreds of people have used the system to capture their family's stories and many thousands of books have been created.

'Starting a new business for the very first time was terrifying, exciting and incredibly challenging. I was used to having a team around me and now it was just me. I was the chief designer, marketing director, sales director, copywriter, accountant, paymaster, the works.'

As I was writing this, Bryher was about to celebrate her seventieth birthday and autodotbigraphy.com had just had its tenth birthday. I asked her what tips she would give other budding entrepreneurs. Here is the advice she shared:

- Have a clear vision of what you want your business to be and do in the future – and why. Believe in this vision and keep referring to it. It will be your guiding star.

• Stories are powerful. Develop the story about how and why your business came into being.

• Think big but start small. While I was always thinking big, I took it slowly to begin with, which I think you have to do with online businesses. Start small, test, change, test again.

• Listen to your clients. Spend as much time as you can listening to clients – and keep refining your service accordingly.

• Keep operating costs to a minimum, especially in the beginning.

• Leverage your strengths, skills and contacts. I have leveraged my contacts mercilessly from the beginning.

• Know what you are not good at. Don't try to do everything yourself.

• Remember that you are always marketing your business, always selling. If you don't have customers, you don't have a business; you have a hobby that costs you money.

CHAPTER 15:

Transitioning from full-time employment

'The time when we stop living at work and start working at living.'
Nursebuff.com

'Transitioning from full-time employment' is a far better term than 'retirement' – a little long-winded I admit but far more accurate.

For the vast majority of us, it is inevitable that our last day as a full-time employee will eventually dawn. For some of us, that day will only be recognisable in the rear-view mirror, but it will come. And for an increasing number of us, that day is happening earlier and earlier in our careers.

Making the transition from full-time employment, like any change, can be quite a challenge. Even those who may have been lucky enough to make this transition with a whopping financial buffer can find it tough. One day they are a captain of industry, the next they are not even captain of the SS *Minnow*,[1] feeling shipwrecked and more than a little lost. Their career has been a significant part of their identity for decades; their self-esteem intrinsically intertwined with their role at work and the responsibility that went with it. They fear that the only thing they will be responsible for in the future is putting the bins out once a week.

The fact we have spent thirty, forty years or more knowing that this day would come somehow doesn't make it any easier, because traditional retirement is so often portrayed as a cliff edge. It is binary; we go from being a somebody to a nobody. At least that's how we fear it will feel.

But we don't become a nobody. Far from it. Leaving full-time employment, at whatever age that may be, heralds a new era of options

---

[1] The 'tiny ship' that was shipwrecked on *Gilligan's Island*, the 1960s American sitcom. It shames me to say that I could still sing you the theme tune if you like.

and opportunities. As we have discussed, we are living so much longer than previous generations. The average sixty-five-year-old British man can now expect to live to eighty-four, according to the Office of National Statistics. Fifty years ago, the average was seventy-six. A sixty-five-year-old British woman can now expect to live to eighty-six. And, pandemics aside, these numbers look set to increase.

A great number of opportunities await us beyond that fateful 'R' day.

Some life coaches recommend easing the transition from full-time employment; doing the job part-time as the end nears so that when the guillotine does fall, it is less of a shock. Working three days a week, say, for the last year or two can ease the transition and give you time to prepare for your life after full-time employment.

I'm not so sure.

In my humble opinion, there are several downsides to this plan. First, as any working mother would attest (or 'working primary caregiver' to be slightly less accurate but a great deal less stereotypical), working three days a week often means doing the same amount of work as you would in five but for 60 per cent of the pay. Even those two days you have 'off' are spent thinking about work or on the phone or email. Many people who have adopted this strategy have found that they did very little preparation for their future lives during these days anyway. They were neither one thing nor the other.

When it comes to organisational change, I tell leaders that they have a choice when it comes to managing the pain of restructuring: they can either 'pay now' or 'pay later', and they will always pay more if they choose to pay later. In other words, sometimes it is better to just rip the plaster off quickly rather than trying to prise it loose in small, painful stages. By all means prepare yourself mentally for the changes and challenges that lie ahead. But dragging out your full-time employment end date can sometimes be akin to lowering yourself into a cold pool slowly, experiencing every millimetre of cold water as it rises up your body with excruciating slowness while you tiptoe cautiously towards the deep end.

Jump in. The water's fine.

Transitioning to what?

Let's be honest. Full-time employment is not something that many of us wish to do through the entirety of our Part Two. Spending five days a week working for someone else with just two days off to get everything else done and only a handful of weeks holiday a year to recover before doing it all over again – that isn't an arrangement that many of us wish to continue into our dotage, however much we may enjoy the benefits of work. Yes, more than a few of us want to keep working well into our Part Two, but at some point the majority of us will want to transition to some other sort of arrangement.

I also appreciate that starting your own full-on business is not going to be everyone's ideal vision of how they wish to spend their second act. While the hours are flexible, in my experience they are long, and, especially if you love running your own business, it can be awfully difficult to switch off (says Campbell sitting at his laptop writing this sentence at 2:15am on a wintry Tuesday).

Other options may feature in your plans for Part Two: working part-time, perhaps for several employers; freelancing; caring for parents; looking after grandchildren; giving something back; investing; volunteering. As we saw back in Chapter 5 (p.44), volunteering is not only a wonderful thing to do, it also reduces stress, slows cognitive decline, and can help us to live happier, healthier and longer.

Part Two may also be the chance for you to follow your heart; to do those things you have always wanted to do – write a book, learn to paint, learn a new language or a musical instrument, travel, and yes, gardening if you really must ...

And for a significant number of us, our second half will also be the time when we will need to address the emotional and financial challenge that our parents aren't getting any younger.

PART FOUR:

Our parents aren't getting any younger

'I am incapable of conceiving infinity, and yet I do not accept finity. I want this adventure that is the context of my life to go on without end.'
Simone de Beauvoir, *The Coming of Age*[1]

Too many of us wait too long to have *those* conversations with our parents

You know the ones I mean. The conversations about where they would like to live when they get old. The conversations about powers of attorney, adapting their home, moving to a house without stairs or perhaps an apartment. About moving into a 'granny' flat, getting assistance at home or moving into a purpose-built retirement or assisted living community. Conversations about care homes. Conversations about funerals.

Sixty per cent of UK adults don't even have a will, according to Family Risk Management (FRisk), a business that specialises in helping people to avoid 'disorganised deaths', which means that up to 30 million Brits leave a parting gift of delay and in-fighting in their wake. It is a similar story across the rest of the world. FRisk Founder and CEO, Martin Holdsworth, is a contentious probate specialist, a specialist in inheritance dispute resolution. 'In virtually every dispute I have dealt with, there comes a realisation by the affected family that, if only their loved one had put plans in place during life, then all the financial,

[1] French writer, intellectual, existentialist philosopher, political activist and feminist (1908–1986).

emotional and litigious suffering could have been avoided.'

This is especially true in situations that involve multiple marriages or unmarried couples. One example Martin speaks of is an unmarried couple who had lived with one another for fifteen years and had three children aged between three and nine. The man died without a will and without life insurance or pension nomination in place. Under the intestacy rules that apply in the absence of a will, his partner received nothing: the house and all assets passed to her three young children, who weren't old enough to legally agree anything. Four sets of lawyers and a court hearing later wiped out the £40,000 of cash savings from the estate, only to end up with an unsatisfactory solution where his partner had 100 per cent responsibility for the mortgage but only 25 per cent ownership of the house. The whole thing could have been avoided by a simple will.

After decades of many such stories, Martin decided to tackle the problem 'at source' and created FRisk to help people get their affairs in order quickly and easily online. With a few simple questions, FRisk generates a personalised interactive Family Risk Report that tells the user exactly what would have happened 'if they had died yesterday'. The report covers a host of factors including which family members would and wouldn't have inherited, property ownership, inheritance tax liability, funeral costs, guardianship, parental responsibility issues and a host of other relevant issues. Frisk can also introduce their users to a panel of vetted providers who can deliver the services they need. You will find more detail on FRisk and a link to the FRisk website at www.you-part-two.com.

When we do finally have the conversations with our parents, they sometimes can be a little superficial. We may organise a lasting power of attorney (although only 10 per cent of us get around to this, according to Martin), but have we discussed the sort of event that would trigger it and how this would be done? We snatch a moment to talk about future care arrangements and then the conversation swiftly turns to lunch or politics or bridge or the grandkids or golf – anything. It is almost as though the very act of talking about these things will make them happen sooner. Either we or our parents don't want to dwell on their mortality, so the conversations remain unfulfilled.

Which is why so many of these important decisions end up being made as distressed purchases in moments of high emotion. A care home has to be found suddenly and swiftly when a father is found rambling semi-naked in the middle of town, having broken out of hospital in the middle of the night. The man in question was coping well living on his own, even with increasing dementia, until a bad fall changed everything. This is very common. Craig Swanger, Co-Founder of Care360, a company we will meet later, estimates that around two-thirds of care home places are filled in a panic with little prior planning after a fall or medical emergency. Funeral parlour profits wouldn't be the same if everyone had the whole thing planned in advance; no one chooses the cheapest coffin for their parent two days before the funeral.

It just shows how strangely complicated we humans are. We all know we will die. The world would be a tad over-populated if that wasn't the case. We have attended funerals for friends and relatives. We know how long, on average, people our age live for and we can do the mental arithmetic. Death is the only thing on the road ahead about which we can have 100 per cent certainty. What is not certain is when it will happen, how it will happen or the stages of the ageing process we will experience en route.

We all know we will age, too, and that one day we are likely to need assistance. Logically, therefore, we should make some plans. Parents should discuss scenarios and options with their children well in advance. We should encourage our parents to have these conversations with us. We want to avoid the situation where a confused parent feels as though they have been dumped into a care home, eternally resentful.

But before we have those conversations, we need to do our homework. Forewarned is fore-armed. And while the subject of aged care could fill a volume of books, the following two chapters are my ten-thousand-foot, seagull-eye's view of the subject. For some readers, the detail will be much too little, for some it will be way too much. I apologise profusely to both groups in advance. But, hopefully, a few Goldilockses among you will think it's just right.

Anyway, I hope it helps.

CHAPTER 16:

Caring for an ageing population

In less than thirty years from now, more than 1.5 billion people on this little planet of ours will be aged sixty-five or over. Soon, one in four people in the West will be older than sixty-five and this ratio is only going one way.
Source: United Nations World Population Prospects 2019[1]

Let's stand back and approach this subject from a macro level for a few minutes. I am a firm believer in the value of understanding the big picture of a problem before diving into the detail.

In this chapter we are going to take a look at one of the world's biggest issues – caring for an ageing population that is living so much longer. It is a global phenomenon, and we can learn a great deal from how different nations are tackling the same problem.

How to organise and fund aged care is a challenge that politicians and civil servants across the globe are grappling with – or at least talking earnestly about grappling with. Like a slow-motion train crash, it is an issue that we have all seen coming for decades, and yet, inexplicably, it is also one that so many governments have repeatedly kicked into the long grass or made incredibly complicated, or both.

None more so than the USA, a country that 'has never had a broad public program covering long-term care', according to the *New York Times*. Consequently, too many older Americans are sicker, and poorer, than their counterparts in other developed countries: 36 per cent of older Americans have three or more chronic conditions versus only 13 per cent of New Zealanders.[2]

[1] UN World Population Prospects 2019. https://population.un.org/wpp
[2] 2017 Commonwealth Fund International Health Policy Survey of Older Adults.

Too many elderly Americans also struggle to afford life's basics. Thirty-one per cent of American high-need elderly struggle with costs compared to only 2 per cent in Sweden. 'Let's face it, long-term caregiving for elderly people can be seriously expensive,' states Aging.com, and the situation looks set to get even worse: 'A decade from now, most middle-income seniors will not be able to pay the rising costs of independent or assisted living.'[3] Which is why in April 2021, President Biden pledged hundreds of billions of dollars more for in-home elder care.

Aged care funding in the US is fragmented and confusing. Almost four hundred programmes exist across federal, state and local governments, Veterans Affairs, non-profits, private organisations and dozens of other agencies – with different and often conflicting qualification rules that can make 'determining one's eligibility a challenge' as payingforseniorcare.com understates. Aging.com recommends US residents head to www.benefits.gov or www.benefitschekup.org to find out what assistance they are entitled to receive.

Australia and the UK have taken the first step in the right direction and admitted that the problem exists. Australia, a nation that introduced compulsory superannuation (pension) three decades ago in a large and purposeful stride towards affording the inevitable costs associated with an ageing population, seems to have underperformed against its own high standards when it comes to aged care. As I write this paragraph in March 2021, a Royal Commission into the state of the Australian aged care system has just been completed and the nation is beginning to digest its stark findings and far-reaching recommendations. An interim report was published in late 2019 and a few of the opening paragraphs are well worth sharing, for the situation it describes is not unique to Australia. The authors could have been describing the aged care situation in any number of countries. Usually government reports are bone-dry, written in formal pseudo-academic legalese designed to obfuscate rather than clarify. This report is different. It uses potent and compelling language from the title onwards, leaving the reader in no doubt as to what the authors are saying.

Read the following and I am sure it will resonate no matter where you happen to be living.

[3] https://www.nytimes.com/2019/05/10/health/assisted-living-costs-elderly.html

Executive Summary: 'A shocking tale of neglect'.

'It's not easy growing old. We avoid thinking and talking about it. As we age, we progressively shift our focus from work to the other things that give us purpose and joy: our children and grandchildren, our friends, our holidays, our homes and gardens, our local communities, our efforts as volunteers, our passions and hobbies. The Australian community generally accepts that older people have earned the chance to enjoy their later years, after many decades of contribution and hard work. Yet the language of public discourse is not respectful towards older people. Rather, it is about burden, encumbrance, obligation and whether taxpayers can afford to pay for the dependence of older people.

As a nation, Australia has drifted into an ageist mindset that undervalues older people and limits their possibilities. Sadly, this failure to properly value and engage with older people as equal partners in our future has extended to our apparent indifference towards aged care services. Left out of sight and out of mind, these important services are floundering. They are fragmented, unsupported and underfunded. With some admirable exceptions, they are poorly managed. All too often, they are unsafe and seemingly uncaring. This must change.

Australia prides itself on being a clever, innovative and caring country. Why, then, has the Royal Commission found these qualities so signally lacking in our aged care system? We have uncovered an aged care system that is characterised by an absence of innovation and by rigid conformity. The system lacks transparency in communication, reporting and accountability. It is not built around the people it is supposed to help and support, but around funding mechanisms, processes and procedures.

We have found that the aged care system fails to meet the needs of our older, often very vulnerable, citizens. It does not deliver uniformly safe and quality care for older people.

It is unkind and uncaring towards them. In too many instances, it simply neglects them.

This cruel and harmful system must be changed. We owe it to our parents, our grandparents, our partners, our friends. We owe it to strangers. We owe it to future generations. Older people deserve so much more.'[4]

Powerful stuff from a formal public enquiry! And this is from a nation that I assumed had got so much right when it came to aged care. The emotional tone of the report reflects the underlying expectations of the majority of Australians that, in return for the taxes they have paid all their working lives, their government should provide a quality safety net for their elderly. Not such a radical idea, is it?

Soon after the release of the interim report, which declared that 56 per cent of aged care homes were unprofitable and therefore at varied risk of closing, the Australian government announced an increase of more than AUD$1bn in funding for aged care, taking the budgeted annual amount to more than AUD$21bn. More funds were pledged upon receipt of the full report. But as the Royal Commission pointed out, much more money, and much more than money, is needed to transform aged care from its current position where one in three elderly Australians receive sub-standard care and 18 per cent of aged-care residents report they have been sexually or physically assaulted.

The first requirement of any aged care system that actually works is a proper strategy – followed by effective regulation, central coordination, local delivery, an abundance of qualified staff, and a mix of public and private providers of different variations of home care. It needs to be straightforward, yet comprehensive and easy to communicate. But most of all, it requires politicians who care and are capable of taking a long-term view. Petty partisan politics need to be removed from the discussion entirely. Political ideologies need to be discarded and all parts of the political spectrum need to focus on delivering the required outcome of uniform, safe, humane and dignified care for our elderly citizens.

The UK conducted its own review of aged care more than a decade ago. Sir Andrew Dilnot was asked by the new coalition government to

[4] https://agedcare.royalcommission.gov.au/publications/Pages/interim-report.aspx

lead a cross-party commission on 'Funding for Care and Support' in 2010. His proposals for change, submitted the following year, were finally approved by the Queen in 2015 but the Prime Minister, David Cameron, and his Chancellor of the Exchequer, George Osborne, decided to postpone implementation of the recommendations after cynically, and successfully, branding the opposition's ideas to increase funding for aged care 'a death tax' in the years leading up to the 2015 election. In 2016, Cameron held, and lost, *that* referendum on the UK's membership of the EU and subsequently the British Parliament did very little about anything other than argue about Brexit for the following four and a half years. After winning the 2019 election, Prime Minister Boris Johnson declared: 'This [aged care] has been shirked by governments for thirty years. Because we have the majority that we need, we're going to get on and deal with this so people get the care that they need in their old age but don't have to sell their home to pay for their care.'

While the promised cross-party talks on the subject are yet to materialise as at the time of writing, Britain's latest Prime Minister has at least appointed a qualified and experienced professional to finalise plans for aged care reform, Camilla Cavendish, who was head of the Number 10 Policy Unit under David Cameron before accepting a lifetime peerage as part of Cameron's resignation honours list. 'If how we treat our frail elderly is a measure of a civilised society, we are failing,' Baroness Cavendish wrote in the *Financial Times* on 9 November 2018.

Towards the end of 2020, Jeremy Hunt, ex Health Secretary and now Chair of the Commons Health and Social Care Committee, called for an extra £7 bn a year to be allocated to aged care, funded by a tax on anyone over the age of forty along the lines of Germany and Japan, because 'the way we treat older people in this country has neither kindness nor decency'. To put that figure into perspective, the annual budget for the Department of Health and Social Care in England alone was £212 billion in 2020/21.

While the UK government has a lot on its plate over the next few years trying to address the colossal economic and social fallout from both COVID-19 and Brexit, an expensive high-speed rail link from London to northern cities, and seriously understaffed National Health Service and police forces, let's hope aged care can makes its way up the government's lengthening to-do list as swiftly as possible.

I also hope Camilla Cavendish and her Australian equivalent take a look at how other nations tackle the problem.

Across Europe, most nations fund aged care through dedicated taxation and co-payment – poorer citizens pay nothing while wealthy citizens pay more, but the amount is capped.

Japan, with more people aged over sixty-five and whose population is living longer than any other, may be the nation from which we could learn the most. The Japanese government acted to get ahead of the problem more than twenty years ago by establishing a specific national long-term care insurance system into which every taxpayer over forty pays. What a sensible idea. Further financing comes from general taxation and user co-payments of 10 per cent of the cost of the care, although these are capped for low earners, who also have their accommodation costs paid for.

The Nordic countries, as in so many things, also seem to get it right. The thing I love about what they have done is that they have a genuine strategy that begins with a clear statement of the outcomes they are seeking to achieve: 'Equality of people regardless of limitations; self-determination and independence; being able to (continue to) live independently; affordability of care for everyone; solidarity with vulnerable fellow citizens; an accessible society; a caring government that guarantees that people can receive good care and can participate in society.'[5]

Generally, large-scale residential facilities have been phased out throughout Scandinavia and care has been integrated into society, mainly under the supervision of municipal authorities. But then social welfare is important to Scandinavians. Community is important. The state plays a much bigger role in the lives of its citizens than it does in many other Western nations, the US especially. Scandinavians feel solidarity with the vulnerable people in their society and their governments accept a high degree of responsibility for the welfare of its people. Obviously, this requires higher taxes.

Aged care is a complex and expensive issue no matter where you live in the world as it cuts across numerous government departments

[5] https://www.vilans.org/app/uploads/2019/05/long-term-care-in-scandinavia.pdf

from health to tax to immigration, but it must be tackled. Now. Because the problem is only set to get worse.

Since the beginning of recorded history, young children have outnumbered their elders. Not anymore. The number of people aged sixty-five or older now outnumbers the number of children under five across the world, even though infant mortality is a tiny fraction of what it once was. Driven by falling fertility rates and remarkable increases in life expectancy, population ageing will continue.

By 2050, less than thirty years away, it is expected that more than 1.5 billion people on this little planet of ours will be aged sixty-five or over. That will be one in six of us (16 per cent), compared to one in eleven in 2019 (9 per cent).[6] Four hundred and twenty-six million people will be eighty or older.

Across Western Europe, Northern America, Australia and New Zealand, we have already exceeded one in six. Very soon, one in four of us will be aged sixty-five or over and the ratio will continue to worsen. In the future, there will be even more of us who will need looking after – and far fewer working-age people to both fund, and provide, the services we will need.

And to add insult to injury, over a quarter of us have no idea how we will pay for our long-term care. Twenty-eight per cent of Brits in their sixties and seventies will be relying on state provision to fund their care into old age, according to a 2019 study by Fidelity.

This situation is mirrored across much of the West. To say that is less than ideal would be a classic British understatement, as we will discover in the next chapter when we attempt to navigate the bamboozling labyrinth that is aged care.

[6] UN World Population Prospects 2019. https://population.un.org/wpp

CHAPTER 17:

Navigating the aged care labyrinth

It is far better to be in the know than in the dark.

It is now time to take a deep breath before we dive into the deep and murky waters of aged care. We have focused this chapter on the pressing matter of providing aged care for our parents, as so many of our friends have already had to do. But of course, we should all have one eye on the fact that in a few short decades, we may be looking to do the same for ourselves. A sobering thought, I know.

But first, a word of warning: if you are arriving to this subject afresh, this chapter may come as a bit of a rude shock. Some of the numbers are bound to be more than a little daunting and while we have tried to soften the reality as much as we can 'it is what it is' to quote many a politician. The unfair reality that lies at the heart of this emotional and complicated subject is that with money, old age can be comfortable and enjoyable, uplifting even. Without money, well, that can be a different situation entirely. This may be stark, but it is true. So, in the belief that it is far better to be in the know than in the dark, let's gird our loins and get started.

There are three main options when it comes to aged housing and care:

Option 1: Adapt the home to better accommodate the needs of the elderly

Option 2: Move to a type of 'retirement living'

Option 3: Care homes and nursing homes

This chapter explores each one in enough detail to whet your appetite. It is not meant to be even close to a definitive guide. We have included detail on the UK, Australia and the US, but the themes are universal.

OPTION 1: ADAPT THE HOME

The majority of elderly people live at home.

According to UK charity, EAC FirstStop, who provide 'advice and information about care and housing choices in later life', only a small proportion of older people live in specially built, age-specific housing. Nine out of ten stay in their own home and adapt it to make it safer and more functional for them as they age – reconfiguring a bathroom, removing steps and those annoying parts of doorframes that are so easy to trip over or even renting or buying a stairlift. Installing a panic button is a good idea for emergencies. So are wearable emergency buttons. Whether people agree to wear them is another matter entirely.

The first step is to carry out an assessment of the care that is required. In Britain, 'Care Needs Assessments' are conducted free of charge by the social services department of your local council, regardless of your income or savings or whether the council thinks you will qualify for assistance, although they will obviously prioritise the more urgent cases. In Australia, assessments are also free. The starting point is a dedicated federal government web portal (www.myagedcare.gov.au), where you can apply for an assessment and a local assessment team will be despatched to conduct it.

Most countries offer some sort of financial assistance for home adaptations, but it is likely to be limited. In the UK, any adaptations or equipment under £1,000, such as fitting lever taps in the kitchen or handrails, will be paid for by the government, irrespective of your financial situation. Means-tested grants, insensitively named 'Disabled Facilities Grants', of up to £30,000 in England (£36,000 in Wales and £25,000 in NI) are also available from the government to help with the costs of more expensive modifications, installing a downstairs shower room, widening doorways, lowering the work tops in your kitchen, installing a stairlift, but the qualification criteria are very strict. However, if the council deems that your parent could afford to service a loan to cover the costs of the modifications (whether or not a bank would actually agree to provide them with such a loan), they will be ineligible for a grant. In Australia, home modifications can be included as part of the federal government's Home Care Packages that we discuss below, but there are limits to the types of modifications that the government will subsidise.

In-home care

A Care Needs Assessment goes beyond making changes to your home; it is a chance for your parent/s to discuss what they may need help with and to start to plan. If they need help with daily tasks such as getting dressed or undressed, washing, getting in or out of the bath or shower, eating and drinking, taking medication, going to or using the toilet, getting in or out of bed, or even telling people what they need or making themselves understood (and there will come a time when the majority of us will need help with at least some of these), they may be able to receive help from the government, irrespective of what they earn or how much they may have in the bank. But in the UK, it's not much. They would be eligible to receive around £60 a week for day care or roughly £85 a week for day and night care. This will translate to between just three and five hours a week of care.

Australia appears to be more generous when it comes to helping people receive care in their homes. With its Commonwealth Home Support Programme, the federal government helps to finance the provision of four levels of home-based care services in the form of Home Care Packages – from basic services such as transport, shopping, domestic assistance, meal preparation, simple home modification and maintenance to the highest-level services including things such as help with showering, getting dressed, feeding, getting into and out of bed, nursing and allied health support. A professional needs assessment is conducted by an ACAT assessor (Aged Care Assessment Team) and the services are means-tested but subsidised, costing the individual between $10 and $42 a day depending upon income, with annual and lifetime caps on both contributions.[1]

[1] https://www.myagedcare.gov.au/home-care-package-costs-and-fees

Twenty-four-hour in-home care

At the top end of the scale, twenty-four-hour live-in care can be very expensive, no matter where you live. One Australian provider, DaughterlyCare.com.au, claim they charge only AUD$3,645 a week after taking a government subsidy of AUD$875 into account, but other providers quote costs that are twice that figure.

Meanwhile in the US, Genworth's 2019 Cost of Care Survey[2] bases the costs of care on an assumed forty-four hours a week and reports that the average monthly cost for in-home care to help with basic cooking, cleaning and household chores in the US is $4,300. A week. This figure could be doubled if you add enough health professionals into the mix, and even tripled for twenty-four-hour care, seven days a week.

At £25 an hour (a figure that is slightly higher than the government's suggested rate but not as much as some private providers will charge), forty-four hours of care a week would cost £1,100 in the UK. Twenty-four-hour care, seven days a week could cost more than £4,000. Every week.

Which is why one in five Britons between the ages of fifty and sixty-four are carers – that's 2.5 million people, according to the Office of National Statistics.

The full and alarming impact of this is reflected in a recent report by Carers UK: 'unpaid carers saved the UK state £530 million every day of the COVID-19 pandemic'.[3] Half a billion pounds every day. As we saw, Jeremy Hunt was asking for £7bn to fill the funding gap for aged care. That may be just a drop in the ocean.

Okay. That was a whistle-stop tour of 'adapting your home'. Let's take a little look at the next option – moving to a type of 'retirement living' (yes, there's that word again!), where residents could be as young as fifty-five.

Marvellous.

OPTION 2: MOVE TO A TYPE OF 'RETIREMENT LIVING'.

Every country uses slightly different terms but there are fundamentally three different types of 'retirement living' options available. They all

---

[2] https://www.genworth.com/aging-and-you/finances/cost-of-care.html
[3] https://www.carersuk.org/news-and-campaigns/news/unpaid-carers-save-uk-state-530-million-every-day-of-the-pandemic

involve moving into purpose-built communities, providing either an instant social life and new friends or a feeling of being trapped in a living hell surrounded by people you don't like. It all depends on the luck of your draw and the attitude of the elderly person in question. The vast majority of people find that it is the former, by the way. And remember that fewer than one in ten people currently opt for any of these options.

Let's start with the most expensive, five-star option.

Retirement villages

Retirement villages are purpose-built 'independent living' communities that offer a mixture of houses, single-storey homes and apartments in a village environment. The top of the range communities are designed to be like living on a cruise liner without the sea sickness and golden candelabras. I spoke to the CEO of Richmond Villages, Philippa Fieldhouse, as part of the research for this section and she explained to me that the most common comment she hears from people who have moved into one of their developments is that they wished they had done it sooner. The villages give their residents a sense of community and boast their own private amenities such as doctors' surgeries, gyms, pubs/bars, restaurants, community halls, pools plus easy access to public transport. To enhance and in fact widen social interaction, many retirement villages offer access to their social facilities to non-residents. The social aspect of these communities is not to be understated: we are social beings after all. My grandmother lived in a similar community for almost fifteen years after my grandfather died, and while her sense of humour wasn't exactly on the same wavelength as every one of her neighbours, she thoroughly enjoyed the fact she had her independence yet with a social life on tap.

Twenty-four-hour domiciliary care is also often available, providing peace of mind in case of emergencies, while many villages have assisted living options and even care homes as part of the complex.

Sheltered housing

This may be a cold and unwelcoming term but it 'does what it says on the tin', I suppose. They are individual properties grouped together into a small complex, usually consisting of a group of self-contained one- or two-bedroom apartments that have been purpose-built or adapted to meet the needs of older people, especially if they want to live in a smaller home that is easier to manage. Typically, sheltered housing schemes come with a twenty-four-hour alarm system, a manager or warden on-site or nearby and a variety of communal facilities such as a lounge, laundry, guest flat and garden. Some may also have a restaurant and even shops such as hairdressers or convenience store, depending on the size of the facility.

Perhaps the greatest advantage of sheltered housing is the close presence of neighbours, and yet everyone maintains their own privacy and independence. The ninety-year-old mother of a friend of ours tripped and knocked her head inside her apartment a few years ago and was unable to right herself, let alone make it to the phone. Her son and daughter-in-law were unable to get hold of her all day. When she missed a hairdresser's appointment, a neighbour knocked on her door. Eventually, the manager was called and they unlocked her apartment to find her prostrate on the floor, semi-conscious. She had been lying there for more than twenty-four hours. Living in 'sheltered housing' probably saved her life.

Assisted living

Assisted living facilities are sheltered housing schemes with care staff or nurses onsite twenty-four-hours a day.

It pays to do your homework. The best assisted living facilities and care homes are those whose managers realise that their residents need independence and purpose, not merely safety and sedatives, as Atul Gawande explains in his book, *Being Mortal* (Profile Books 2014). Assisted living should be about living well for the rest of their lives, not just waiting to die. Good operators treat every single resident as an individual and realise that our elderly deserve to live a fulfilling life with as much independence as possible. They treat their residents as customers, as people, not patients. They hire staff members who genuinely care about the physical and mental health of each of their residents. The bad operators focus on drugs and control. Their over-riding purpose appears to be keeping their patients safe and quiet, rather than helping them to live the remainder of their lives to the fullest.

Of course, the good ones are bound to have waiting lists; so, it pays to do your homework and, if at all possible, to plan ahead. I appreciate that is not always as easy as it sounds.

Buying a 'retired living' property

As of 2020, a one-bedroom self-contained apartment in a sheltered housing complex on the south coast of England cost around £300,000. A typical two-bedroom retirement home in Fairford, Gloucestershire, was in the vicinity of £375,000. Richmond Villages also offer assisted living apartments within their retirement villages at a cost of around £350,000–400,000, while an independent living apartment or townhouse in a Richmond Village retirement village can cost anywhere from £250,000 to £750,000 depending upon size and location. As with so many things in life, you get what you pay for.

All of these properties are 'leasehold' purchases rather than 'freehold', which means legally your parents won't own the property per se. What leaseholders buy is the right to occupy the building for a given length of time, and this right can be on-sold. Mind you, most leases are 125 years or longer in duration and when the lease is this long, it feels much like buying the property outright ('freehold').

Why do the providers sell their properties on a leasehold basis? They say it is to ensure continuity of standards and quality of buildings, the estate and associated services – which makes some sense, to be honest. The way they ensure these high standards is through the charging of regular upkeep, maintenance and service fees; and if a leaseholder doesn't pay the fees, the freeholder can take the property back and sell it to someone else. Twenty-six per cent of leaseholders feel their freeholder overcharges but are unable to do anything about it.[4] Or to put it another way, three-quarters of people are happy with the arrangement and the costs.

Because they don't own the property per se, leaseholders also have to pay an annual 'ground rent' to the freeholder. It is usually small but there have been stories over the years about unscrupulous owners increasing ground rents every year by ridiculous amounts until they become untenable. Be sure to check the contract for the rules around how

[4] 2019 Annual Homeowner Survey. hao.org.uk

much the owner can increase any ground rents. The reputable providers will cap increases at c.2.5 per cent per annum or some inflation index, whichever is higher.

Selling the property

In the UK, there is often a fee payable when the property is sold. A number of sheltered housing or assisted living providers charge a normal fee akin to an estate agent of 1.5–2 per cent on the sale of the property. But premier retirement village providers can charge a 'transfer fee' of up to 10 per cent. (Richmond Village charges between 6 per cent and 10 per cent depending upon how long your parents have owned the property.) The existence of this fee was a surprise to me. I have never seen or heard of such a thing in the world of real estate outside of purpose-built 'retirement villages'. It doesn't exist when you sell a holiday villa or apartment, but it does for this part of the market. The providers insist that this helps keep the quality of the grounds and facilities at a high standard, and that the purchase price of the properties would be higher without this sort of exit fee. While the fee may be high, it is completely legal and certainly not hidden; just one to keep an eye out for. The good news is that your parents or their estate get to keep any capital gains. Some countries allow the accommodation providers to take that, too.

Renting a 'retired living' property

If renting is the only option, then one place to go is your local council, often in conjunction with a housing association. In the UK, each council has its own housing allocation policy and stock of aged care housing available. Quality varies but they will still be council-provided properties, so don't expect the Ritz Carlton! There are very few private properties available to rent in the UK and because the demand is so high, they go rather quickly. Richmond Villages has recently begun to offer rental contracts on some assisted living apartments, priced at around 8 per cent of the apartment's value per annum (i.e., around £2,500 a month).

Ongoing costs

Running costs vary, too. The £300,000 sheltered housing apartment discussed above came with monthly running costs of around £600. The property in the Fairford village was a little less.

Retirement villages' ongoing costs are another scale entirely, especially with one of the premier providers. Costs include:

- A service charge for ongoing upkeep maintenance, repair and cleaning of all communal areas and services – c.£500 a month.
- Ground rent, as discussed previously – around £25 a month.
- Lifestyle packages. These are packages of optional services for residents who don't wish to self-cater. Either through need or choice, they want everything done for them – laundry, food and drink, housekeeping, utilities, post, newspaper delivery ... the list is lengthy. The costs of these lifestyle packages in a premier retirement village can be between £2,600 (for one person) and £4,000 (for two people) a month. Premier service certainly doesn't come cheap!

OPTION 3: CARE HOMES AND NURSING HOMES

Care homes are there for when people have got to that stage of their life when they simply can't cope on their own and need round-the-clock care. The good ones are part hospital, part hotel and part home. Nursing homes are care homes with nurses available onsite twenty-four hours a day.

And while it may be true that only 10 per cent of elderly people live in such homes, this is still a large number – more than 500,000 in the UK alone.

Even though care homes are regulated by a government body (The Care Quality Commission in the UK, the Centers for Medicare & Medicaid Services in the US, the Aged Care Quality and Safety Commission in Australia, the Retirement Homes Regulatory Authority in Canada), quality varies considerably from region to region, no matter which country you happen to be living in. While the regulators publish formal inspection regimes, use them as a guide. In the inimitable words of Sonia Nuttall, who did the lion's share of the research on this topic and had personal experience in finding a care home for her dementia-suffering father: 'In my experience the regulator's ratings do not necessarily match the reality of the homes I visited, nor did they take into account the smell of boiled cabbage and worse!' She also found that just because the home was rated as being able to cope with dementia, this was not necessarily the case; it depended upon the extent of the condition and the effect it had on the patient.

Costs can be higher than expected and decisions are too often made in the midst of emotional panic, delivering sub-optimal results, so it pays to plan ahead. It pays to do your homework in advance – work with your parents well ahead of time to form a joint plan together. Online services exist to help you do this such as which.co.uk and ageuk.org.uk in the United Kingdom, assistedlivingcare.com and care.com in the US, and myagedcare.gov.au in Australia. But often, these types of sites simply provide checklists of questions and alphabetical listings of local care homes. An excellent new Australian online business, Care360.com.au, goes much further – helping you to find the care home that is right for your loved one with additional services to make the entire angst-ridden process as stress-free as possible. It is such a good idea that other similar businesses are bound to spring up across the globe. A list of resources on this subject can be found on www.you-part-two.com.

Most nations subsidise care home costs to varying degrees on a means-tested basis, but it is rarely straightforward, and each country has its own set of biases and blackspots, intended or otherwise.

Australia does things a little differently than many other nations, but the model seems to make some sense (if you are a homeowner), because you effectively buy the room. The average cost of a care home room is around AUD$350,000, about half the national average house price. But you can pay more than $1 million in some parts of Sydney – indeed, I have heard of rooms priced as high as $2 million. So, your parent sells their home and stumps up the cash for the room. This cash payment is called a Refundable Accommodation Deposit (RAD). If you don't have enough for the full amount, a payment of 6 per cent per annum is charged on any shortfall. This is called a Daily Accommodation Payment (DAP) – Australia loves its acronyms – and it is deducted from the RAD on a monthly basis. Stay with me. If your parent's income is below $70,000 a year and they have assets below $172,000, the government says it will pay for some or all of the accommodation costs.

Okay, that pays for the room. Now the care needs to be paid for.

All residents are charged a basic daily fee of $52.50 a day to cover meals, cleaning, facilities management and laundry. This figure is set at

85 per cent of the single person rate of the basic age pension. A means-tested 'care fee' of up to $260 a day is also charged to cover personal and clinical care, but these costs are capped at $28,000 a year or $67,500 in a lifetime (as of 2020). If your parent qualifies for any state pension, this will be used as payment, otherwise the cost of care is deducted from the Refundable Accommodation Deposit. Whatever is left in the RAD is refunded or transferred to the estate when a resident leaves the home.

It is worth bearing in mind that only 200,000 Aussies were permanent care home residents in the 2017/2018 tax year while 900,000 people received some sort of assistance to live at home.

In the US, the average cost of a private room in a nursing home was US$1,960 a week according to the Genworth Study cited earlier.

In Britain, the average cost of a nursing home is around £900 a week, but top end homes can cost £1,700 a week, some even more. If a person qualifies for financial assistance (and not many do qualify), the government will subsidise the cost of a care home bed at around £600 per week for care homes and £800 per week for nursing homes. These are the 2020 averages across England, and they vary from county to county.

But, as is so often the case, the care home or nursing home that you want for your parent will most likely cost more than this figure and the deficit will need to be funded by you and your brothers and sisters if you have them. A deficit of £400 a week is not uncommon, and it could be much higher. Again, these are conversations to have with your siblings as early as possible because it can be the source of incredible acrimony. A friend of ours recently placed her mother into a home that costs £1,200 a week. Her mother qualifies for financial assistance, so she receives £700 from the council to help with this cost, leaving a deficit of £500 a week to fund. She initially thought that her mother's pension would cover the difference, but the council takes this. And for some reason, her brother refuses to part with a penny towards the extra £500 a week. Families.

By the way, under the current rules, most people in Britain don't qualify for any government assistance when it comes to care or nursing home costs. The £600/£800 a week subsidy I discussed above is only available if your parent's total capital, including savings, investments and the value of their home, is below £23,250, which rules out 99 per cent of homeowners, seeing as the average UK dwelling is worth c.£250,000.

So how does your parent or parents afford the cost of a care or nursing home, which as we have seen could be anywhere between £3,000 and £7,000+ a month? Well, first they use up their savings and then they sell their home. Care home providers effectively hold an IOU over your parent's house until it is sold. A decade ago, The Dilnot Commission suggested that the amount of money that anyone should have to spend on care costs should be capped at approximately £46,000 in today's money. Beyond this figure, the government would be required to pick up the tab. But at the time of writing this chapter, there is no cap, which means that the cost of the care home could whittle your parent's capital all the way down to their last £23,250, at which point the government subsidy kicks in and any deficit will then need to be funded by the family.

The mathematicians among you will have your calculators poised and will be wondering what the average duration of tenure in a care home actually is. Obviously, it depends upon the age and health of the person at the time that they move into the care home – and fate. Not only do averages vary from country to country (Israelis spend an average of sixty-three days in a care home while people in Luxembourg can last more than two thousand days![5]) but means and medians can be misleading.

A study of 11,565 residents in BUPA care homes in the UK a decade ago found that the average length of stay was 114 weeks (twenty-six months). At a weekly cost of say £1,200, that would add up to a total cost of £137,000. But this is an average – half of the residents died within fifteen months of their arrival at the home and around a quarter lived for more than three years. The longest-staying resident lived in their lovely BUPA care home for twenty years. Twenty years at £1,200 a week . . . I think my calculator just froze.

DYING WELL

I was going to end this chapter with the enduring image of a frozen calculator, but then I realised that I had neglected a vital and all too often overlooked part of end-of-life care: hospices. Hospices help people to die with dignity; arguably one of the greatest services of all. The problem is

[5] 'Factors associated with length of stay in care homes: a systematic review of international literature.' *Systematic Reviews Journal.* 20 February 2019.

that government only covers up to a third of their costs, usually less. They are dependent upon charitable donations to survive.

Every year in the UK, hospices transform the lives of more than 225,000 people with terminal or life-limiting illnesses plus several hundreds of thousands of family members and loved ones. Hospices are there for us through life, through death and through grief. From managing someone's pain, to looking after their emotional, spiritual and social needs, hospice care supports the whole person, helping them to live the last days of their life to the full.

The last paragraph was an edited quote from the Hospice UK website, www.hospiceuk.org, the national charity for end-of-life care that sits across all of the UK's hospices. They are driven by one fundamental belief: that everyone, no matter who they are, where they are or why they are ill, should receive the best possible care at the end of their life.

The service that hospices provide is simply wonderful and the life-changing stories that every hospice worker could tell would fill a library. One such tale simultaneously put a smile on my face and brought a tear to my eye. It was of an elderly man who was coming to the end of his life. I have forgotten his name, so I am going to call him Bill. One day, as one of the 'hospice angels' sat with him holding his hand, he was reflecting on his time and remarked that he had lived a great life and felt blessed. His nurse asked him if there was anything he regretted; anything at all. Bill stared into space in quiet contemplation and finally said softly, 'Yes. Just one thing.' He paused before continuing. 'I regret that I didn't marry Else. I met her soon after my wife died, and I have been with her for so long. We never saw the point in getting married, but now I wish we had. I wish I had formalised our relationship and showed her just how much she means to me.'

His nurse said nothing, but her mind went into over-drive. Two days later, Else arrived at the hospice in her best outfit, flanked by close family and hospice workers, while a celebrant officiated over one of the most heart-warming marriage ceremonies that the hospice staff had ever seen. Bill was beaming throughout as his sole, lingering regret evaporated; his last wish had been fulfilled.

Bill passed away a few days later.

We all know that death is inevitable and yet most of us don't talk about it in the way that perhaps we should. Our society often talks about 'quality of life' but rarely do we discuss 'quality of death'. And yet death is very much a part of life. 'Dying matters' to quote the eponymous website and community established by Hospices UK in 2009 to help kick-start conversations about dying, death and bereavement, and to help change society's attitude to this entirely natural subject; a subject that every single one of us has in common.[6]

The care that hospices provide is frankly invaluable, and yet they desperately need funds and support. To find your local hospice, to make a donation or to leave something for them in your will, visit hospiceuk.org, hospicefoundation.org, palliativecare.org.au or search for hospice care in your country. Your donation will change lives.

WHAT HAVE WE DISCOVERED ABOUT AGED CARE?

Aged care is confusing, expensive and overladen with emotion, so the sooner you start planning the better. To help you to do your homework, you will find links to all of the charities, associations, government bodies and service providers that we have mentioned throughout this section on the website www.you-part-two.com.

The most important step of all is to have those conversations with your parents now. Discussing the inevitable does not make it happen any sooner. It just makes sure everyone is prepared. There is nothing more inevitable than old age or death, and so many of us will experience both. One day your parents, or parent, will have to follow one or more of the paths we discussed in this chapter. They will have to adapt their home; move into a form of 'retirement living' whether it be sheltered housing, assisted living or a retirement village; or move into a care home or nursing home. It needs to be done with grace and dignity – and it will all need to be funded.

It is also worth pausing to reflect upon how you may end up funding your own aged care. I know that it is several decades away, and your focus right now is on the beginning of your Part Two, not the end of it, but it may be worth a few minutes of your time one rainy Sunday afternoon.

And speaking of Part Two, how *are* you going to fund it?

---

[6] https://www.dyingmatters.org

PART FIVE:

Money

'Money doesn't solve all problems. But it would solve my money problem.'
Minion.com (I know, but it was too good)

Okay. We have skirted around this subject throughout the book. It is now time to address the thorny and often emotional subject of money. After all, our Part Two needs to be funded, no matter what we wish it to look like.

Some people find the subject of money to be mind-numbingly dull. If this is you, or if you are simply not in the mood for a chat about finances right now, or perhaps this topic is not the reason you picked up this book in the first place, I suggest you skip this section and head straight for Part Six: You (p.215).

If you are a seasoned investor and have your finances completely sorted, you may decide to do the same. Although, before you do, I suggest taking a peek at Chapter 23, 'Where are the customers' yachts?' (p.200). It is about where and why the financial services industry has got it so wrong, so often, in the past.

I have written these chapters for everybody else: for those of us who find the subject of money interesting but not all-consuming; for those of us who know we need to make the sums add up and wouldn't mind chatting it through; for those of us who find the whole subject to be far more convoluted than it should be; and for those of us who aren't seasoned investment experts but know that we need to dig a little deeper into the subject than perhaps we have in the past.

In other words, I have written it for people like us.

I have been working in, with or for the financial services industry since the mid-1990s. I have worked with independent financial advice networks, restricted financial advice firms (wealth managers), pension providers, superannuation providers, life insurers, general insurers, active fund managers, passive fund managers, investment platforms, pension platforms, private equity firms, banks, sovereign wealth funds, even fintech firms – in the UK, Australia, Europe, US, Asia and the Middle East. Along the way, I have learnt one or two things about how different parts of the industry work and have formed firm views about how they *should* work. I have also gathered a few thoughts about financial services and investing that I think are worth sharing.

To aid both momentum and digestion, I have broken this part of the book down into a number of bite-sized chapters that do not need to be consumed all at once. Feel free to graze through the following smorgasbord at your leisure.

Together, we will explore:

Chapter 18: And then a miracle happens (financial planning in the second half)
Chapter 19: Pension? What pension?
Chapter 20: Tips from a financial services insider
Chapter 21: Pay attention to fees
Chapter 22: Find an adviser you trust
Chapter 23: 'Where are the customers' yachts?'
Chapter 24: What good looks like in financial services

Like Part Four (p.149), this is not meant to be even vaguely close to a definitive guide, and like any good discussion, if you take away just one or two useful nuggets, it will have been a valuable use of your time.

Please let me be crystal clear about something before we begin. Throughout these chapters, I am making observations, not providing recommendations or giving any sort of financial advice. I am not a financial adviser. My expertise is not in investing. I am a strategy and change guy, not a chartered financial planner. This section is merely designed to start a discussion.

Anyway, enough with the caveats and preamble; it's time to crack on with the amble itself. Let's break open the piggy bank and get started.

CHAPTER 18:

And then a miracle happens
(financial planning in the second half)

'Your portfolio looks fine. It's your dreams we need to talk about'
Mike Baldwin[1]

Whenever I have been presented with a personal financial planning report there always seems to be a big gap in the middle.

On the far right-hand side of the page is a picture of a future where Jane and I are living high on the hog in a beautiful house and with post-full-time-work earnings that will keep us comfortably in the lifestyle to which we wish to become accustomed. The financial planner then asks me a few questions concerning the size of the assets we want to leave behind and turns this lovely vision into a whopping 'total capital required' figure.

On the far left-hand side is a description of the reality of our net assets today and some assumptions about earnings, savings and investment returns over the ensuing years. The wide chasm between the two sits arrogantly, yet silently, mocking me with its vastness.

'Oh, that's okay,' I once said, in a futile hope that humour would defuse the situation and magically make the numbers add up. 'There's a special step in the process that you seem to have missed.' The adviser's eyebrows rose as I leaned over, politely pulled the presentation towards me, took out my pen and in the middle of the gulf between today's reality and tomorrow's dream, I drew a neat little box into which I wrote 'and then a miracle happens'.

He wasn't amused.

Neither was I to be honest. I needed to work out how to bridge that gap . . .

[1] Cartoonist (1954–) from his 'Cornered' Series.

FINANCIAL PLANNING IN THE SECOND HALF

The first step in any planning process is to articulate what it is you are seeking to achieve. This is as true in life as it is in business. So, when it comes to funding your second half – what does good look like to you?

And while we are all different, when it comes to financing the second half, we all pretty much fall into one of three camps:

1. We want to avoid running out of money;
2. We want to maintain a particular lifestyle, or, if we are really fortunate;
3. We want to increase our wealth, perhaps to leave something behind for future generations.

Which camp are you in?

Of course, we each have our own unique set of financial circumstances. Some of us are homeowners. Some own more than one. Some don't own any. In fact, the proportion of fifty-five- to sixty-four-year-olds who rent has doubled in the last decade. Some will benefit from final salary pensions. Most of us won't. Some have been diligent savers throughout their lives. Most of us haven't. Some plan to rely on inheritance – actually a third do. Others plan to leverage the equity in their homes and downsize as their second half progresses. Some of us have even put money aside for our own old-age care. Actually, I don't personally know a single person who has done that, but they must be out there.

We also have our own differing attitudes to the subject of money. Some of us love it, others find it incredibly boring. Some of us fear the whole subject and prefer to stick our heads in the sand. Others simply assume it will always be there. So many of us don't know where to turn.

Mind the gap

But whether we like to think about it or not, most of us could do with working out how much we are likely to need in the future and the size of the probable shortfall, before then moving on to tackle the question of what we may have to do to save and invest to fill the gap.

Unfortunately, there is no straightforward answer to these

questions. Nor are the answers quick or permanent – financial situations, valuations and performance are always moving, always changing.

Which is frustrating, as the high-level logic of determining the answers appears to be quite simple:

1. Make a list of the assets you have today and make some assumptions about how much each one is likely to appreciate in the future.

2. Make some assumptions about how much you should be able to put aside in either savings or pensions in the ensuing years – and for how long.

3. Add on any potential windfalls you may be expecting, such as inheritance or downsizing. It seems that one in three of us are counting on some form of inheritance to fund us through the latter stages of our second half.[2]

4. Pick an age where you think your income from working is likely to decline or cease.

5. Make an assumption regarding the investment income or percentage of your assets you could withdraw every year to live on – and when this may start.

6. Work out how much you would *need* to earn to live on.

7. Work out how much you would *like* to earn to live on.

8. Deduct any private or state pension you may receive to work out the earnings gap that your investments will need to fill.

9. Analyse the differences between 5, 6 and 7, and start playing around with all of the assumptions that lie behind each of the above to create a myriad of 'what if' scenarios to determine what you may need to do about it.

Hmm. Maybe it's not so easy after all.

The majority of us will need a little help with the above calculations. If the thought of getting lost in a plethora of financial permutations and combinations is your idea of hell – hire a financial adviser to run the numbers for you. But don't put it off – clarity can be far

---

[2] Sanlam UK Limited report – 'spreading the love' conducted by Atomik Research, 20 December 2018.

more blissful than ignorance, no matter how uncomfortable the answers turn out to be.

If you are a do-it-yourself kind of person who enjoys playing around with spreadsheets, and think that you would rather tackle the above financial planning challenge on your own – move away from Excel as I have found an alternative solution that you may find rather interesting: RetireEasy.

RetireEasy is an online subscription service that does all of the above far better than the vast majority of us could ever do ourselves.

There is no possible way that I could have built a spreadsheet to do a fraction of what their system does. In fact, it would have taken multiple spreadsheets and the kindergarten-level nature of my Excel skills would have become painfully obvious and almost certainly would have produced disastrously incorrect results.

The trigger for building the system was the moment that RetireEasy founder and CEO, Richard Collinson, left full-time employment, just four days shy of his sixtieth birthday. He was suddenly struck by a nagging fear that he may not have put away enough money to fund the rest of his life. 'I had some cash to add to a few small properties I owned and a SIPP [self-invested personal pension]. Not a bad situation, I felt, and one that could give me security and a comfortable life. But then I looked at the income those assets would generate, and the penny dropped – it would not on its own be nearly enough to give me the lifestyle I had imagined.'

Either he was going to have to use up a little of his hard-earned capital every year to top up the income he wanted, reduce his lifestyle aspirations, or continue working in some fashion to create another source of income. Perhaps all three.

'The obvious and immediate problem was that I had no way of knowing how long my assets would last, particularly if values fell,' Richard explained. 'Being a confirmed Excel junkie, I started to develop a set of spreadsheets to cash-flow model the next thirty to forty years. As always with Excel, these spreadsheets got more and more complex, and with complexity comes errors, so it was like painting the Forth Bridge: it would never be completely finished, or completely correct.'

But, even with its admitted inaccuracies and inadequacies, Richard's self-built system provided him with one enormous benefit –

the invaluable gift of peace of mind. His convoluted spreadsheets told him that his funds were likely to 'see him out'. He could relax and stop worrying.

But then 2008 arrived and he watched the mayhem unfold. 'I guess I lost a third of my portfolio's value in short order,' said Richard. 'At least with the system I had built, I was able to see exactly how my annual spending would be impacted. It wasn't great news, but it meant that I understood exactly what I needed to do to make the funds last.'

Richard's wife and chair of RetireEasy, Naomi, saw the potential of the Excel program he had created but recognised that it needed to be easier to use – and online. They looked for products that could do the same thing and couldn't find any, so they had one built using Richard's spreadsheets as the prototype.

And it works. Really well. The system is intuitive, easy to use and allows for any number of 'what if' scenarios. For more information about RetireEasy, and a link to the service, go to www.you-part-two-com.

Now you know the size of the gap, it is time to focus on saving and investing to try to bridge it. Some of us will use a financial adviser to do this, some of us will opt to manage our investment directly via any number of direct investment platforms.

And the moment the discussion turns to investing for our second half, one word inevitably pops into our heads – complete with a host of unfortunate associations: pensions.

CHAPTER 19:

Pension? What pension?

'From a retirement income perspective,
many Gen Xers are, frankly, screwed.'[1]
David Sinclair, Director of the UK's International Longevity Centre

A fifth of today's 'retirees' are not relying solely on their pensions and life savings, according to SunLife, the insurance company.

Many thousands of people who have ceased their main job have gone on to start their own businesses, while others keep themselves active and supplement their incomes in all sorts of ways: buying and selling on eBay, Amazon or Facebook Marketplace, renting out property, renting out rooms, private tutoring, exam invigilating, working as an extra for film or TV, mentoring younger people, interim work, part-time public appointments, non-executive directorships, paid work for charities, becoming a carer, becoming a tour guide, house sitting, teaching English to refugees – the list is long and limited only by your imagination.

Which is just as well, because our generation has been rubbish at saving. One in three people in the UK who were born between the early 1960s and the late 1970s (i.e., 4.3 million Generation Xers) are set to retire with meagre pension pots. Something like 2.3 million Brits who are yet to retire will end up relying predominantly on the state pension – which, to be frank, isn't enough to live on. David Sinclair summed it up rather bluntly in the quote that opened this chapter. When it comes to retirement savings, many Gen Xers have a great deal of work to do if they wish to maintain their current lifestyle.

As a generation, we will have to find ways of putting more aside

[1] https://ilcuk.org.uk/2-6-million-gen-xers-retirement-savings-disrupted-by-covid-19-pandemic-and-many-more-at-risk-of-facing-financial-hardship-in-retirement

than we have been doing to date or lowering our lifestyle expectations to a degree that we may not want to contemplate.

It's up to us.

The previous generation, the much-touted Baby Boomers born between the Second World War and the early sixties, are the wealthiest generation that the world has ever seen. They are also the wealthiest retirees, many leaving full-time work with final salary pension schemes that provide them with 75–100 per cent of their final salary for the rest of their days.

Things are very different today. Only nineteen companies in the FTSE 100 continue to provide defined-benefit (also known as 'final salary') pension schemes to their employees, according to employee benefit provider JLT, and seventeen of those have significantly reduced the amount of money they will pay out. None of them are open to new employees. When I was employed by Zurich Insurance more than a decade ago, the company reduced the future benefits of its final salary scheme overnight by 25 per cent[2] and closed it to future employees. Companies can no longer afford final salary pension schemes for the simple reason that we are living so much longer. Something had to give.

What 'gave' is that the burden of saving for our retirement was dumped squarely into our own laps. Consequently, our generation and those following us are on track to have significantly reduced incomes in the latter part of their lives than the Boomers who went before us – unless we do something about it.

A few people in their fifties today may still enjoy the benefits of a final salary pension but the pay-out is likely to be around 50 per cent of their final monthly pay-cheque or less due to reducing benefits discussed earlier. That is, of course, as long as their employer pension scheme has been well managed, which may not necessarily have been the case. A 2018 PBS Frontline documentary, *The Pension Gamble*, reported that half of US states have public pension schemes that are only 70 per cent funded or worse. Some US thinktanks calculate that private union workers and state employee pensions funds are only 43 per cent and 35 per cent

---

[2] Just for the sake of clarity, employees did not lose any of the pension entitlement they had already accrued. Up until 1 January 2008, employees had accrued an entitlement 1/48 of their final salary for every year they paid into the pension scheme. After that date, they accrued an entitlement every year of 1/60 of their final salary.

respectively.[3] The stories of business leaders raiding or neglecting employees' pension funds could fill many a page and would be well known to employees of countless organisations worldwide.

For many of us in our fifties and pretty much anyone in their forties and younger, the size of our pension pot will be entirely dependent upon how much we put into it and how well our investments perform. And of course, the earlier you start saving for the future, the better your future will be – financially at least. Try selling that to your average twenty-two-year-old!

But even a 'direct contribution' pension is still a good way to save, as it comes with distinct tax advantages and often includes additional money from employers. In Australia, 'superannuation' is compulsory and has been for more than thirty years, which is one of the main reasons why the current Australian pension system is ranked number three in the world behind the Netherlands and Denmark.[4] Every employer is required by law to place an additional amount equivalent to 9.5 per cent of every employee's gross salary into their personal superannuation account – and this amount is legislated to increase to 12 per cent by 2025.

In the UK, if you put 5 per cent of your before-tax salary into a pension, your employer must contribute a further 3 per cent, which is a relatively new development. Whereas Australia made superannuation compulsory in 1992, Britain's lighter-touch version, which is very much like the 401(k) system that has been running in the US for a while now, only came into existence in 2014.

But saving for our second act is not solely about pensions. Britain's excellent ISA (Individual Savings Accounts), where you can put up to £20,000 a year into shares or cash with no capital gains tax, is just one example of other ways that governments all over the world are encouraging people to save. And of course, we save for the future in all sorts of ways: we invest in our property, our businesses, other people's businesses, shares directly, funds directly, corporate debt, savings accounts; not only via a pension.

---

[3] https://www.heritage.org/social-security/commentary/major-threat-us-economy-unfunded-retirement-deficits-theyre-almost-big
[4] Melbourne Mercer Global Pension Index 2019.

But for many of us, no matter how we save and invest for the future, the numbers don't quite seem to add up as well as we would have wished. Even if we wanted to stop working completely, fewer and fewer of us will be able to afford to do so – and more of us, perhaps even most of us, will need to find other forms of income in our second half.

A friend of mine told me how his father had been a stressed and hardworking policeman and had retired more than thirty years ago at the tender age of forty-three on a police pension. He had worked hard on a public sector salary, paid his taxes and reckoned he was entitled to free healthcare and a good pension for the rest of his life. While we may raise an eyebrow at the young age at which he was able to do this, I too would like to think that we live in a society where its citizens can pay their taxes throughout their working lives and that would indeed entitle them to retire on a reasonable pension from the state.

But we don't.

Our governments simply can't afford it. Forty years ago, there were two people older than sixty-five for every ten people of working age in the OECD.[5] That number is now three and it is projected to reach almost six out of ten by 2060. Nations simply can no longer afford to provide generous state-funded pensions.

In the UK, the basic state pension is not means-tested – every worker qualifies for it no matter how much they earn or own. The amount you receive is based on the number of years you have been working and paying National Insurance, which, of course, adversely affects a significant number of women. Mind you, the state pension is not much to write home about. The average weekly state pension in the UK during 2018 was just £143.82 a week. (Interestingly, the UK government's 'Guarantee Credit' exists to ensure that every UK retiree receives a minimum of £173.75 a week but a third of people who are eligible don't apply for this extra cash!) £173.75 a week is £9,035 a year. How on earth is someone supposed to live on that? But people do. Seven per cent of pensioner couples and 22 per cent of single pensioners have no source of income other than the state pension and benefits, according to the Department of Work and Pensions in 2018.

---

[5] http://www.oecd.org/els/emp/Brochure per cent20OW per cent2028-08.pdf

In the US, as in the UK, everyone qualifies for an age pension. This surprised me. Americans are eligible for Social Security payments from age sixty-five, calculated using the thirty-five highest earning years of your career and adjusted for inflation, subject to a cap. There is also a minimum monthly state pension, which differs from state to state. The average weekly pay-out in early 2020 was US$347.[6]

In Australia, because saving into a pension has been compulsory for every worker for the last thirty years, the government pension is now means-tested. If you earn more than AUD$1,000 a week, you are not eligible for the state pension. If you earn less than $85 a week, you will receive a pension from the government of between AUD$430 and AUD$472 (figures as of 2020).

I am going to go out on a limb here and suggest that £174, US$347 or AUD$472 a week will not be enough for you to live on.

[6] https://money.usnews.com/money/retirement/social-security/articles/how-much-you-will-get-from-social-security#:~:text=The per cent20average per cent20Social per cent20Security per cent20benefit,age per cent20is per cent20 per cent243 per cent2C011 per cent20in per cent202020

CHAPTER 20:

Tips from a financial services insider

*'The individual investor should act consistently
as an investor and not as a speculator.'*
Ben Graham[1]

I have been working in and around financial services for several decades, and while I am not a qualified financial planner nor a financial adviser, I have repeatedly been reminded of a few investment fundamentals that are relevant for institutions and individuals alike.

My top three are:

- Keep things simple
- Mix it up (diversification)
- Don't panic (trust the markets)

None of these is rocket science but amateur and professional investors alike ignore them at their peril. When combined they form a key plank of pretty much any successful portfolio, so they are worth exploring in a little detail.

Sometimes, we all need to be reminded of a few of the basics.

I know I do.

KEEP THINGS SIMPLE

'Keep it simple and focus on what matters. Don't let yourself be overwhelmed.'—Confucius

I am a big fan of keeping things simple. My first recommendation when it comes to financial planning is to find someone you trust to give

---

[1] A British-born American economist, professor and investor, widely known as the 'father of value investing' (1894–1976).

you advice; someone who is as impartial as humanly possible. You need a good accountant and most likely a financial adviser, but no matter who you choose, keep them on their toes. Wanting to trust them is not enough. Keep asking them questions, no matter how daft you think the questions may be, and make sure you understand everything they say.

My parents lived the first seventy-eight years of their lives avoiding the stock market. They didn't trust it, nor did they trust the industry that fed off it. But then for most of their lives, they didn't have any spare cash lying around either. Whenever they did 'invest', they invested in their home or they invested in themselves, starting several businesses including their last one, which they built over thirty years and then sold when they were in their late seventies. Was this a high-risk strategy? With the benefit of hindsight, perhaps not. But, yes, they did have everything in one big basket: their business. With a mixture of hard work, risk-taking, skill, luck (although you often make your own luck) and timing – it worked. So, approaching their eighties, they turned to the stock market for the very first time. Consequently, they thought it sensible to get some advice, so in 2015 they organised a meeting with the wealth management arm of their bank and met with their designated financial adviser, who asked all the right questions and took copious notes – all of which he duly ignored. After proposing an outrageous advice fee of many thousands of dollars, an investment plan was compiled that could have been put together by a semi-intelligent algorithm designed by a sixteen-year-old intern.

The outrageously expensive investment plan that came back almost entirely comprised high fee-paying active funds, almost every one of which was managed by the fund management arm of the bank, with initial setup fees and high ongoing management charges. He wasn't an adviser; he was a salesman, and not a very good one at that. My parents refused to pay the balance of the so-called 'advice fee' and instantly moved their money to another bank.

They have since chosen to manage their foray into investing themselves with the help of a good accountant and a highly knowledgeable stockbroker, both of whom they trust implicitly. The last few words were the most important ones in this entire chapter.

Their stockbroker charges a small transaction fee for every buy or sell order plus a small pre-agreed fee based on assets under management for access to an online platform through which they can view and manage their investments. The fees they pay are clear, straightforward and fair.

Given their age and financial needs, they invest in a blend of dividend-paying stocks, well-rated corporate debt and bank loans. When it comes to shares, they focus on the earnings from their investments rather than capital gain. Yes, it is gratifying if the shares increase in value, but the dividends are by far the more important component. It certainly helps that Australia is the highest paying dividend country in the G20 group of major global economies, with average dividend yields of c.5.6 per cent – almost three times that of the US and 50 per cent higher than the UK. COVID-19 certainly put their sworn dividend focus to the test – and they passed with flying colours. When share markets tanked in 2020, my parents remained calm and didn't sell anything. They were genuinely focused on the dividends rather than the capital value and believed that the share market would eventually bounce back. Which is exactly what happened.

Their attitude also mirrors the approach of the late Jim Schiro, CEO of Zurich Insurance, during the 2008 crash, which was to avoid any investment product that you can't understand quickly and easily. When asked why Zurich had almost zero exposure to the collateralised debt obligations that had sent several banks and insurers to the wall, Jim replied something along the lines of, 'I couldn't get my head around them.' If something seems too good to be true, it usually is.

The moral of this story is: keep it simple and be clear about what you are trying to achieve, and why.

Please do not think that the moral is to do it yourself. This is definitely not what I am saying. Find someone you trust and when it comes to fees, as long as you believe they are fair, proportionate and clear, they are well worth paying – as we will discuss.

MIX IT UP

'Do not put all your eggs in one basket.'—Warren Buffett[2]

Without diversification, investing can feel a little too much like gambling. Although I do know of one multi-millionaire who said to me in

[2] American investor, billionaire and philanthropist (1930–).

2015, 'I only own one stock. All of my equity investment is with one company: Amazon.' That was back when its share price was bumping along at $500 a share, having never recorded a profit, let alone given any consideration of ever paying a dividend. My friend has increased his net worth by a factor of six since then – and counting. Why don't I listen to these people?!

But we all know exceptions that prove the rule. Generally, diversification is a highly sensible idea.

When it comes to shares, we could split our investments between active funds and passive funds. We could even split the active portion with more than one active manager. And why all in funds? How about some direct investments? We may even look to spread the risk across several sectors, geographies and currencies. Always be conscious of your home currency – I have seen currency fluctuations wipe out substantial investment returns. We could even consider diversifying among dividend paying companies and non-dividend payers, across large companies and mid–small cap firms.

When it comes to living off a fixed income, we could stick to zero interest savings accounts and government debt or invest in corporate debt as well – directly or via a fund.

Don't forget about real estate. The house you live in, the holiday home you may be lucky enough to own: throw them into the mix, too. However, while most of us tend to think of real estate as safe investments ('safe as houses'), professional investors put real estate in a similar risk category to shares, albeit with different characteristics. They understand the sector experiences wild swings in sentiment and value, and it can sometimes be difficult to sell your assets if you need to. Real Estate Investment Trusts (REITs) are a simple way to invest in this sector and in the past have often outperformed active real estate portfolios – although we may want to wait to see which ones survive the inevitable post-COVID shakeup of that particular industry. Several real estate funds halted trading during 2020 to prevent a flood of outflows that could have ruined them.

One interesting way to diversify is to invest in ready-made model portfolios with pre-ordained percentages split between shares and fixed income. e.g., you could invest in a 60:40 fund that is 60 per cent shares and 40 per cent bonds. Most wealth managers and fund managers offer such a product. For example, Vanguard LifeStrategy funds let you choose from five variations of portfolio from 100 per cent shares to 20 per cent shares, with the balance a mix of government and corporate bonds. They have been providing them in the UK for a decade and in the US for much longer – with ultra-low costs that no wealth manager, and few other fund managers, could ever afford to replicate. In 2019, BlackRock launched a rival to LifeStrategy called 'MyMap' with annual charges that were even a little lower than Vanguard's.

Diversification is a key part of any investment strategy. No one can predict the future. Even the highest paid professional investors can get it spectacularly wrong.

DON'T PANIC

'Don't Panic. It's the first helpful or intelligible thing anybody's said to me all day.'—Douglas Adams, *The Hitchhiker's Guide to the Galaxy*[3]

Managing our investment portfolio ourselves can be fraught with risks. One of the biggest risks is the temptation to panic-sell when markets take a dive, thereby cementing our losses. This happens to so many self-managed pension owners whenever there is a financial crisis.

Once we have sold in a bit of a panic, we are often uncertain and hesitant about when to get back into the market, desperately seeking the right moment to press that 'buy' button. Vanguard did some analysis of the small subset of their customers who decided to sell their funds as soon as the pandemic hit in early 2020 in the hope of timing the market and buying back in at rock bottom. While this sounds logical, timing the market successfully is incredibly difficult to achieve. Vanguard found that 80 per cent of these investors would have been better off if they had not sold and had simply waited for the market to rebound.

Timing the market is even difficult for professional institutional investors. The investment committee of Cambridge University's Clare College was advised by some of the university's leading minds on long-term investing; professors who had published countless books on the subject.

---

[3] Spoken by Arthur Dent upon seeing the front cover of The Hitchhiker's Guide to the Galaxy for the first time.

After a number of detailed and informed debates, the investment committee decided to borrow £15 million shortly after the 2008 crash when interest rates and stock markets appeared to have reached an all-time low. Their initial plan was to invest the entire amount during the last quarter of 2008, but in November the investment committee was suddenly struck by a serious case of cold feet as equity prices continued to fall. Consequently, only 40 per cent of the cash was invested by the end of 2008 and only a little more than half of the £15m had been invested by mid-2009.

Then prices began to rise. Nervous that this may have been a blip before another downturn, they held off to see what would happen. The stock market kept going up and by late 2011, only two-thirds of the cash had been invested. Yes, they made a handsome profit, but nowhere near as much as they had originally planned. It just shows that even experts who study this for a living can find timing the market to be nigh impossible.

Some of the best exponents of the 'don't panic' mantra can be found among the world's largest sovereign wealth funds. From October 2007 to February 2009, global stock markets fell 43 per cent (as reflected by the MSCI World Index), but many of the large sovereign funds were able to hold their nerve. One year after the crash, share markets had recovered more than half of their losses. By late 2013, markets had fully recovered and would rally quite spectacularly for a further six years.

In 2020, the MSCI World Index plunged 30 per cent in March. It had fully recovered by October and by December it was 10 per cent above its February peak. By May it had risen a further 10 per cent.

Not panicking can sometimes be the best investment decision you will ever make.

CHAPTER 21:

Pay attention to fees

'Most people, even highly educated ones, are bad at percentages.'
Pierre Chandon[1]

Fees are a necessary part of financial planning and investing, in the same way that they are a necessary part of accounting, recruiting, gardening, consulting, building or any type of service industry. Financial planners, stockbrokers and investment managers need to be paid for the service they provide. Fees are good.

But they can be so confusing! No matter how hard financial regulators have tried to simplify matters, the whole subject of fees can be a labyrinthine nightmare. The fee documents of the most compliant financial adviser can run to sixteen pages or more: transparency and clarity rarely go hand-in-hand.

Unfortunately, for too many of us, the full impact of fees may only be truly understood in hindsight. If you aren't careful, they can significantly erode your investment returns, as we will discuss shortly. This is true whether you use a financial adviser to manage your money or manage your investments yourself.

To make the achingly dull but really important subject of fees a little easier to absorb, I have split them into four distinct buckets:

1. Upfront advice fees: Fees that your financial adviser will charge you to establish your financial plan and design your investment plan. Some advisers charge a flat amount for

---

[1] 'So, You Think Your Customers Understand Percentages?' Pierre Chandon, The L'Oréal Chaired Professor of Marketing, Innovation, and Creativity at INSEAD and Director of the INSEAD-Sorbonne Behavioural Lab, 10 March 2015.

these services, which is in line with the spirit of the regulations. However, more than a few, perhaps even most, charge a percentage of the amount you are investing with them, no matter how onerous or simple your financial plan may be to construct. In the UK, it is common for Independent Financial Advisers to charge a fee of around 3 per cent, but it varies. Obviously, if you don't use a financial adviser, these fees won't apply.

2. Upfront investment fees, which include:

• Initial product fees. These are rare but some pension products or insurance bonds do come with an upfront fee, so watch out for them. One particularly large and well-known wealth manager declares that it charges an upfront product fee of a massive 1.5 per cent (on top of a 4.5 per cent initial advice fee!). More about them in a minute.

• Initial fund fees. Very few fund managers charge an upfront fee for their investment funds, but a handful still do. I wish they wouldn't.

3. Ongoing Advice fees: Charges for your adviser's ongoing time and advice. Most Independent Financial Advisers charge 0.5 per cent per annum for this valuable service, but, again, it varies.

4. Ongoing investment fees, which you will incur whether you manage your own investments or use a financial adviser to do it for you. They include:

• Annual management charges: The annual fees charged by both the product provider and fund managers. Most annual product charges such as those for a self-invested pension are small (usually 0.1–0.2 per cent). Ongoing fund charges can range from 0.06–0.25 per cent for tracker funds to up to c.1.25 per cent for some actively managed funds.

• Ongoing transaction costs: The costs of buying and selling underlying shares within the product or fund. Often small, but they can add up.

• Other ongoing investment fees. Often you will be charged a small platform fee of around 0.2–0.45 per cent per annum of your investments for access to a trading and service platform, and perhaps a custody fee of 0.10–0.15 per cent to ensure your underlying investments are safe. Both are well worth paying.

• Exit fees. These are fees for withdrawing your own money. I have yet to hear a credible justification for these. Even though regulators have been threatening to ban them for many years, some forms of exit fees persist in a few dark corners of the industry. Look for them, preferably to avoid them.

How much do all these fees add up to? Make sure you look closely at every one of the above, because they can sure add up if you are not vigilant.

What do wealth managers charge?

Most wealth managers charge 1–2 per cent for upfront advice depending upon the size of your investment and up to 2.4 per cent per annum (figures from Brewin Dolphin, a UK wealth manager).

But one wealth manager has a far more complicated approach. It also happens to be the biggest and most successful wealth manager in the UK. FTSE 100 member St James's Place (SJP) takes a unique, schizophrenic approach to fees that in some circumstances can appear to be weirdly customer-centric once you retune your brain accordingly. I must admit, I give them credit for trying so desperately to achieve the seemingly impossible – give the regulator the transparency it demands while providing customers with the clarity they crave. Transparency is not the same thing as clarity. In fact, when it comes to financial services, the opposite can quite often be the case.

Let me explain.

In 'transparency' mode, the SJP website, as of May 2021, stated very clearly that 6 per cent of your investment would be taken on day one to pay for initial advice and product charges if you invested via their Self-Invested Personal Pension or an Insurance Bond. (Up to 5 per cent would be taken if you invested via an ISA or Unit Trusts.) The site was also clear that if you withdrew any of your money out of SJP within the first six years, you would be charged an 'early withdrawal fee' of 6 per cent in year one tapering to 1 per cent in year six. Annual advice fees of 0.5 per cent, product fees of 1 per cent and average fund fees of c.0.5 per cent would also be charged on the remaining investment pot (although the 1 per cent product fee would be waived during the first six years, as the tapered early withdrawal fee reduced during the same period . . . you can see why I needed to place a cold towel over my head at this point!).

But in 'clarity' mode, the SJP website then implied that all of the fees mentioned above were the equivalent of the customer paying no upfront fees at all and a total of c.2 per cent per annum on the entire investment amount – as long as they invested for more than six years. In the right set of circumstances this could, I guess, work out cheaper than several other wealth management firms, but the caveats are significant, and it is a regulatory minefield to articulate.

SJP is able to achieve this seemingly impossible feat because it uses its own life insurance company to manage its clients' pension investments. To go into any more detail than that would require a stiff drink, trust me. To my knowledge, no one else has tried to replicate this fee structure.

An alternative is to keep things simple. Active investment firm, Fisher Investments, does this, charging between 1 per cent and 1.5 per cent upfront depending upon the size of investment, and a total all-encompassing fee of 1.63 per cent pa (or 1.74 per cent if your investment is in a SIPP). These are UK figures. They may differ if you are investing with them in the US or Europe.

Vanguard and BlackRock don't provide advice. They both charge zero upfront, only 0.06–0.22 per cent per annum for their passive funds, and around 0.45 per cent per annum for their active funds.

What do IFAs charge?

If you use an IFA, you will usually pay around 3 per cent upfront for financial planning advice and then costs of around 0.5 per cent per annum for ongoing advice plus the usual ongoing investment costs we mentioned earlier that should range from 0.75 to 1.5 per cent per annum depending upon what you invest in.

Some IFAs, though, one of whom I mention in Chapter 24 (p.209), take a different approach and may be cheaper, charging flat upfront advice fees that can equate to less than 1 per cent of your investment, plus total ongoing advice, product and investment fees that can average out to less than 1 per cent.

It pays to shop around and do your homework.

DIY costs

If you manage your investments yourself, you will only pay the ongoing investment fees mentioned above. But, here, too, it pays to shop around to find the trading platform or service that you feel most comfortable with.

Net returns after fees

Of course, net returns after fees are what we are really looking for.

Fees of 2 per cent or even 2.4 per cent sound small, until we realise the impact that they can have on investment returns. Let me give you an example. If you invested $10,000 for fifty years at 7 per cent annual return, your savings would have grown to almost $300,000. Einstein once remarked: 'Compound interest is the eighth wonder of the world. He who understands it, earns it. He who doesn't, pays it.'

Now let's say that you paid 2 per cent in fees every year, resulting in a 5 per cent net return. How large do you think your nest egg would be fifty years later? Not $300,000, obviously. It wouldn't be $200,000 either. It would be just $115,000 – almost a third of the size!

'Fees can be exceptionally corrosive,' explained James Norton of Vanguard during our interview. 'Costs are one of the few things that investors can control – future returns are uncertain; fees are not. Investing is highly counter-intuitive. In most other areas of life, the more you pay for something, the better it is. This is not always true when it comes to investing.'

This is because wealth managers and active fund managers charge fees irrespective of whether they make you money or lose it for you, whether they outperform the index or not.

Allow me to illustrate with a few simple scenarios:

Let's say we have invested $100,000 with our favourite wealth manager and the total of all of their fees has come to 2.4 per cent per annum.

Scenario 1

Let's assume our investment increases by 10 per cent in its first year. We now have $107,360 in our pot ($110,000 less fees of $2,640), after having paid our wealth manager more than a quarter of our investment return.

Scenario 2

Investment returns of 5 per cent. In this scenario, we are left with $102,480 ($105,000 less fees of $2,520), having paid our wealth manager more than half of the gains.

Scenario 3

Zero capital gain. If our investment pot doesn't increase at all in 12 months, we still pay fees of $2,400 and our overall pot shrinks to $97,600.

Scenario 4

Now, let's assume that our investment falls by 10 per cent. In this scenario, we still pay our wealth manager $2,160, reducing our pot even further to just $87,840.

Notice there is not all that much difference in how much the wealth manager earns in the best and worst scenario above. In the scenario where our portfolio went up by 10 per cent, the wealth manager took $2,640. In the scenario where our portfolio fell by 10 per cent, the wealth manager still took $2,160 in fees – meanwhile we are almost $20,000 poorer.

Performance after fees is the main reason why investors across the world have been flocking to low-cost passive index funds rather than paying active fund managers and wealth managers to pick stocks for them. Since August 2019, more money is now held in low-cost index-tracking US equity funds than in active US funds. As I mentioned in *The Change Catalyst*,[2] most active fund managers rarely outperform their index on a regular basis – even though that is precisely what we pay them to do.

As a general rule, most of us don't pay enough attention to percentages, fees or net returns after fees.

We really should.

[2] *The Change Catalyst: Secrets to Successful and Sustainable Business Change.* Wiley 2017.

CHAPTER 22:

Find an adviser you trust

The adviser you should hire is the one you trust the most.

Nobel Prize winner William Sharpe[1] described retirement income planning as 'the hardest and nastiest problem in finance.'

So, perhaps the most important thing of all is to find an adviser you trust. The adviser you should hire is the one you trust the most.

If you are looking for a financial adviser, find someone who will help you develop a clear and sound financial plan and investment plan, and continually remind you of your strategy, what you designed it to achieve – and why. Someone who will review it regularly. Someone who will help you 'know when to hold 'em and know when to fold 'em', to quote the late, great Kenny Rogers.[2]

But, more than anything, someone who will give you peace of mind.

There are countless dedicated and professional financial advisers out there. All you have to do is look for them. And if you do want to engage a financial adviser, these are some of the characteristics I think you should look for:

- A dedicated professional who has taken the time to obtain the highest levels of professional qualifications. Financial advice is a profession. Hire a professional.
- Someone whose fees are crystal clear and easy to understand. Don't only ask them about the fees they charge, ask them why.

[1] William Forsyth Sharpe (1934–) is an American economist. He is the STANCO 25 Professor of Finance, Emeritus at Stanford University's Graduate School of Business, and the winner of the 1990 Nobel Memorial Prize in Economic Sciences. He is most famous for the creator of the Sharpe ratio for measuring risk-adjusted investment performance.
[2] One of the best-selling recording artists of all time (1938–2020). His signature tune, 'The Gambler', won a Grammy award in 1980.

Spend a great deal of time understanding these fees. Use Chapter 21 (p.191) as a guide. Ask them whether you will be able to withdraw your money at any time and if there any penalties for doing so. If you can't get your head around their fees or still feel a little uncomfortable once you do understand them, pause and reflect whether you should put your money with them.

• Ask to see their menu of fees. Ask if their fees are calculated on a fee-for-service basis and check that you are very clear about precisely what you will get for each service. If the charge for their services is calculated as a percentage of the amount you are investing, ask why, and precisely what services they will, and won't, deliver for this percentage. Are there other services that their clients tend to require that cost extra?

• Some advisers, such as Jane Hodges, founder of Money Honey Financial Planning, the award-winning IFA I reached out to for help with this chapter, allow their clients to pay only for the advice that they want. She charges flat fees for her initial financial planning advice and only switches to a small percentage of their investment if they wish her to design an investment solution for them. Some clients simply want information, planning advice and reassurance; they manage the investing themselves. And that's fine by Jane. Others use her for everything, and there are numerous shades of grey in between. It is entirely up to the customer. For more about Jane and other trusted advisers, head to www.you-part-two.com.

• But some advisers and wealth managers provide a significant number and depth of services for their percentage-based fee, which could perhaps work out better value if you have complex needs. Do your homework. Get some quotes.

• Find a financial adviser whose business model is genuinely aligned to you. Ask them to explain their business model to you – how they build their own wealth and how they make their money. Ask them what they are trying to achieve with their business and what drives the value of their firm. Ask them how they are going to make sure that their business is sustainable and going to be there for the long term.

• Ask them about their future plans – personally and for their business. Ask them what will happen to you if their firm becomes too big – will the level of service you receive decline? Ask them who will actually be looking after you.

• Ask them who holds your money. This may sound daft, but this was one of the key issues behind Madoff's brazen Ponzi scheme – his victims wrote cheques out to his investment company and he could do anything he liked with the money. Many investment managers safeguard your money by using a professional third-party custodian such as Fidelity or State Street that keeps custody of your investments on your behalf. Effectively all the investment manager does is instruct the custodian on what and when to buy and sell.

• Ask them what makes them special. Ask them for a break-down of the types of clients they serve – and what is the ideal client that their firm is best set up to serve. Ask to speak to some of their current clients. Ask them if customers have left their firm, and why.

• Find a financial adviser who genuinely cares about achieving the best possible outcomes for you. Ask them why you should trust them and their firm.

Some of my colleagues in the industry may have a minor conniption at my next comment, but I don't think it matters whether your adviser is 'independent' (i.e., able to recommend any financial product from any provider) or 'restricted' to a smaller universe of products and funds. The most important thing is that you have confidence in them.

I prefer to free myself of obfuscation. I value straightforward services, straightforward fees and an uncomplicated approach. Others value prestige and size; they are happy to overlook convoluted fee structures because the entire experience of being with their wealth manager gives them the peace of mind they need.

If you are looking for a financial adviser, find one who knows what they are doing, who genuinely cares about you, and whose business model is clear and has you at the centre of it. Someone whose charges are reasonable, transparent and you believe are fair.

Most of all, find an adviser you trust.

CHAPTER 23:

'Where are the customers' yachts?' [1]

'The evidence of culture is how people behave
when they think no one is watching.'
Bob Diamond, CEO of Barclays

The point of this chapter is to help you understand where the money is made in financial services so that you can engage with the industry with both eyes wide open. The industry is so awash with money that sometimes the professionals within it seem to have forgotten that it is our money they are awash with.

From the moment I started working with the financial services sector back in the nineties, it was painfully obvious that this was an industry that too often placed the needs of its executives and shareholders, in that order, above the needs of its customers – sometimes without even realising it.

I have sat in boardrooms where the only subject under discussion for the entire meeting was the executive bonus plan. I have seen leadership teams continually accept chronic and abysmal customer satisfaction scores that in any other industry would have seen them sacked. The leaders of a global insurer used to refer to the customer-facing parts of the business as 'the balance sheets'. I have seen exec teams renege on promises to share proceeds of the pending sale of the business with their core customers simply because they wanted to keep more of the money for themselves.

Too many previous generations of financial services leaders have paid lip service to the concept of 'customer first'. Assets Under Management (AUM) has been at the heart of the industry and attracting

[1] Fred Schwed Jr. *Where Are the Customers' Yachts? or A Good Hard Look at Wall Street* (Wiley, 1995).

customers' money has often been possible without paying undue consideration to the actual customer, as I will explain.

But there are myriad exceptions to this rough and ugly generalisation, and in the next chapter I talk about what good looks like in this industry and feature a few of the financial services firms that I admire that, in my humble opinion, 'get it'. There are numerous signs that the industry as a whole is changing. One of the reasons for the change is generational. A new generation of leaders is coming to the fore across the industry; leaders who have seen how the industry has behaved in the past and are coming to prominence determined to place the customer firmly at the centre of everything they do.

I was invited to speak at the Financial Services Forum's Annual Mortgage Summit in St Paul de Vence in the foothills above Nice soon after the publication of *The Change Catalyst* back in 2017. The topic of my speech was 'Change is inevitable. Successful change isn't.' The audience was the great and the good of the £280bn UK mortgage industry. With the title of the speech displayed in large letters on the floor-to-ceiling screen behind me, I began by asking everyone in the audience who was my age or older to raise their hands. Roughly half the audience did so. I then waved them aside, declaring: 'This speech is not for you. You are never going to change. The status quo suits you just fine. You have been far too successful to change the way the industry works this late in your career. And you have the final salary pension schemes that the generations coming up behind you can only dream of.'

It was a risky opening.

I then turned to the rest of the audience and said, 'Can you believe what these guys have been doing?', before displaying a slide with the results of the 2017 Gallup Business Sector & Industry Ratings in which 'Banking' had come a dismal eighteenth out of the twenty-five sectors in its annual survey of consumers' perceptions of trustworthiness.

Half the audience chuckled uncomfortably. Half squirmed in their seat. Fortunately, no one left. My next slide posited: 'Maybe the next generation will change our industry for the better.' We then launched into an energising treatise on how to lead successful and sustainable change.

'*But is financial services all that different from any other sector?*' I hear you ask. After all, if you dig around any industry, you will find innumerable examples of executives ripping off shareholders, boards viewing employees as expendable, unscrupulous owners plundering employee pension funds and numerous companies treating customers as an annoying necessity, as data to be mined or as wallets to be looted. The problem is global and a list of corporate hubris could run for a depressingly large number of pages.

But financial services is different. It *is* special. For one fundamental reason, the same reason that infamous bank robber, Willie Sutton, once gave for robbing banks: 'Because that's where the money is'.

It's where *your* money is.

THE NEED FOR CHANGE

Banks deserve a special mention, here, for they have been keeping financial regulators in every part of the world very busy indeed.

Who lent now defunct US energy trader Enron billions of dollars in loans and turned several blind eyes as Enron executives committed brazen fraud during the last five years of the last millennium? The banking industry. Some banks were found to be complicit in hiding debt from investors and financial regulators.[2]

And who was to blame for the 2008 crisis that brought the global economy to its knees, reduced the standards of living of the average worker and left savers floundering from more than twelve years, and counting, of non-existent interest rates? Yep, the banks again. This time, they saw an 'opportunity' to sell mortgages to people who couldn't afford them (let's just pause to let that sink in for a second) and then package up these nonsensical loans and sell them on to investors as magically AAA-rated investment products with the promise of fairy-tale returns. What could possibly have gone wrong with that?

And we could rattle off scores of further banking scandals in the last few decades: from the Savings and Loan crisis in the eighties to the Madoff Ponzi Scheme in the noughties that defrauded investors of an incredible $65bn[3], and on to Wells Fargo Bank creating two million fee-generating bank accounts and credit cards without customer approval only a few years ago.[4]

[2] https://www.baltimoresun.com/business/bal-bz.banks24sjul24-story.html
[3] https://www.reuters.com/article/us-madoff-idUSTRE52A5JK20090313
[4] https://www.nbcnews.com/news/all/wells-fargo-pay-3-billion-over-fake-account-scandal-n1140541

In 2018, the FS Forum asked me to return to St Paul de Vence, this time to speak on 'Meeting the Change Challenge in Financial Services' at their European Executive Summit. The theme of the conference that year was 'Leadership and Re-establishing Trust in Financial Services'. I began my speech with a telling 2014 statistic from The Economist Intelligence Unit: 53 per cent of financial services executives believe that career progression at their firm will be difficult without 'flexibility over ethical standards'.

That simple statement says it all. If you haven't done so already, read it again. And then maybe a third time. The problem within the financial services industry was cultural; deep-rooted and endemic. After pausing to let the significance of the statement to sink in, I then clicked on to my next slide to share the best definition of corporate culture I had ever seen: 'The evidence of culture is how people behave when they think no one is watching.'

Everyone agreed. Some even chuckled. Then I revealed who said it: Bob Diamond, the CEO of Barclays, in the BBC's inaugural Today Business Lecture in November of 2011, eight months before he was forced to resign when Barclays was fined more than $400 million for its role in the Libor-fixing scandal.[5] When viewed through that lens, the definition of culture took on a completely different hue.

But the Barclays fine wasn't an outlier. UBS, Citicorp, RBS, JP Morgan, Bank of America and Barclays were collectively fined almost US$6 billion for foreign exchange manipulation.[6] A few months after the summit, Standard Chartered was fined more than a billion dollars for a combination of lax money laundering controls and breaching US sanctions against Iran.[7] Global banks have paid a total of $36 billion in fines since 2008.[8]

---

[5] https://en.wikipedia.org/wiki/Libor_scandal#:~:text=On%2027%20June%202012%2C%20Barclays,the%20Libor%20and%20Euribor%20rates.
[6] https://www.abc.net.au/news/2015-05-21/us-britain-fine-top-banks-nearly-6-bn-for-forex-libor-abuses/6485510
[7] https://www.theguardian.com/business/2019/apr/09/standard-chartered-fined-money-laundering-sanctions-breaches
[8] 'Banks have paid $36bn in fines since the 2008 financial crisis' Yahoo Finance 29 January 2020.

Australian banks and financial institutions were also placed on the naughty step after a 2017 Royal Commission was established to investigate 'Misconduct in the Banking, Superannuation and Financial Services Industry'. The CEOs and chairs of Westpac,[9] AMP[10] and National Australia Bank[11] were all forced to step down. The CEO of the Commonwealth Bank[12] had already been forced to resign a few years earlier.

Meanwhile, the UK banking and insurance industry was found guilty of mis-selling Payment Protection Insurance to mortgage customers and interest-rate swaps to business customers. To date, the industry has been forced to pay out £2.4bn due of the latter[13] and more than £38bn due to the former.[14]

The amount of money involved in all this malpractice has been staggering.

ADVISERS OR SALESPEOPLE?

Less than a decade ago, commission was king. Then, from 1 January 2013, commission on the sale of investment products was banned in the UK. Australia had banned it the year before. The US still allows investment commission to be paid and articles continue to be written about why it is important to hire a fee-only financial adviser.[15]

Incentives drive behaviours and commission drives the most predictable behaviours of all. When I was a board member and HR director of the UK's largest Independent Financial Adviser network back in the mid-2000s, I stood on stage in front of a few thousand advisers and

[9] https://www.theguardian.com/australia-news/2019/nov/26/westpac-chief-executive-brian-hartzer-resigns-over-money-laundering-scandal

[10] https://www.theguardian.com/australia-news/2018/apr/30/amp-chair-catherine-brenner-resigns-scandals-banking-commission

[11] https://www.theguardian.com/australia-news/2019/feb/07/nab-shares-put-in-trading-halt-pending-announcement-regarding-leadership#:~:text=National%20Australia%20Bank's%20chief%20executive,departure%20after%20the%20market%20closed

[12] https://www.theguardian.com/australia-news/2017/aug/14/commonwealth-bank-ceo-ian-narev-to-step-aside-by-july-2018-chairman-says

[13] 'Hundreds of businesses are trying to figure out whether UK banks defrauded them via LIBOR manipulation', Business Insider. 13 July 2015.

[14] https://www.fca.org.uk/data/monthly-ppi-refunds-and-compensation. 7 May 2020.

[15] https://www.businessinsider.com/personal-finance/fee-only-vs-commission-based-financial-advisor?r=US&IR=T

asked them why the sales of a certain savings bond had gone through the roof: 'Could it possibly have anything to do with the fact that the product provider increased its commission during that quarter?'

'What's wrong with that?' an adviser asked me in the break. 'Why shouldn't I sell the one that pays me a little more commission?' There were so many things wrong with the question, I didn't know quite where to start. I could completely understand his argument, but it was a crystal-clear example of why and how the industry needed to change.

And the banning of commission did change a large swathe of the UK financial advice industry. Many clients with less than £50,000 to invest were effectively abandoned by advisers as they were too costly to serve. Banks got out of the financial advice business entirely and a quarter of advisers retired from the industry.

It isn't only the big end of town that has been caught 'taking the Mickey'; the financial advice end of the market has also been culpable.

From endowment mortgages, which were mis-sold by countless advisers in the 1990s; to the 'precipice bonds' scandal, which decimated retirees' savings plans between 1997 and 2004; to today's latest scandal: pension mis-selling. Innumerable advisers have been convincing their clients to transfer their pension money out of a final salary scheme and into a SIPP, forgoing a guaranteed income in retirement for the risk of managing their own lump sum. A whopping £37bn was transferred in 2017 alone.

Don't get me wrong, under the right circumstances transferring your pension in this manner can be a perfectly sensible thing to do, but too often it seems the advice has been inadequate, and the fees sometimes obscured – and these fees can be sizeable and continue for years. £40m was paid in compensation to investors in 2018 alone for pension mis-selling.[16]

That figure will surely continue to grow. Why? Because the big money is made in financial services by moving a client's investments from wherever it is currently into the pot that the financial adviser or wealth manager controls – and then clinging onto it for dear life. And the money 'trapped' in final salary pension pots is significant: a £9,000 a year

[16] 'Pension mis-selling payouts double in 2018' FT.com. 6 January 2019.

annual pension can transform itself into a £250,000 lump sum, adding very nicely to the overall sum that your adviser controls or influences.

ASSETS UNDER MANAGEMENT: THE KEY TO WEALTH IN FINANCIAL SERVICES

Your financial adviser has the same objective as you do; they need to fund their second half as well.

Their wealth is tied up in their business, and the best way for them to build the value of their business is to maximise the Assets Under Management (AUM) that their firm influences or controls. The value of your adviser's wealth management or advice firm is almost entirely dependent upon how much of their client's money they are able to amass. If they manage to corral £100 million of their clients' money into their firm, they could expect to sell their financial advice business to a larger wealth manager for almost £4 million in cash. If a wealth manager amasses £100 billion under management, their market cap is likely to be north of £5 billion. Swap the pound sign for any denomination you like and the above figures will be fairly accurate no matter where you live in this world.

As well as charging fees based on assets under management, many large wealth managers also act as wholesalers, benefiting from their scale to extract a margin from the funds that they on-sell to their customers. They agree to buy funds from the likes of Invesco, L&G or Aviva Investors at discounted annual management charges (let's say 0.15 per cent for illustration purposes), to which they add an enthusiastic margin and on-sell to their clients (at say 0.5 per cent).

It's not all that different from a wholesaler buying baked beans from Heinz and then selling them on to supermarkets – at a considerable mark-up. If you multiply my illustrational 0.35 per cent profit by tens or even hundreds of billions of Assets Under Management, it adds up to significant revenues. For example, collecting a margin of 0.35 per cent on $100 billion of assets would produce annual revenue to the wealth management firm of $350 million from this wholesaling activity alone. Now I have your attention!

In fact, the business models of some of the wealth managers are so good that the best investment decision you could have made may have been to buy their shares. Take SJP for example: I have no idea whether their investment performance has been good, middling or awful. In fact, I can find reports to prove each one. It completely depends upon which of their funds you invested in, over what period and what you compare them to. But what I do know is if you had been a shareholder in St James's Place, you could have quadrupled your money between January 2010 and January 2020. When you include dividends, I calculate that this would have been an average annual return in the vicinity of 18 per cent every year for ten years. Their business model has been that good.

The successful wealth managers are also exceptionally good at customer retention, marketing, communication and making their customers feel proud to be with the firm; at creating a sense of exclusivity and privilege at which Ivy League and Oxbridge universities have been excelling for centuries.

WHERE IS THE CUSTOMER IN ALL THIS?

Over the years, financial regulators across the globe have tried to nudge, coerce and fine product providers, wealth managers and financial advisers to 'Know Your Customer' and 'treat customers fairly'.

These are the actual instructions contained in the UK regulator's 2007 Money Laundering Regulations and in many other countries' regulations several years earlier. Can you imagine any other industry needing to be convinced and coerced into thinking that 'knowing their customers' and 'treating their customers fairly' may be a good thing, let alone forced to do it by the authorities?!

Sometimes it feels as though the financial services industry just hasn't been able to help itself, and I can't help but conclude that the root cause of all of this historic mis-selling and blind-eye-turning has been because the primary focus of too many firms has been making money for itself rather than the financial welfare of its customers.

Business schools, marketing agencies and management consultancies alike all preach that business success starts with the customer. Why the company exists, who it exists to serve, how this is to be done and why – this should lie at the centre of every successful company's strategy and plans. But it appears that too many financial services leaders in the past haven't believed that this charming customer-centric view of the world applied to them or their industry.

They were far more interested in amassing as much of their customers' money as possible and holding onto it for dear life.

But the industry isn't all hubris, greed, glossy marketing and assets under management.

The financial advisers, wealth managers, investment platforms, pension firms and fund managers who plan for sustainable success fully realise that placing the needs, wants and aspirations of their customers at the heart of their business is the only route forward; that their success is intertwined with the success of their customers.

It may not be rocket science, but a burgeoning number of financial services firms genuinely understand the value of putting the customer first. Of course, some of them have been doing this for decades. That is why they have been so successful.

Let's meet a few.

CHAPTER 24:

What good looks like in financial services

'A customer is the most important visitor on our premises.
He is not dependent on us.
We are dependent on him.'
Mahatma Gandhi[1]

I would like to have a brief chat about what good looks like in financial services – and to highlight a few of the firms I believe are getting it right, because there is also a great deal to admire within the financial services industry.

Yes, I have witnessed some despairingly self-centred and short-term behaviour in this industry, but I have also met some wonderfully talented and committed people working for well-run companies who understand the fundamental tenet that successful, sustainable business starts with the customer. And I am meeting more of these people every day.

Genuinely putting the customer at the heart of the business is the first and primary feature of any company – including financial services firms. Looking after the customer is the only way to deliver long-term, sustainable shareholder returns. Of course it is important that the business is financially healthy and sustainable – it is in the customers' best interests for their financial adviser, wealth manager, fund manager and insurer to be in business for the long term – but it is a matter of balance. We don't want our financial services firm to be successful at the expense of us, the customer. We want their success to be intertwined

---

[1] Indian lawyer who employed non-violent resistance to lead the successful campaign for India's independence (1869–1948).

with, and built upon, our success. We want firms who treat the money that they invest as though it was ours – because it is.

Financial services companies are in a unique position to be able to lead the way in addressing social and environmental sustainability, too, seeing as this $25 trillion industry controls or influences most of the money in the world.[2] Financial services firms have the opportunity, responsibility even, to use their influence and the capital at their disposal to make this world a better place. To invest in clean energies, disease eradication, later-life care, physical wellness and mental well-being. They can invest to make our lives healthier as well as longer.

They can channel their funds away from tobacco, a product that, as we have discussed, kills 8 million people every year. They can enable us not to invest in the likes of gambling or arms or coal if we so desired.

They can use their power to coerce other organisations to be responsible capitalists – build long-term, sustainable businesses that put people first and realise that shareholders and executives are only two of the stakeholders that companies need to look after. (The other five are customers, employees, suppliers, partners and the communities in which the company operates. If you would like to read my essay on responsible capitalism, you will find it on www.you-part-two.com.)

I would now like to introduce you to a few of the companies that I admire, because they do one or several of the things I have talked about above. They are a mix of privately-owned firms, partnerships, mutuals and listed companies, and each of them has an approach to business that is customer-centric and sustainable.

The firms highlighted in this chapter are merely a tiny subset of the myriad firms that, in my humble opinion, 'get it'. This chapter could be a book in its own right and the small sample below will undoubtedly grow over time – in print and online.

In the interest of space, I have only provided a brief summary of each firm in these pages. More detail about what I admire about each one, and why, can be found at www.you-part-two.com.

And let me state very clearly for all sorts of legal purposes, I am not recommending any of them. They are merely some of the firms that I have

[2] https://www.investopedia.com/ask/answers/030515/what-percentage-global-economy-comprised-financial-services-sector.asp

seen exhibit some of the characteristics that I admire.

If you work for a firm that you believe should be featured in one or more of the categories below, go to www.you-part-two.com and let us know.

Culture drives everything

If you want to get an idea of whether you should place your money with a financial services firm, my advice is to try to understand their culture. Talk to employees past and present to get an idea of how the business works, which behaviours are encouraged, either implicitly or explicitly, how their leaders lead, and whether the leadership team genuinely cares about their people and their customers.

In my line of work, I am able to observe the leadership teams and cultures of so many financial services firms up close, and one organisation in particular impressed me so much that I have used them as a case study in my Leading Change workshops and speeches ever since. Wellington Management Company is a $1 trillion+ global active fund manager headquartered in Boston, whose ethos is simply three words: 'Client, Firm, Self.'

Their culture is based on the all-too-rare concepts of stewardship and genuine collaboration. Every single leader and manager is driven by the desire to leave their part of the business in a better state than they found it. Every one of their investment analysts is taught and encouraged to engage constructively with their peers, even when they disagree with them. This way, everyone learns from one another, for the benefit of the customer and the firm. I witnessed all of this in action and it stood out for me because, while these traits should be commonplace, in my experience, they aren't.

Wellington manages active funds for some of the world's largest institutional investors and on behalf of several of the world's largest fund managers. Look a little closer at the next fund your adviser recommends or that you are about to buy yourself. It may be managed by Wellington.

Keeping costs low

Vanguard Asset Management shares many of the same cultural values as Wellington because its founder, Jack Bogle, left Wellington to establish

Vanguard in 1975. Jack's founding principle was that instead of paying dividends to external shareholders, he would direct the new business's surplus profits back to investors in the form of lower fees. To this day, Vanguard has not listed. It is a mutual, effectively owned by its funds.

Vanguard is the founder of passive investment; inventing the index fund to 'democratise investment'. It is known for its low-fee passive funds and has been a major force in driving fees lower across the industry since inception. With c.$7 trillion under management, Vanguard is the second-largest fund manager in the world. You can invest with them directly, via your adviser or from any investment platform worth using. And you can find out more about them at www.you-part-two.com.

Using their power to keep boardrooms honest and sustainable

BlackRock was an eight-person start-up three decades ago. Today, it is the largest fund manager in the world with more than $8.6 trillion under management. What I was surprised to discover when I met with the global leadership team of BlackRock was their genuine commitment to the principle of 'investment stewardship': working to improve the way that listed companies are run by directly engaging with their leadership teams. It uses its considerable voting rights and significant influence to hold corporate executives to account.

CEO and founder Larry Fink is a firm believer in both 'responsible capitalism' and 'investing for the long term', and the firm has been a founding member of the industry associations created to address both of these philosophies and change the world of business for the better. His annual 'Letters to CEOs' simultaneously chide and encourage corporate leaders to build long-term, sustainable businesses that put people first, put customers first and take climate change seriously.

Active investors who keep it simple

Fisher Investments is a global active fund manager with $140bn under management with an impressive track record and a straightforward approach. They have just two funds for individual investors, a global equity fund and a global fixed income fund. They also employ a simple all-encompassing fee structure with no hidden extras – no additional trading commissions, platform fees, lock-in periods, exit fees, early-withdrawal fees or additional costs – and investment counsellors who guide investors through their highly compliant process.

Investing to make life better for their community – and for second halfers in particular

I did not expect to be talking about Legal & General in this chapter or on my website. I had always thought they were just another faceless insurance and investment behemoth. But then I discovered two things that changed my perception of them entirely: first, one of their top team is assigned the genuine role of Group Customer Champion, whose job it is to ensure the customer is at the centre of every decision, and; second, rather than simply placing educated bets on public share markets, they invest their own money to benefit the real economy, the communities they serve and specifically to meet the needs of second halfers. They have invested in medical technology firms and retirement villages, and even used their money to explore the creation of 'the care home of the future'.

Taking care of second halfer employees as well as clients

And, as we discussed in Chapter 11 (p.112), Aviva not only realises that second halfers like you and I are their core customers, they are also their core employees – so they help them plan to thrive in their Part Two.

On www.you-part-two.com you will find a full description of each of the companies above, including a deeper look at why they made this list.

These few are merely the tip of the iceberg. This is an exciting time in the world of financial services. More and more companies are genuinely putting the customer at the heart of their businesses, becoming ever-more-responsible capitalists and cajoling the companies in which they invest to do the same. They are giving investors the ability *not* to invest in tobacco, arms, gambling or coal. They are investing to improve the lives of second halfers and in clean technologies, future cities, immunology, next generation antibiotics, biotech and infrastructure to make our worlds better places in which to live. This chapter has merely scratched the surface.

Head to www.you-part-two.com to explore this subject matter in more detail and to let us know of other organisations that you believe should be listed on the site.

PART SIX:

You

'The privilege of a lifetime is to become who you truly are.'
Carl Jung[1]

We have reached the pinnacle of the book. After all, this is your Part Two we are talking about.

These last two chapters focus on the star of this show. We discuss finding your purpose, your relevance, your *ikigai* (more about this in a moment). We talk about harnessing your many strengths, celebrating your 'allowable weaknesses' and defining You Tomorrow.

This last part is about you.

---

[1] Carl Gustav Jung (1875–1961) was a Swiss psychiatrist and psychoanalyst who founded analytical psychology.

CHAPTER 25:

Meaning, purpose and relevance

'We have two lives and the second life begins
when we realise we only have one.'
Confucius

A wise and enigmatic man, that Confucius. Just saying his name makes me write as if I'm Yoda. I think what the ancient Chinese philosopher was trying to say in the quotation above is that the first part of our life is not really living; it is spent busily existing. It isn't until we pause and start to search for meaning, purpose or relevance that our 'real' life begins.

This was always going to be a tricky chapter, skirting nervously around matters such as spirituality, meaning and purpose. But we couldn't possibly write a book about the second half of our lives without at least penning a few thoughts on this fundamental and highly subjective subject. After all, this time of life is indeed the ideal time for reflection, as Confucius wisely remarked. So, let's tiptoe through the minefields and see how we go.

MEANING

To be honest, the first thought that entered my mind when sitting down to write this chapter was, *Am I qualified to write about finding meaning in life?* My instinctive response was, *No!*, but then, perhaps the fact I don't have all the answers actually makes me more qualified than someone who fervently believes that they do.

Spirituality is obviously a topic that has filled many a library. The feeling that there is more to life than merely existing is one of the driving forces behind every major religion and philosophy. Devout Christians, Jews and Muslims alike find meaning in a life dedicated to the worship of a single, omnipotent God, the creator of all things. All three groups also believe that this life is a prelude to a heavenly life-after-death that will start with some form of Judgement Day – 'The Last Judgement' (Christianity), 'The Day of The Lord' (Judaism) or the 'Day of Resurrection' (Islam). The Christian Bible calls this event the Rapture, a time when Jesus will appear to resurrect Christians and take them to heaven. For some followers, this belief can lead to a dangerously nihilistic view of their comparatively sub-optimal current life on this planet, perhaps even a desire to hasten the end of days forecast in The Book of Revelation. But I would suggest that the vast majority of Christians opt for the view that this life *before* death of ours is precious and something to be cherished.

Hinduism, Jainism, Buddhism and Sikhism have a completely different take on life and death. Followers of these faiths believe in reincarnation and the eventual attainment of enlightenment through the understanding of karma: that the sum of a person's actions in this and previous states of existence will determine their fate in future existences.

At times, I can feel a little envious of people who are deeply religious. I imagine such total faith must lead to a sense of great inner calm from 'knowing' that through a combination of worship and good deeds you will either move a rung or two further up the ladder of reincarnation or will be able to live in heaven for eternity, and that living a good and honourable life based on the teachings of the prophet Muhammad or Jesus of Nazareth or following the rituals and rules of the Jewish Torah will give your life its purpose.

Of course, this all hinges on belief. If you don't believe that Jesus was the son of God, that He was sent to this planet to die for the sins of *Homo sapiens* and came back to life after a horrible death by crucifixion before transcending to heaven, thus paving the same path for all believers, then an eternity of damnation lies ahead. Similarly, if you don't believe that Muhammad was the chosen prophet to whom God spoke at length, several times, to reveal the secrets of life and the afterlife, the same fate awaits you.

A different view of divinity is that perhaps the divine lies within; a concept to which several religions, and philosophies including yoga, subscribe. As BKS Iyengar said, 'One of the purposes of yoga is to kindle the divine fire within yourself. Everyone has a dormant spark of divinity in him which has to be fanned into flame.' Whether you decide that it is *the* divine that lies within you or simply something divine, I find the concept to be heart-warming and life-affirming.

PURPOSE

But no matter what we may believe about the nature of divinity, one thing we could all agree on: having a purpose is not only good for our mental health and well-being, it is good for our physical health, the quality of our sleep and even how long we live, as innumerable research studies have shown.

'Helping people cultivate a purpose in life could be an effective drug-free strategy to improve sleep quality, particularly for a population that is facing more insomnia,' concluded one of the authors of a study of 825 people by BioMed Central in the US in conjunction with the Minority Ageing Research Study and the Rush Memory and Ageing Project.[1] The report goes on to say: 'Purpose in life is something that can be cultivated and enhanced through mindfulness therapies.'

And as Confucius implied, real life begins when we seek to find our purpose.

Inspired and informed by a conversation and exchange of emails with Huw Williams, a good friend and advertising creative who came up with the superb title of this book, the following is our attempt to elaborate on what the ancient Chinese philosopher may have been trying to tell us two and a half thousand years ago – framed in a modern context. Here goes . . .

When we were young, our thoughts rarely extended in any meaningful way beyond ourselves and our friends. We believed that right would always win in the end and, at least when we were very young, that our parents were close to infallible. We believed in our teachers. We may even have believed in our government.

We believed all of these things until we didn't.

We lose many of these beliefs as we age. We learn that we are mortal, that people die, that people lie and that not everything is as it seems or as we wish it to be. We learn that life isn't fair: good things

[1] https://sleep.biomedcentral.com/articles/10.1186/s41606-017-0015-6

happen to bad people and bad things happen to good people. We learn there is no such thing as a free lunch and that if something looks too good to be true, it usually is. We learn that our actions have consequences.

We learn that life is rarely easy, nor is it meant to be. We learn that everything worthwhile in life requires effort. We learn that the destination is rarely as important as the journey, so it pays to pause once in a while to appreciate the voyage.

But it isn't until we work out who we are and what our purpose is that our real life actually begins. Until that moment, we are simply rushing around aimlessly. Our real life begins when we start to become our best self, and that requires experience. The self who understands what we are going to do with our life, even if we have trouble articulating it. The self with a purpose, a relevance and an inner strength that can enjoy the beauty and majesty of living while riding with the inevitable punches and bouncing back even stronger.

Looking outwards

'If you want happiness for an hour, take a nap. If you want happiness for a day, go fishing. If you want happiness for a year, inherit a fortune. If you want happiness for a lifetime, help somebody.'—Chinese proverb

A strong and sustainable purpose is outward facing. This is as true for individuals as it is in the world of business. If a company's sole purpose is to make money, maximise profit or maximise shareholder returns, it is a hollow organisation that is ultimately doomed to irrelevance. The same goes for us, too. As we saw in Chapters 5 and 9, our lives are so much richer and, well, more purposeful, when we are able to let go of our ego and help others, without thinking of ourselves. And, if our altruism is genuine, it also makes us happier and healthier, as we have seen.

Of course, how and how much we give back will be different for all of us. Some dedicate their entire lives to helping others. Others help others through their businesses. Some focus on helping their children or spouse or family. Some help others financially; others help by donating with their time – both are invaluable.

Finding your ikigai

Your purpose doesn't have to be grand. It simply has to be genuine and relevant to you.

It could simply be finding solace in nature. It is a well-observed fact that appreciation and enjoyment of the great outdoors reduces stress levels considerably. People find purpose in gardening. In being a grandparent. They find purpose in building a business. They find purpose in philanthropy. Purpose is not a one-size-fits-all deal. And it is certainly not a 'my purpose is better than your purpose' deal. Purpose is personal and there is no such thing as a bad purpose, a poor purpose or an inferior purpose – as long as it is real and meaningful to you.

Unless it does significant harm to others, even unintentionally. Then it's a shocker of a purpose.

'Fulfilment is a right and not a privilege,' is Simon Sinek's opening refrain in his book, *Find Your Why*.[2] 'Fulfilment is not a lottery. It is not a feeling reserved for a lucky few.'

In other words, we all have a Why; we just may need some help in working out what it is. To do that we have to be completely honest with ourselves. You can't fudge a purpose. And for help in finding your purpose, it may be hard to find a better place to start than the ancient Japanese philosophy of *ikigai*.

'Less stress, better health and greater happiness: it's all about the Japanese life philosophy *ikigai*,' read a headline in *The Times* in 2017.[3]

Ikigai means 'reason for being' and it is accompanied by a superb model that anyone could use to help unlock their very own 'Why'.

Japanese people live longer on average than anyone else in the world. While diet is a key reason for this, it is becoming widely regarded that fulfilment through *ikigai* is also one of the other secrets to their longevity.

Contentment through purpose helps us to live longer.

To find your *ikigai*, start with asking yourself:

1. What do I love?

2. What am I good at?

---

[2] Penguin Random House 2017.
[3] *The Times,* UK, in its review of Ken Mogi's book, *The Little Book of Ikigai* (Quercus, 2017).

3. What can I be rewarded for?

4. What does the world need?

Once you have done that, you can plot them on the following diagram. The magic of *ikigai* lies in all the places where your four answers intersect.

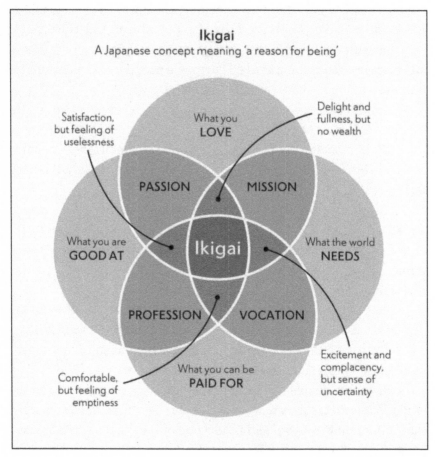

Your 'passion' can be found in the intersection between what you love and what you are good at. Your 'profession' should be located at the intersection of what you are good at and what you can be rewarded for. Your 'vocation' is described as being rewarded for doing something that the world needs, and your 'mission' is doing something you love that the world needs.

But the empty spaces in this diagram are the most profound. Read the following explanations of each one slowly and deliberately.

If we are doing something that we are good at, but the world doesn't really need it, we will achieve a superficial level of satisfaction, but we won't feel useful.

If we are doing something that we are well rewarded for, but it isn't what we love, we may be financially comfortable, but we will feel empty and unfulfilled.

If we are doing something that the world needs but we aren't very good at it, we will feel uncertain and insecure.

If we are doing what we love but aren't getting properly rewarded for it, we are unlikely to feel content; we could even begin to resent the way the world works.

We all know people who are in every one of these intersections and, if you are anything like me, you have spent time in each one yourself.

Ikigai is to be found at the centre of this diagram – when you are doing what you love and are good at it, the world needs it and you are being well rewarded for it: where your passion, your mission, your vocation and your profession all collide.

Japanese neuroscientist, broadcaster and author Ken Mogi says that *ikigai* is 'about discovering, defining and appreciating those of life's pleasures that have meaning for you.' He describes it as 'a frame of mind where people feel that they can build a happy and active life.'[4]

Mogi has identified five 'pillars', which he describes as the foundations that will allow your *ikigai* to flourish:

1. Starting small

2. Accepting yourself ('a low-budget, maintenance-free formula for being happy' declares Mogi)

3. Harmony and sustainability through connecting with the world around you

4. The joy of little things

5. Being in the here and now

We like these pillars. They are very yogic.

[4] https://ikigaitribe.com/ikigai/the-5-pillars-of-ikigai

RELEVANCE

If 'meaning' and 'purpose' aren't your bag, perhaps what you most want in your Part Two is to become, or remain, relevant. 'Relevant to whom?' should perhaps be the first question to ask. 'Why?' would be the second.

'Relevance' is about adding value and feeling valued. It is about finding your role – at home, within your family, in your community, at work, in life. You have already had a vast number of roles throughout your life so far, several of them at the same time. Your roles, your identities, have changed over the years and they will continue to change throughout your Part Two.

'One of the challenges of aging is the shift in roles that helped define our identity,' said Markus Schafer, Associate Professor of Sociology at the University of Toronto in an article published for the *American Sociological Association*.[5] 'They take time and energy and an emotional commitment. When we lose those roles, there can be quite a hole, leaving us to wonder where our significance is now.'

Our identity and other sources of relevance are always changing. Completely different things made us feel 'relevant' when we were a small child compared to when we were teenagers, or young adults just starting to make our own way in the world. Different things make us relevant today and the sources of our relevance will continue to change throughout our lives.

As we proceed further into our Part Two, we will need to find new forms of relevance, based on our ever-changing situations. Ideally it will be based around what we like doing, what we are good at and what we can do to help others, but it will change over time – again and again.

But one thing that will always be important is the relationships that we form: our social connections and connectedness. Our relevance is often linked to our sense of belonging; we are social beings after all. We need to belong.

Many of us badly want to remain relevant at work or to the job market, and the solution to this is quite straightforward – never stop learning, stay up to date with tech, never stop networking, understand and appreciate modern culture and ways of thinking, see the positives

---

[5] https://journals.sagepub.com/doi/full/10.1177/0190272516628297

and the opportunities in what the younger generations are trying to do and the different ways they are going about it, mentor or join forces with younger people, and never think of yourself as irrelevant. If you know you are relevant, you will be. If you think you're not, you won't be. It's a self-fulfilling kind of thing.

You may find relevance in still being able to play your favourite sport or hobby to a high standard – or trying a new one. Or as a member of the community at your golf club, bridge club, church, mosque or synagogue. Your purpose may be based on supporting your partner or helping family members when they are in need. It may be through philanthropy, from helping others. It may be from the work you do in your community or 'simply' in your role as a father, mother, grandfather, grandfather, wife, spouse, partner or child.

Others find relevance in their business. Or in family. Or in yoga. In writing and speaking and running workshops that help people. These are all important and valid sources of relevance.

But as I write this chapter, I can't help thinking that perhaps meaning, relevance and purpose actually begin from within.

Yes, they need to be outward facing, but to be genuine they also need to be built on strong foundations. Because the sports, hobbies, work or external activities that may currently fuel your purpose and relevance are most likely, one day, to come to their natural conclusion – and then what will you be left with?

Your Self.

CHAPTER 26:

You Tomorrow

> Be yourself; everyone else is already taken.
> Oscar Wilde[1]

There is literally no one quite like you, which is a fact that fully deserves to be cherished and celebrated. Whatever 'You Tomorrow' looks like, you can't possibly hope to build it on quicksand, on baseless wishes. You will need to build it on something solid, on something real. You will need to base it on the fact that your inner self already contains the fundamental building blocks you need; the DNA of You Tomorrow already exists.

You Tomorrow needs to be far more genuine and much longer lasting than a New Year's resolution, which tend to come from a position of unworthiness and negativity. 'You Tomorrow' needs to start from a place of positivity, from the realisation of your strengths, and the value that lies within.

Speaking of New Year's resolutions, yoga has a far better version, a *sankalpa*: an expression of the heartfelt desire that already lies within us. So, rather than a resolution such as 'I will lose weight' – the classic empty promise uttered by countless millions of people in the first few minutes of each new year – a *sankalpa* is a statement that is self-affirming rather than self-critical. It looks behind the resolution for the source, the key driver, of the outcome we desire. A key driver of improving our health and weight is 'loving and respecting our body' – if we do this, we will care about what we put into it and how we treat it. To give them real power, and to remove any little last vestiges of derision, *sankalpas* are stated in the present tense – and made personal. Rather than 'I will lose weight',

[1] Irish poet and playwright (1854–1900)

your *sankalpa* becomes: 'I love and respect my body': a positive affirmation that is real, right now. Not an 'I will' at some future point in time. It is your truth, right now.

YOU TOMORROW STARTS WITH YOU TODAY

'What are you seeking to achieve?' and 'Why?'

These are the first two questions I ask my business clients, whether I am helping them to clarify their strategy, redesign their organisation, energise their leadership team, transform their company's culture or plan their own career.

They are also ideal questions to ask of ourselves as we plan our Part Two.

When asking yourself these questions, remember that 'What you are seeking to achieve' often comes in two forms: numbers and narrative. Think about both. There are often two forms of 'why' as well: a 'real' reason and a 'right' reason, as we discussed in Chapter 13 (p.131). Think about both forms of these, too. The real reason for wanting to achieve the outcomes you desire is often an internally focused one, while the right reason tends to face outwards. Both are valid and useful, but they must be genuine.

A look in the mirror

The next step is to take stock: to pause and assess what you are good at, what you would like to be better at, how, what's holding you back and the opportunities you could create; in other words, your personal SWOT. But in this context, we are going to replace the traditional 'T' (Threats) with 'O' (Obstacles) and we have added a couple of questions about Values and Essence. So, actually, we will be conducting our very own SWOOVE analysis!

Strengths

What am I good at? What are my key skills? What do I excel at? What do I do better than most? What am I passionate about? When am I at my most confident? What do I like most about myself? Why? What puts a bounce in my step? Your many strengths are the ones to capitalise on, to grow, to leverage in your Part Two.

Weaknesses

What am I not so good at? What are my 'allowable weaknesses': those things that I will never be very good at but are important enough for me to find someone who can do it – to plug my weakness with their strength? Which key skills should I improve and sharpen? What new skills should I try to develop? How?

Obstacles

Think back to Chapter 9 (p.89). What are the barriers that are getting in the way of you achieving the Part Two you desire? List them. Rank them in order of impact. What can you do to overcome them? What help do you need to overcome them? How are you going to get that help?

Opportunities

What are the potential opportunities that you may be able to engineer or take advantage of, at work and in life? Make a list. Brainstorm ideas – the crazier the better. Then pick the ones that appeal the most, either because they are revelatory, or they are pragmatic. Then ask yourself the question, 'What do I have to do to transform these opportunities into realities?'

Values

How would you describe your values? What is the ethos that you would like to underpin everything you do? What matters most to you? Why? Does this revelation mean you may want to change some of your previous answers?

Essence

When are you your best self? What gives you the deepest satisfaction and makes you feel energised and excited? What is your 'anandamaya kosha': that layer at the heart of your very soul that makes you bubble up with bliss? To some people it is God, for others it is nature, for others it may be their partner, or something else altogether. What is yours? This is the essence that should fuel and guide your Part Two.

Which is a perfect place to bring the book to a close.

If you wish to dive into planning your Part Two in greater detail, please go to www.you-part-two.com, where you will find a 'You Tomorrow' planning template to download and use to your heart's content.

You will also find tips from the extraordinary life and executive coach we mentioned back in Chapter 8 (p.88), Sharon Hall, as well as numerous articles, tools and links to a host of useful websites and life-planning tools, along with details of the full 'You: Part Two Online Programme'.

In fact, you will be able to delve deeper into every subject contained in this book – from ageism to attitude, menopause, enhancing our ability to accept and embrace change, reaching a state of radical acceptance and contentment. You will find information and links about working in the second half, changing careers, starting your own business and navigating the aged care labyrinth. You will also find more detail and links to all of the organisations and services we discussed in the Money part of the book (p.173).

We have covered a great deal of ground together, travelling between the covers of this book. Thank you so much for joining us.

We wish you all the best in defining what your Part Two looks like and feels like – and most important of all, living it to the fullest.

Focus your energy and resources, garner the support you need – and make it happen.

For this is your time.

Life is exquisitely and achingly
short.
Too short to waste regretting the past.
Too short to waste worrying about the future.
Your time is now.
Cherish and nurture your family, your friendships;
all the relationships that are important
to you.
Find good tribes.
Like yourself. Treat yourself with kindness. Believe in yourself.
Breathe.
Laugh well, love well, live well.
Give back.
Become the person you always wanted to be; the one that has been within
you all this time.
Accept and embrace the changes that come your way
and thrive.

Campbell and Jane Macpherson   www.you-part-two.com

Acknowledgements

There are so many people to thank for transforming this book from an idea into reality, and the first is our agent, Jonathan Hayden, for believing in it and pitching it to Hachette. The second is Tom Asker, Commissioning Editor at Little, Brown, without whom *You: Part Two* would not have come together anywhere near as well as we hope it has.

Thanks to Sonia Nuttall and Jo Evans, our intrepid researchers who broke the back of the vast amount of research we required, and to Huw Williams for the inspired book title, the Confucius quote that was perfect for Chapter 25 and his collaboration in helping us to put the ancient philosopher's saying into a modern context.

Special thanks to the unstoppable Louise Johnson for her invaluable input to several key parts of the book.

Thanks also to so many other friends for letting us know what they would like to see in *You: Part Two* – Nigel Johnson, David Pitman, Tony Wright, Mark Mostyn, James Howarth, Ant Borgman, Jim and Laura Cleary and a host of others.

To Sean Russo, Trisha Wilcox, Bryher Scudamore and Gaele Lalaly for allowing us to tell their stories. To Katische Haberfield for permitting us to use her interview with Jane as the basis for the chapter on menopause.

To Simon Taylor of the UK's Professional Players Federation, Lisa Delaney of the Jockeys Education and Training Scheme, Natasha Oppenheim from No Desire to Retire, Mary MacLeod of Korn Ferry, Emma Jones of Enterprise Nation, Rob Smith, Olivia Anderson and Martin Holdsworth of Family Risk Management, Philippa Fieldhouse of Richmond Villages. To Leanne Tuckfield for helping us to begin to understand the Australian approach to aged care and Anthony Dee for making us aware of the incredible life-affirming service that hospices provide.

To IFA, Jane Hodges; financial adviser, Sandro Forte; Ruston Smith, Chair of JP Morgan Asset Management, the Tesco Pension Fund and the AEG Pension Fund; Simon Chrystal of WPS; Peter Hobbs and George Prior of The Devere Group; Susan McMurry of Wellington; Jonathan Goodstone and James Norton of Vanguard; Kirsty McBride and Marko Penko of Fisher Investments; Chris Knight, Millie Hyde-Smith and Jess McCreadie of Legal & General; Alistair McQueen of Aviva; Ryan O'Keefe of BlackRock and Richard Collinson of RetireEasy.

To PR professional Alexia Latham, who helped secure many of the contacts above, and Sharon Hall of River Deep Coaching for introducing us to Gaele and for her deep insights on coaching.

And finally, to the taxi driver Campbell met in Vegas: we hope you were able to save up for those teeth.

Index

acceptance, 83–4, 99–104

Adams, Douglas, 189

Aged Care Quality and Safety Commission, 167

aged care, 5, 151–72

    see also care homes and nursing homes; hospices; retirement living

ageism, 4, 24–31

air pollution, 41

Airbnb, 17

alcohol, 37, 62

All Blacks, 116

Alzheimer's, 38, 42–3

Amazon, 17, 135, 180, 188

American Association of Retired Persons, 52

American Heart Association, 39

American Psychological Association, 32, 95

American Psychologist, 41

American Sociological Association, 224

Angelou, Maya, 32

anger, 81–2, 91

antibiotics, 19

anti-depressants, 53–4, 67, 101–2

anxiety, 45, 50, 53–6, 58, 69, 76, 89, 96, 119, 121

apprehension, 85

Aristotle, 103

Assets Under Management (AUM), 200, 206

assisted living, 164–6

attitude, 32–5

Australia, 20, 30, 141, 204

    aged care, 153–5, 157–8, 161–2, 167–9